Archaeologies of Memory

Archaeologies of Memory

Edited by
Ruth M. Van Dyke
and Susan E. Alcock

Blackwell
Publishing

350 Main Street, Malden, MA 02148-5018, USA
108 Cowley Road, Oxford OX4 1JF, UK
550 Swanston Street, Carlton South, Melbourne, Victoria 3053, Australia
Kurfürstendamm 57, 10707 Berlin, Germany

First published 2003 by Blackwell Publishers Ltd

Library of Congress Cataloging-in-Publication Data
Archaeologies of memory / edited by Ruth M. Van Dyke and Susan E. Alcock.
    p. cm.
Includes bibliographical references and index.
    ISBN 0-631-23584-1 (alk. paper) – ISBN 0-631-23585-X (pbk. : alk. paper)
    1. Social archaeology.   2. Memory–Social aspects.   I. Van Dyke, Ruth.
II. Alcock, Susan E.
    CC72.4 .A733 2003
    930.1–dc21
                                                                    2002009132

A catalogue record for this title is available from the British Library.

Set in 10.5 on 12.5 pt Bembo
by SNP Best-set Typesetter Ltd., Hong Kong
Printed and bound in the United Kingdom
by MPG Books Ltd, Bodmin, Cornwall

For further information on
Blackwell Publishing, visit our website:
http://www.blackwellpublishing.com

Contents

Plates

Figures

Maps

Notes on the Contributors

Susan E. Alcock (Ph.D. Cambridge 1989) is John H. D'Arms Collegiate Professor of Classical Archaeology and Classics at the University of Michigan. Her recent major publications include: *Graecia Capta* (1993); *Placing the Gods: Sanctuaries and Sacred Space in Ancient Greece* (co-editor, 1994); *The Early Roman Empire in the East* (editor, 1997); *Pausanias: Travel and Memory in Roman Greece* (co-editor, 2001); and *Empires: Perspectives from Archaeology and History* (co-editor, 2001).

Susan M. Alt is a graduate student in anthropology at the University of Illinois, Urbana-Champaign, where she is the recipient of a National Science Foundation Graduate Research Fellowship. Her recent major publications include: "Spindle Whorls and Fiber Production at Early Cahokian Settlements," *Southeastern Archaeology* 18 (1999); and "Cahokian Change and the Authority of Tradition," in *The Archaeology of Traditions*, ed. T. Pauketat (2001).

Emma Blake (Ph.D. Cambridge 1999) is a Postdoctoral Fellow in Humanities at Stanford University. Her recent major publications include: "Sardinia's Nuraghi: Four Millennia of Becoming," *World Archaeology* 30 (1998); "Identity Mapping in the Sardinian Bronze Age," *European Journal of Archaeology* 2 (1999); and "Constructing a Nuragic Locale: The Spatial Relationship between Tombs and Towers in Bronze Age Sardinia," *American Journal of Archaeology* (2001).

Richard Bradley is Professor of Archaeology at the University of Reading. His recent major publications include: *Rock Art and the Prehistory of Atlantic Europe* (1997); *The Significance of Monuments* (1998); *An Archaeology of Natural Places* (2000), and *The Past in Prehistoric Societies* (2002). In 2002, he was awarded an honorary doctorate from the University of Lund, Sweden.

Rosemary A. Joyce (Ph.D. Illinois-Urbana 1985) is Professor of Anthropology at the University of California, Berkeley. Her recent major publications include: *Women* *in Prehistory: North America and Mesoamerica* (co-editor, 1997); *Social Patterns in Pre-Classic Mesoamerica* (co-editor, 1999); *Beyond Kinship: Social and Material Reproduction in House Societies* (co-editor, 2000); *Gender and Power in Prehispanic Mesoamerica* (2001); and *The Languages of Archaeology* (2002).

Katina T. Lillios (Ph.D. Yale 1991) is Associate Professor of Anthropology at Ripon College. Her recent major publications include: *The Origins of Complex Societies in Late Prehistoric Iberia* (editor, 1995); "Objects of Memory: The Ethnography and Archaeology of Heirlooms," *Journal of Archaeological Method and Theory* 6 (1999); "A Biographical Approach to the Ethnogeology of Late Prehistoric Portugal," *Trabajos de Prehistoria* 57 (2000).

Lynn M. Meskell (Ph.D. Cambridge 1997) is Associate Professor of Anthropology at Columbia University. She is the founding editor of the *Journal of Social Archaeology.* Her recent major publications include: *Archaeology Under Fire* (editor, 1998); *Archae-ologies of Social Life: Age, Sex, Class etc. in Ancient Egypt* (1999); and *Private Life in New Kingdom Egypt* (2002).

Amy Papalexandrou (Ph.D. Princeton 1998) is an independent scholar based in Austin, Texas. Her recent major publications include "Text in Context: Eloquent Monuments and the Byzantine Beholder," *Word & Image* 17 (2001); and "Conversing Hellenism: The Multiple Voices of a Byzantine Monument in Greece," *Journal of Modern Greek Studies* 29 (2001).

Timothy R. Pauketat (Ph.D. Michigan 1991) is Associate Professor of Anthropol-ogy at the University of Illinois, Urbana-Champaign. His recent major publications include: *The Ascent of Chiefs: Cahokia and Mississippian Politics in Native North America* (1994); *Cahokia: Domination and Ideology in the Mississippian World* (co-editor, 1997); and *The Archaeology of Traditions: Agency and History Before and After Columbus* (editor, 2001).

Mieke Prent is a Ph.D. candidate at the University of Amsterdam. She has published articles on excavation and survey projects in Crete and on the Greek mainland. "Cretan Early Iron Age Hearth Temples and the Articulation of Sacred Space" and "Cult Activities at the Palace of Knossos from the End of the Bronze Age" are sched-uled to appear in the British School at Athens Supplementary Series.

Carla M. Sinopoli (Ph.D. Michigan 1986) is Associate Professor of Anthropology and Associate Curator, Museum of Anthropology at the University of Michigan. Her major publications include: *Approaches to Archaeological Ceramics* (1991); *Pots and Palaces: The Earthenware Ceramics of the Nobleman's Quarter of Vijayanagara* (1993); and *Empires: Perspectives from Archaeology and History* (co-editor, 2001).

Ruth M. Van Dyke (Ph.D. Arizona 1998) is Assistant Professor of Anthropology at Colorado College. Recent publications include: "The Chaco Connection: Evaluating Bonito Style Architecture in Outlier Communities," *Journal of Anthropological Archaeology* 18 (1999); "A Space Syntax Analysis of Guadalupe Ruin," *American Antiquity* 64 (1999); and "Chacoan Ritual Landscapes," in *Great House Communities across the Chacoan Landscape*, ed. J. Kantner and N. Mahoney (2000).

Preface

This collaboration was originally conceived at a roundtable luncheon during the 1999 Society for American Archaeology meetings in Chicago. Sue Alcock had been working on monuments and memory in Roman Greece, and Ruth Van Dyke had been thinking about memory from the standpoint of Chacoan roads running to abandoned sites. In our conversation that day, we agreed that the uses of archaeology in the politics of the present were receiving quite a lot of attention, but not so the equally fascinating political uses of archaeology in the past. We also realized that we were coming at similar issues from different, if overlapping, contexts of study. To bridge the still too familiar gap between classical and anthropological archaeology, we surmised that it might be useful to bring people from these disparate backgrounds together to discuss common interests in archaeology and memory.

Pooling our energies amidst a flurry of e-mails led to two co-organized conference sessions – one in an anthropological and one in a classical context. In 2000, we organized "Archaeologies of Memory: Case Studies, Comparative Perspectives" at the 65th Annual Meeting of the Society for American Archaeology in Philadelphia; the following year saw us responsible for "Mediterranean Memories: Archaeologies of the Past in the Past" at the 102nd Annual Meeting of the Archaeological Institute of America in San Diego. A variety of very interesting papers emerged from these two sessions; many of which now appear in this volume. To amplify our coverage, in the end we invited Richard Bradley, Rosemary Joyce, Lynn Meskell, Tim Pauketat and Susan Alt to make contributions as well.

The resulting volume has benefited from the enthusiastic energy of Jane Huber at Blackwell, as well as the Blackwell production staff. Ruth wishes to express her appreciation to the National Endowment for the Humanities and the School of American Research for support during her tenure as Resident Scholar in 2000–2001. Ruth would also like to thank the Department of Anthropology at Colorado College, particularly Heather Gerhart, who helped with formatting. The ideas in this book have benefited from discussions with many people. Ruth especially appreciates intellectual contributions and support provided by Rebecca Allahyari, James Brooks, Gary Gossen, Joshua Jones, Gabrielle Katz, Jane McDougall, Marni Sandweiss, and Louise Senior.

Sue Alcock would like to acknowledge the support offered by her Arthur F. Thurnau Professorship, as well as the encouragement of John F. Cherry.

Both editors would like to thank all the participants in the two conference sessions, as well as their attentive audiences. Most importantly, our heartfelt gratitude to our wide-ranging cast of contributors, who were both responsible and good-humored about this entire endeavor, and who – like us – are firm believers in the ability of archaeology to address the problem and the power of memory.

Ruth M. Van Dyke
Colorado College
Susan E. Alcock
University of Michigan

1
Archaeologies of Memory:
An Introduction

Ruth M. Van Dyke and Susan E. Alcock

> The past is everywhere. All around us lie features which, like ourselves and
> our thoughts, have more or less recognizable antecedents. Relics, histories,
> memories suffuse human experience. . . . Whether it is celebrated or
> rejected, attended to or ignored, the past is omnipresent. (Lowenthal
> 1985:xv)

In a scene that may resonate with contemporary archaeologists as uncannily familiar, a sixth century BC cuneiform tablet from Larsa, in modern Iraq, testifies to the incipient archaeological investigations of Nabonidus, king of Babylon (Schnapp 1997:13–20). The tablet describes how Nabonidus mobilized workers with picks, shovels, and baskets to excavate in sites already millennia old, seeking to recover and restore past traces of a mighty predecessor. Yet the deeds of Nabonidus offer more than an exceptionally early example of archaeological practice – the king was actively engaged in the construction of social memory.

Today, it is the accepted business of the discipline of archaeology to interpret human pasts, and in the process, to contribute to the construction of memory for contemporary societies. Although we style ourselves as participants in a fairly young academic discipline, the "fascination with the past" or "backward-looking curiosity" that gave rise to the formal practice of archaeology is not a phenomenon specific to the post-Enlightenment era. Like the Babylonian ruler Nabonidus, past peoples knowingly inhabited landscapes that were palimpsests of previous occupations. Sites were built on sites; landscapes were occupied and reoccupied time and again. Rarely was this a meaningless or innocent reuse. Like us, past peoples observed and interpreted traces of more distant pasts to serve the needs and interests of their present lives.

This collection of essays is intended to explore these uses "of the past in the past" from a wide range of archaeological perspectives. The papers that follow are drawn from a spectrum of cultures and chronological periods: from prehistoric to early modern times, from the American Southwest to southern India. The peoples involved in each case study accessed the past through different means, employing varying combinations of texts, oral traditions, iconographic representations, heirlooms, and visible remains on the landscape.

In spite of this diversity, the papers share certain common themes. All engage with *social memory*, the construction of a collective notion (not an individual belief) about the way things were in the past (Connerton 1989; Halbwachs 1975 [1925], 1992 [1950]; Hutton 1993). Social memory is nowhere here perceived as monolithic, but as variable by gender, ethnicity, class, religion or other salient factors, allowing for a multiplicity, and possible conflict, of memories in any society. Also central to the volume is the acceptance of social memory's mutability, the recognition that it emerges and evolves from acts of both remembering and forgetting. Investigating the pressures and desires behind those acts became a chief task for all the book's authors. Finally, the essays are committed to the notion that archaeology, and in some cases *only* archaeology, can do much to illuminate how people in the past conceived their past, and perceived their present and future.

In some senses, this volume is leaping onto a well-established bandwagon. Memory currently possesses a robust hold on the scholarly imagination, a development traced back by some to Sigmund Freud (1966–74 [1914]) and his interest in uncovering childhood events during psychoanalysis. In 1925, the sociologist Maurice Halbwachs (1975 [1925]) moved the discussion of memory beyond the bounds of the individual and the personal, arguing instead that memory must be taken as a social, or group phenomenon. Since Halbwachs' death in World War II, memory has only gained ground as a topic of discourse in popular culture and literature, accelerating especially as the twentieth century drew to a close. Part of this can no doubt be related to the self-reflective frame of mind that characterized the end of the millennium. Simon Schama's *Landscape and Memory* (1996), for example, dissected the relationships between Western cultural values and our visions of the natural world. Marcel Proust's *A la recherche du temps perdu*, published between 1913 and 1927 and so often taken as "the" novel about memory, was released as a film (*Le Temps retrouvé*) in 1999 (see Bradley, this volume); the 2000 film *Memento* in turn explored the role of memory in the construction of reality. Two recent issues of the interdisciplinary journal *Representations* have been devoted to memory in history and the social sciences (see Davis and Starn 1989; Laqueur 2000). Genealogy sites proliferate on the internet as disenfranchised or dislocated suburban Americans seek their family roots. Cultural critics have noted the flowering of a post-modern nostalgia for an imagined simpler past (e.g., Nora 1989). Innumerable other examples of a western near-obsession with memory and with wars over memory could be cited, from Holocaust commemoration, to the display of the Enola Gay, to the ongoing debate over memorializing the events of 9/11 (e.g., Baer 2000; Linenthal and Englehardt 1996; Zerubavel 1995).

Where have archaeologists stood in all of this? Obviously, they have been directly pulled into museum controversies or arguments over the role of heritage management; they have been actors in the recovery of lost objects (or human remains), such as the work of forensic archaeology on the "disappeared" of Argentina (Crossland 2000). Other authors, notably David Lowenthal (1985), have considered the unique, and uniquely complex, contributions of archaeology to accessing the past. Archaeologists have also joined with historians and social scientists in recognizing the potential of memory to illuminate the pasts of marginalized groups (Alonso 1988; Blight 2001). Memory has been "claimed by the heretofore silenced and oppressed as the gateway to a past that history had closed" (Laqueur 2000:1). To that end, explicit attention has been paid to the juxtaposition of present–day oral narratives with archaeological epistemologies (e.g., Echo-Hawk 2000; Mason 2000). Finally, the role of archaeology in commemorative manipulations in aid of nationalist or other political agenda has been scrutinized, and often condemned (Arnold 1990; Bender 1998; Dietler 1998; Gero and Root 1990; Trigger 1984).

Given the backward-looking nature of the archaeological enterprise, it is hardly surprising that memory should increasingly form a focus for our attention, and from many directions. This collection concentrates upon one particular domain – the awareness and construction of the past in the past. Although this arena of inquiry has been somewhat slower to emerge than concern over the uses of archaeology in the present, there is a growing body of literature on memory and the past in archaeological contexts (e.g., Alcock 2002; Bradley and Williams 1998; Chesson 2001; Joyce and Gillespie 2000; Lillios 1999; Meskell 2002). Peoples in the past shared memories too – memories that archaeologists have the potential to recover and consider, if sometimes only in partial or shadowy form.

Social Memory in Archaeological Contexts

"Memories are not ready-made reflections of the past, but eclectic, selective reconstructions . . . " (Lowenthal 1985:210). People remember or forget the past according to the needs of the present, and social memory is an active and ongoing process. The construction of social memory can involve direct connections to ancestors in a remembered past, or it can involve more general links to a vague mythological antiquity, often based on the re-interpretation of monuments or landscapes (Gosden and Lock 1998; Meskell, this volume). Obliteration of the past rather than connection to it may also be involved, as pasts may be subsumed and dominated, conquered and dismantled (Manning 1998; Papalexandrou, this volume).

The construction of memory can symbolically smooth over ruptures, creating the appearance of a seamless social whole. Social memory is often used to naturalize or legitimate authority (e.g., Alcock 2002; Hobsbawm and Ranger 1983; Jonker 1995). "Collective memory . . . is one of the great stakes of developed and developing societies, of dominated and dominating classes, all of them struggling for power or for life, for survival and advancement" (Le Goff 1992:97–8, cited in Laqueur 2000:2). A related and common use of social memory is to create and support a sense of individual and community identity (Basso 1996; Blake 1998). Although in archaeological contexts it is easiest to see the top-down machinations of elite groups using memory to these ends, memory is also employed in the service of resistance. However, these processes are not straightforward, simple, or monolithic. Memory's mutability makes it possible for multiple and conflicting versions of events to co-exist, sometimes in the interests of competing parties (Alonso 1988).

All in all, it is clear that the creation and re-creation of social memory is an active and ongoing process . . . yet how does that process work? Anthropologists and archaeologists have offered various categories of practice. Rowlands (1993) makes an archaeologically useful distinction between inscribed memory practices, characterized by repetition and public access, and incorporated memory practices, characterized by opaque symbolism and secrecy. Inscribed memory is manifested in materially visible commemorative activities such as the construction of monuments, whereas incorporated memory lends itself to obliterative or fleeting acts that leave few archaeological traces (Bradley 2000:157–8). In his influential work *How Societies Remember* (1989), Connerton distinguishes between inscribed memory, involving monuments, texts and representations, and embodied memory, encompassing bodily rituals and behavior. Similar distinctions between prescriptive, formulaic, repetitive, and materially visible acts on the one hand, and performative, mutable, transitory behavior on the other, have been made by Bloch (1985) and Sahlins (1985).

It is easiest for archaeologists to access the inscribed, material end of the spectrum of memory practices. Although embodied, performative, incorporated practices are more difficult to study archaeologically, we do see "footprints" left by these activities. We possess four broad, overlapping categories of materially accessible media through which social memories are commonly constructed and observed: ritual behaviors, narratives, objects and representations, and places. To some extent, all of these are elements in the papers to follow, although the last two categories engage the most attention.

Ritual behavior is materially visible through evidence for activities such as processions, mortuary treatments, abandonments, feasting, and votive deposition, although untangling the relationship of such behavior to commemorative patterns can be challenging. Avenues, tracks, and cursuses enable the re-enaction of prehistoric movements that in some cases may have involved ritual processions (Barclay and Harding 1999; Barrett 1994; Roney 1992; Tilley 1994:173–200). Mortuary practices, long of great interest to archaeologists, are a growing venue for memory studies (e.g., Barrett 1988; Chesson 2001; Jonker 1995; Kuijt 1996). Some of the most visible commemorative ritual activities revolve around veneration of ancestors (Chang 1983:33–43; McEnany 1995). Many of the authors in this volume deal with commemoration of the dead in some form or another. Humans are not the only recipients of ritual treatment after their passing; in the American Southwest, Walker (1995) interprets the intentional conflagration of structures and the deposition of votive objects just prior to abandonment as evidence for rituals of closure. Cult activities such as feasting (Hamilakis 1999; Prent, this volume; Toll 1985) and votive deposition (Bradley 1990) often have to do with the celebration of memory. Despite the destructive intentions of prehistoric actors who set fire to buildings and tossed bronze objects into the Thames, such activities have left us with intriguing and interpretable archaeological traces.

Narratives, stories or other forms of information about the past, may be transmitted onwards either in oral traditions or as more fixed textual accounts. A number of the authors in this volume are working, to some degree, with the benefit of textual information. The written word, of course, has many alluring qualities: it seems secure and reliable. Yet it is important to bear in mind that texts, especially in the pre-modern societies discussed here, are the work of a certain class of people – normally elite, educated, wealthy, and politically invested – with resulting particular agendas and biases. This undeniable fact, of course, makes archaeological investigation all the more attractive, and essential, for studying the past of the marginalized, the resistant, the non-literate.

Representations and *objects* include such items as paintings, masks, figurines, rock art, and other representational media that often possess commemorative functions. Rock art panels, for example, may depict ancient mythic events while locating them on the landscape (Bradley 1997; Taçon 1999). Human bones may have been treated as commemorative objects in some Neolithic European settings (e.g., Barrett 1988). Objects provide graphic but non-linguistic access to the past (Rowlands 1993:144). Following Kopytoff (1986), objects are acknowledged to have life-histories that may be traced to illuminate the variable constructions of memory (Lillios 1999; Walker 1999). Portable objects lend themselves well to purposes of remembering, as well as forgetting (Lillios, this volume). A frequently cited example of the latter is the destruction of carved *malangan* images in mortuary contexts as part of a process of forgetting (Küchler 1993).

Finally, all of the authors in this volume deal, in one way or another, with commemorative *places*. Places are spaces that have been inscribed with meaning, usually as a result of some past event or attachment. Here, this broad category encompasses monuments, landscapes, natural features, buildings, tombs, trees, obelisks, shrines, mountain peaks, and caves (e.g., Alcock 2001; Ashmore and Knapp 1999; Blake 1998; Bradley 1998, 2000; Brady and Ashmore 1999; Holtorf 1998; Williams 1998).

Place, Memory and Phenomenology

Memory is closely integrated with place in the work of major theorists such as Bachelard (1964), Casey (1987), de Certeau (1984) and Nora (1989). Places, meanings, and memories are intertwined to create what some authors have termed a "sense of place" (e.g., Feld and Basso 1996). A sense of place rests upon, and reconstructs, a history of social engagement with the landscape, and is thus inextricably bound up with remembrance, and with time; its construction is tied into networks of associations and memories through a process Basso (1996:107) calls interanimation. As humans create, modify, and move through a spatial milieu, the mediation between spatial experience and perception reflexively creates, legitimates, and reinforces social relationships and ideas. Influential treatments of these ideas include Bourdieu (1977), Foucault (1977) Giddens (1984), Harvey (1989), Lefebvre (1991), and Soja (1996). The recursive role of space in the production of society has, of course, been explored in a number of disciplines (e.g., Cosgrove 1984; Davis 1990; Duncan and Ley 1993; Morphy 1995; Zukin 1991), not least in archaeology (e.g., Bender 1993; Edmonds 1999; Glassie 1975; Miller 1984; Pearson and Richards 1994; Smith and David 1995).

The experiential nature of place provides one starting point to retrieve social memory; this perhaps becomes especially vital in prehistoric studies. Although many culturally-specific contextual meanings can never be known, a *phenomenological* approach in archaeology such as that espoused by Gosden (1994), Thomas (1996) and Tilley (1994) allows us to think about the ways in which landscapes and built forms were experienced, perceived, and represented by ancient subjects, working from the starting point of a contemporary body in the same space. Place, above all, is a sensual experience, with the body, social identity, and shifting perceptions of society intersecting through daily, lived spatial experiences. Lawrence Durrell captures the way in which memory is embedded in daily, lived encounters with place in the following passage from *The Alexandria Quartet* (1960), in which he describes a character's return to the Egyptian city:

> Alexandria, capital of memory! How long had I been away? . . . Once one had left the semi-circle of the harbour nothing had changed whatsoever. The little tin tram groaned and wriggled along its rusty rails, curving down those familiar streets which spread on either side of me images which were absolute in their fidelity to my memories. The barbers' shops with their fly-nets drawn across the door, tingling with coloured beads: the cafés with their idlers squatting at the tin tables (by El Bab, still the crumbling wall and the very table where we had sat motionless, weighed down by the blue dusk). . . . Walking down with remembered grooves of streets which extended on every side, radiating out like the arms of a starfish from the axis of its founder's tomb. Footfalls echoing in the memory, forgotten scenes and conversations springing up at me from the walls, the café tables, the shuttered rooms with cracked and peeling ceilings. Alexandria, princess and whore . . . I could feel the ambience of the city on me once more, its etiolated beauties spreading their tentacles out to grasp at my sleeve. (Durrell 1960:11, 31–2, 63–4)

Durrell's rich description privileges the visual re-encounter with Alexandria, and certainly visual experiences are key to the experience of place and landscape, from the ashlar masonry of Crete (Prent, this volume) to the dramatic landforms of the American Southwest (Van Dyke, this volume) or Australia (Taçon 1999). However, Thomas (1993) points out that contemporary archaeologists also tend to privilege the visual over other ways – such as smells and tastes – of recognizing and remembering the past. Proust's madeleine is a famous case in point. Attempts are increasingly being made to reconstruct sounds, textures, tastes, and smells from archaeological contexts (e.g., Hamilakis 1999; Houston and Taube 2000; MacGregor 1999; Watson and Keating 1999). Emotions and emotional attachments to particular places are also obviously implicated in the construction of memory, and are increasingly sought by anthropologists and archaeologists (Altman and Low 1992; Strauss and Quinn 1994; Tarlow 1997). In the Durrell quotation above, for example, the character's response to Alexandria is colored by memories of a past love affair. Not surprisingly, emotionally charged places – ranging from the predictable (a tomb, a shrine) to the unexpected (a rock, a tree) – are frequent candidates for commemorative appropriation and transformation.

An Overview of the Volume

If social memory can be traced, if in some instances only faintly, through the media of ritual behavior, texts, representations, and places, what good does that do us? What can we learn from this study of past decisions and developments, allegiances and antagonisms? These questions are probably best answered by demonstration, and we can now turn to a review of the papers presented in this collection. These play out – in very different settings and with very different forms of evidence – the twists and turns of social memory; together, they also offer an instructive overview into current archaeological approaches to tracing commemorative activity and its meanings.

With such a temporally and geographically diverse collection of case studies, the "order" of papers could have taken many, equally legitimate, forms. To one extent or another, all papers engage with the twin, inter-related themes of authority and iden- tity, and the role memory plays in their creation, defense and possible transformation. The question of the definition and protection of elite groups is another widely shared element, particularly in the contributions of Meskell, Prent, and Van Dyke. Certain papers (e.g., Pauketat and Alt; Sinopoli) explore the invention of a past "common" to people of diverse backgrounds, while other appeals to antiquity were more exclu- sionary in nature (e.g., Lillios; Papalexandrou; Prent). Finally, the papers elaborate upon the changing character of social memory, arguing profoundly against any static under- standing of the memorial power of artifact or of place (e.g., Blake; Joyce; Meskell; Papalexandrou).

The full spectrum of media reviewed above – ritual behavior, narrative, represen- tations and objects, and place – is, at one point or another, used in this volume to access social memory in the past. The use of objects, or artifacts, in memorialization is most clearly demonstrated by Lillios and Joyce. In this particular collection, as noted above, the concept of place (taken in its broadest sense) is most frequently invoked to discuss trajectories of commemoration. The concept here includes the veneration of antique sites or features (e.g., Sinopoli; Van Dyke): whether they understood what they were or not (Meskell), whether they were "mere fragments" or not (Papalexandrou).

One basic division, however, does separate those studies which could draw on written evidence or literary testimonia (if only indirectly or partially) and those which could not. To that end, the case studies are organized into two broad groups: first, those working within the framework of literate societies (Sinopoli; Meskell; Papalexandrou; Prent; and Joyce); and then those within genuinely prehistoric con- texts (Lillios; Pauketat and Alt; Van Dyke). This is not to claim that texts "solve" all our problems – far from it – but they unquestionably grant some richness and nuance to the relevant analyses. Organizing the papers in this fashion allows readers, if they wish, to sample that richness in order to illuminate, and complicate, the necessarily "barer bones" of the prehistoric case studies.

This particular line-up moves us forward and backward in time, crisscrossing from the Old World to the New. We begin with Carla Sinopoli's investigation of the multi- faceted construction of legitimacy and authority in Vijayanagara, an early modern state in southern India. Over three centuries, the rulers of Vijayanagara consolidated a wide area containing diverse ethnic, linguistic, religious, and occupational groups. They suc- ceeded, in part, through emphasizing associations with past sacred mythic events, not least the Ramayana epic. In addition, Vijayanagara temple architecture imitated the forms of the older, Chola empire to suggest strains of legitimate continuity. After the decline of Vijayanagara, the ancient state and its monuments themselves became fodder for constructed memories used to validate the governments of subsequent, smaller kingdoms.

The deep palimpsest that is the Egyptian landscape provides fertile terroritory for Lynn Meskell to explore memory at two discrete moments in the past. At Deir el Medina, on the west bank of the Nile, Meskell finds evidence for both short-term commemorative practices and long term memorialization. During the New Kingdom occupation of the site as a worker's village, connections with immediate ancestors and with deceased historical figures are evidenced by house design and contents, by stelae, statuary, and texts, and festivals were settings for a variety of mnemonic activities. In the much later Roman period, Deir el Medina was used as a burial place for elites who sought to associate themselves with an unknown but presumably glorious past – revealing their own particular imagining of the site's prior history.

Architecture is the focus of Amy Papalexandrou's study in Byzantine Greece, where *spolia* – fragments of ancient masonry and tombstones – were included as decorative elements in the facades of medieval buildings. The use of spolia both celebrated and neutralized Greek antiquity, connecting Byzantine administrators with a remarkable (and pagan) Greek past which was now dismantled and under Christian control. Some *spolia* contain inscriptions and are themselves written records, providing intriguing examples of Connerton's inscribed and incorporated memory practices. The incorporation of ancient Greek inscriptions would speak to Greek viewers recognizing (however imperfectly) their own language, while simultaneously excluding those who could not understand.

Mieke Prent examines the relationships between early Iron Age Crete and its Bronze Age past. Monumental Bronze Age ashlar structures found at a number of Cretan sites contain evidence – such as votives, animal bones, and cauldrons – for open-air Iron Age cult activities. Prent contends that members of an Iron Age warrior aristocracy associated themselves with the glories of the past by destroying wealth and engaging in ritual feasting at dramatic Bronze Age locations. Some of these activities took place in harbor sites, where the participation of foreign visitors may have added to the prestigious nature of the ritual events.

Rosemary Joyce begins an investigation into memory among the Classic Maya using contemporary psychological insights that parallel and reference the commemorative/embodied memory distinction made by Connerton (1989). She focuses on objects such as ear spools that were inscribed with text, thereby linking bodily practices with histories. These inscribed objects, visible only to certain individuals at certain times, would have cued implicit memories among restricted social groups over generations. In addition, the circulation of curated or rediscovered objects contributed to the creation of disjunctive, generalized connections to the distant past.

Although our prehistoric authors lack the rich detail provided by texts, they successfully argue, using artifacts and architecture, that memory was integral to the construction of authority and identity in prehistoric contexts. Katina Lillios investigates engraved slate plaques found in burials in Neolithic and Copper Age Iberia between 3,000 and 2,500 BC. The plaques, she argues, were used as mnemonic devices to transmit genealogical information. The plaques appear to have reinforced social differences, as not everyone was memorialized in this way, and plaques were placed out of public view inside tombs. Reuse and destruction of some plaques over time suggests changes in social relationships and in the uses of memory.

Tim Pauketat and Susan Alt examine the prehistoric construction of earthworks, such as Cahokia, in the Mississippi valley of the southeastern United States between 1,000 and 1,200 AD. Large four-sided and pyramidal mounds generally have been held to represent shared belief systems within a context of social hierarchy. However, the microscale evidence for construction suggests these mounds were created in multiple series of building episodes by disparate peoples with diverse interests. The Mississippian mounds represent the negotiation of identity as well as authority, with mound making, in part, an appeal to a real or imagined common past.

Ruth Van Dyke investigates the role of memory in fashioning the large-scale masonry architecture at Chacoan sites in the American Southwest between 850 and 1,150 AD. Here, landscape and architecture referenced the past as one way to legitimate social authority and to create a sense of community identity. The great kiva, a built form used hundreds of years before the Chacoan era, was revived and formally incorporated within new buildings. Artificial trash mounds suggested lengthy occupations for new buildings, and road segments tied old and new structures inextricably together.

We conclude the volume with a cautionary tale followed by commentary. Emma Blake's study of the Byzantine reuse of Neolithic hypogea should be heeded by archaeologists concerned with the interpretation of social memory. At Pantalica on Sicily, it would seem logical to assume that Byzantine residents moved into Bronze and Iron Age rock-cut tombs to consolidate communal identity or to evoke connections with a respected past. After a careful examination of this phenomenon, however, Blake concludes that the Byzantine occupants – far from aligning themselves with the past – were actually moving in step with contemporary, pan-Mediterranean trends. At Pantalica, Blake asserts, "retreating into the embodiment of the local past was in fact a gesture of cosmopolitanism." Finally, at the end of this odyssey, we offer commentary by Richard Bradley, a pioneering influence in the study of "the past in the past." Bradley recaps the volume and returns us safely to the twentieth century and the generative musings of Marcel Proust.

This wide-ranging collection unquestionably will serve to raise still more questions about the archaeological study of memory, while leaving others yet unanswered. Not all volume contributors would agree with the concepts we have outlined in this introduction. All are united, however, by the contention that investigations into memory are a provocative and necessary contribution to contemporary archaeological dialogue. The archaeological study of memory is in its relatively early days; this volume is dedicated to airing out both its undoubted problems and its infinite possibilities.

References Cited

Alcock, S. E. 2001: The reconfiguration of memory in the eastern Roman empire. In *Empires: Perspectives from Archaeology and History*, S. E. Alcock, T. N. D'Altroy, K. D. Morrison and C. M. Sinopoli. Cambridge: Cambridge University Press, pp. 323–50.

Alcock, S. E. 2002: *Archaeologies of the Greek Past: Landscape, Monuments and Memories.* Cambridge: Cambridge University Press.

Alonso, A. M. 1988: The effects of truth: re-presentations of the past and the imagining of community. *Journal of Historical Sociology* 1, pp. 33–57.

Altman, I. and Low, S. M. (eds.) 1992: *Place Attachment.* New York: Plenum Press.

Arnold, B. 1990: The past as propaganda: totalitarian archaeology in Nazi Germany. *Antiquity* 64, pp. 464–78.

Ashmore, W. and Knapp, B. (eds.) 1999: *Archaeologies of Landscape: Contemporary Perspectives.* Oxford: Blackwell.

Bachelard, G. 1964: *The Poetics of Space.* Boston: Beacon Press.

Baer, U. 2000: To give memory a place: Holocaust photography and the landscape tradition. *Representations* 69, pp. 38–62.

Barclay, A. and Harding, J. (eds.) 1999: *Pathways and Ceremonies: The Cursus Monuments of Britain and Ireland. Neolithic Studies Group Seminar Papers* 4. Oxford: Oxbow Books.

Barrett, J. C. 1988: The living, the dead, and the ancestors: Neolithic and Early Bronze Age mortuary practices. In *The Archaeology of Context in the Neolithic and Early Bronze Age: Recent Trends*, ed. J. Barrett and I. Kinnes. Sheffield: Sheffield Department of Archaeology and Pre-history, pp. 30–41.

Barrett, J. C. 1994: Moving beyond the monuments: paths and peoples in the Neolithic landscapes of the "Peak District." *Northern Archaeology* 13.

Basso, K. H. 1996: *Wisdom Sits in Places: Landscape and Language among the Western Apache.* Albuquerque: University of New Mexico Press.

Bender, B. 1998: *Stonehenge: Making Space.* Oxford: Berg.

Bender, B. (ed.) 1993: *Landscape: Politics and Perspectives.* Oxford: Berg.

Blake, E. 1998: Sardinia's Nuraghi: Four millennia of becoming. *World Archaeology*, 30(1), pp. 59–71.

Blight, D. 2001: *Race and Reunion: The Civil War in American Memory.* Cambridge, Mass.: Belknap Press of Harvard University.

Bloch, M. 1985: From cognition to ideology. In *Power and Knowledge*, ed. R. Fardon. Edinburgh: Scottish Academic Press, pp. 21–48.

Bourdieu, P. 1977: *Outline of a Theory of Practice.* Cambridge: Cambridge University Press.

Bradley, R. 1990: *The Passage of Arms: An Archaeological Analysis of Prehistoric Hoards and Votive Deposits.* Cambridge: Cambridge University Press.

Bradley, R. 1997: *Rock Art and the Prehistory of Atlantic Europe: Signing the Land.* London and New York: Routledge.

Bradley, R. 1998: *The Significance of Monuments: On the Shaping of Human Experience in Neolithic and Bronze Age Europe.* London and New York: Routledge.

Bradley, R. 2000: *An Archaeology of Natural Places.* London and New York: Routledge.

Bradley, R. and Williams, H. (eds.) 1998: The Past in the Past. *World Archaeology*, 30(1).

Brady, J. E. and Ashmore, W. 1999: Mountains, caves, water: ideational landscapes of the ancient Maya. In *Archaeologies of Landscape*, ed. W. Ashmore and A. B. Knapp. Oxford: Blackwell, pp. 124–45.

Casey, E. S. 1987: *Remembering: A Phenomenological Study.* Bloomington: Indiana University Press.

Chang, K. C. 1983: *Art, Myth, and Ritual: The Path to Political Authority in Ancient China.* Cambridge, Mass.: Harvard University Press.

Chesson, M. (ed.) 2001: *Social Memory, Identity, and Death: Anthropological Perspectives on Mortuary Rituals.* Archeological Papers of the American Anthropological Association No. 10. Arlington, Virginia: American Anthropological Association.

Connerton, P. 1989: *How Societies Remember.* Cambridge: Cambridge University Press.

Cosgrove, D. 1984: *Social Formation and Symbolic Landscape*. Totowa, N. J.: Barnes and Noble.

Crossland, Z. 2000: Buried lives: forensic archaeology and the disappeared in Argentina. *Archaeological Dialogues* 7, pp. 146–59.

Davis, M. 1990: *City of Quartz: Excavating the Future in Los Angeles*. London and New York: Verso.

Davis, N. Z. and Starn, R. 1989: Introduction (Special Issue: Memory and Counter-Memory). *Representations* 26, pp. 1–6.

De Certeau, M. 1984: *The Practice of Everyday Life*, trans. S. Rendall. Berkeley and Los Angeles: University of California Press.

Dietler, M. 1998: A tale of three sites: the monumentalization of Celtic oppida and the politics of collective memory and identity. *World Archaeology* 30(1), pp. 72–89.

Duncan, J. and Ley, D. 1993: *Place/Culture/Representation*. London and New York: Routledge.

Durrell, L. 1960: *Clea*. New York: Dutton and Company.

Echo-Hawk, R. 2000: Ancient history in the New World: integrating oral traditions and the archaeological record in deep time. *American Antiquity* 65, pp. 267–90.

Edmonds, M. 1999: *Ancestral Geographies of the Neolithic: Landscapes, Monuments, and Memory*. London and New York: Routledge.

Feld, S. and Basso, K. H. (eds.) 1996: *Senses of Place*. Santa Fe: School of American Research Press.

Foucault, M. 1977: *Discipline and Punish: The Birth of the Prison*, trans. A. Sheridan. New York: Vintage Books, Random House.

Freud, S. 1966–74: Remembering, repeating, and working-through [1914]. In *The Complete Psychological Works*, Volume 12. London: Hogarth Press and the Institute of Psycho-Analysis, pp. 147–66.

Gero, J. M. and Root, D. 1990: Public presentations and private concerns: archaeology in the pages of *National Geographic*. In *The Politics of the Past*, ed. P. Gathercole and D. Lowenthal. London: Unwin-Hyman, pp. 19–37.

Giddens, A. 1984: *The Constitution of Society: Outline of the Theory of Structuration*. Berkeley and Los Angeles: University of California Press.

Glassie, H. 1975: *Folk Housing in Middle Virginia*. Knoxville: University of Tennessee Press.

Gosden, C. 1994: *Social Being and Time*. Oxford: Blackwell.

Gosden, C. and Lock, G. 1998: Prehistoric histories. *World Archaeology* 30(1), pp. 2–12.

Halbwachs, M. 1975 [1925]: *Les Cadres sociaux de la mémoire*. New York: Arno.

Halbwachs, M. 1992 [1950]: *On Collective Memory*, ed. and trans. L. A. Coser. Chicago: University of Chicago Press.

Hamilakis, Y. 1999: Food technologies/technologies of the body: the social context of wine and oil production and consumption in Bronze Age Crete. *World Archaeology* 31, pp. 38–54.

Harvey, D. 1989: *The Condition of Postmodernity*. Oxford: Blackwell.

Hobsbawm, E. J. and Ranger, T. (eds.) 1983: *The Invention of Tradition*. Cambridge: Cambridge University Press.

Holtorf, C. J. 1998: The life-histories of megaliths in Mecklenburg-Vorpommern (Germany). *World Archaeology* 30(1), pp. 23–38.

Houston, S. and Taube, K. 2000: An archaeology of the senses: perception and cultural expression in ancient Mesoamerica. *Cambridge Archaeological Journal* 10, pp. 261–94.

Hutton, P. 1993: *History as an Art of Memory*. Hanover: University of Vermont Press.

Jonker, G. 1995: *The Topography of Remembrance: The Dead, Tradition and Collective Memory in Mesopotamia*. Leiden: E. J. Brill.

Joyce, R. A. and Gillespie, S. D. (eds.) 2000: *Beyond Kinship: Social and Material Reproduction in House Societies*. Philadelphia: University of Pennsylvania Press, pp. 189–212.

Kopytoff, I. 1986: The cultural biography of things: commoditization as process. In *The Social Life of Things: Commodities in Cultural Perspective*, ed. A. Appadurai. Cambridge: Cambridge University Press, pp. 65–91.

Kuijt, I. 1996: Negotiating equality through ritual: a consideration of Late Natufian and Pre-pottery Neolithic A Period mortuary practices. *Journal of Anthropological Archaeology* 15, pp. 313–36.

Küchler, S. 1993: Landscape as memory: the mapping of process and its representation in a Melanesian society. In *Landscape: Politics and Perspectives*, ed. B. Bender. Oxford and Providence: Berg, pp. 85–106.

Laqueur, T. W. 2000: Introduction. *Representations* 69, pp. 1–8.

Lefebvre, H. 1991: *The Production of Space*, trans. D. Nicholson-Smith. Oxford: Blackwell.

Le Goff, J. 1992: *History and Memory*, trans. S. Rendall and E. Clamen. New York: Columbia University Press.

Lillios, K. 1999: Objects of memory: the ethnography and archaeology of heirlooms. *Journal of Archaeological Method and Theory* 6, pp. 235–62.

Linenthal, E. G. and Engelhardt, T. (eds.) 1996: *History Wars: The Enola Gay and Other Battles for the American Past*. New York: Metropolitan Books/Henry Holt and Co.

Lowenthal, D. 1985: *The Past is a Foreign Country*. Cambridge: Cambridge University Press.

MacGregor, G. 1999: Making sense of the past in the present: a sensory analysis of carved stone balls. *World Archaeology*, 31, pp. 258–71.

Manning, S. W. 1998: Changing pasts and socio-political cognition in Late Bronze Age Cyprus. *World Archaeology* 30(1), pp. 38–58.

Mason, R. J. 2000: Archaeology and Native North American oral traditions. *American Antiquity* 65, pp. 239–66.

McEnany, P. A. 1995: *Living with the Ancestors: Kinship and Kingship in Ancient Maya Society*. Austin: University of Texas Press.

Meskell, L. M. 2002: *Private Life in New Kingdom Egypt*. Princeton: Princeton University Press.

Miller, D. 1984: Modernism and suburbia as material ideology. In *Ideology, Power, and Prehistory*, ed. D. Miller and C. Tilley. Cambridge: Cambridge University Press, pp. 37–49.

Morphy, H. 1995: Landscape and the reproduction of the ancestral past. In *The Anthropology of Landscape*, ed. E. Hirsch and M. O'Hanlon. Oxford: Clarendon, pp. 184–209.

Nora, P. 1989: Between memory and history: les lieux de mémoire. *Representations* 26, pp. 7–25.

Pearson, M. P. and Richards, C. (eds.) 1994: *Architecture and Order*. London and New York: Routledge.

Proust, M. 1983 [1913–27]: *Remembrance of Things Past*, trans. C. K. Scott-Moncrieff and Terence Kilmartin, 3 vols. New York: Penguin.

Roney, J. R. 1992: Prehistoric roads and regional integration in the Chacoan System. In *Anasazi Regional Organization and the Chaco System*, ed. D. E. Doyel. Albuquerque: Maxwell Museum of Anthropology Anthropological Papers 5, pp. 123–32.

Rowlands, M. 1993: The role of memory in the transmission of culture. *World Archaeology* 25(2), pp. 141–51.

Sahlins, M. 1985: *Islands of History*. Chicago: Chicago University Press.

Schama, S. 1996: *Landscape and Memory*. New York: Vintage Books.

Schnapp, A. 1997: *The Discovery of the Past*. New York: Harry N. Abrams.

Smith, A. T. and David, N. 1995: The production of space and the house of Xidi Sukur. *Current Anthropology* 36, pp. 441–71.

Soja, E. W. 1996: *Thirdspace*. Oxford: Blackwell.

Strauss, C. and Quinn, N. 1994: A cognitive/cultural anthropology. In *Assessing Cultural Anthropology*, ed. R. Borofsky. New York: McGraw-Hill, pp. 284–97.

Taçon, P. S. 1999: Identifying ancient sacred landscapes in Australia: from physical to social. In *Archaeologies of Landscape: Contemporary Perspectives*, ed. W. Ashmore and A. B. Knapp. Oxford: Blackwell, pp. 33–57.

Tarlow, S. 1997: An archaeology of remembering: death, bereavement and the First World War. *Cambridge Archaeological Journal* 7, pp. 105–21.

Thomas, J. 1993: The politics of vision and the archaeologies of landscape. In *Landscape: Politics and Perspectives*, ed. B. Bender. Oxford and Providence: Berg, pp. 19–48.

Thomas, J. 1996: *Time, Culture, and Identity*. London: Routledge.

Tilley, C. 1994: *A Phenomenology of Landscape*. Oxford and Providence: Berg.

Toll, H. W. 1985: *Pottery, Production, and the Chacoan Anasazi System*. Ph.D. dissertation (University of Colorado). Ann Arbor, Michigan: University Microfilms.

Trigger, B. G. 1984: Alternative archaeologies: nationalist, colonialist, imperialist. *Man* 19, pp. 355–70.

Walker, W. H. 1995: Ceremonial trash? In *Expanding Archaeology*, ed. J. M. Skibo, W. H. Walker and A. E. Nielson. Salt Lake City: University of Utah Press, pp. 67–79.

Walker, W. H. 1999: Ritual life histories and the afterlives of people and things. *Journal of the Southwest* 41, pp. 383–405.

Watson, A. and Keating, D. 1999: Architecture and sound: an acoustic analysis of megalithic monuments in prehistoric Britain. *Antiquity* 73, pp. 325–36.

Williams, H. 1998: Monuments and the past in early Anglo-Saxon England. *World Archaeology* 30(1), pp. 90–108.

Zerubavel, Y. 1995: *Recovered Roots: Collective Memory and the Making of Israeli National Tradition*. Chicago: University of Chicago Press.

Zukin, S. 1991: *Landscapes of Power: From Detroit to Disney World*. Berkeley and Los Angeles: University of California Press.

Part I
Memory Studies with Access to Texts

2

Echoes of Empire: Vijayanagara and Historical Memory, Vijayanagara as Historical Memory

Carla M. Sinopoli

Introduction

In the early fourteenth century AD southern India was in political turmoil. The sources for this disarray lay, in large part, in the late thirteenth to early fourteenth century incursions of the northern Sultanate of Delhi, as well as in various internal crises. I will not recount the complex political histories of the South Indian Kakatiya, Chola, Hoysala, Pallava, Yadava, Kampili, and Chalukya of Kalyani states – all powerful regional polities of the tenth through early-fourteenth centuries (see Stein 1998). Suffice it to say that by the 1330s, all of these large territorial polities had collapsed.

Emerging from this cataclysmic period was a small military state based at a sacred site on the southern banks of the Tungabhadra River in what is now central Karnataka. The founders of this state, brothers of the Sangama family, proved to be effective military and political leaders, and within a few short decades had consolidated control over a large area of the peninsula south of the Tungabhadra. The empire they ruled was named after their capital: Vijayanagara, Sanskrit for "City of Victory." The Vijayanagara empire dominated Southern India for three centuries under four successive dynasties until its collapse in the late seventeenth century.

The territories claimed by Vijayanagara's rulers were vast (ca. 360,000 sq. km) and diverse, encompassing areas that had been ruled by all of the pre-Vijayanagara states mentioned above. Environmentally, imperial territories included the rich river valleys and seacoasts of the southeastern peninsula, the semi-arid upland zone surrounding the imperial capital, and the mountainous forested zones of the western coastal ranges

My thanks to Sue Alcock and Ruth Van Dyke for organizing the conference session from which this volume derived. My archaeological research at Vijayanagara could not have taken place without the support of the American Institute of Indian Studies, the Archaeological Survey of India, and the Karnataka Department of Archaeology and Museums. My profound gratitude to each of these organizations, and to my collaborator Kathleen Morrison, and my collaborators and mentors John Fritz and George Michell, whose insights from more than two decades of Vijayanagara scholarship provide much of the data for this paper.

– sources of pepper, cardamom, and other spices essential for international commerce. Culturally, the region was even more complex. The empire's subjects (perhaps as many as 25 million people; Stein 1989) spoke the three major Dravidian languages of Kannada, Telugu, and Tamil, as well as other less common languages. They were Jains, Muslims, and Hindus; the latter grouped into numerous sects. Other "tribal" communities followed various local religious traditions. Vijayanagara's subjects also included diverse occupational communities, organized into numerous highly specialized hereditary castes or subcastes. Connections among these various localized occupational communities were forged through multiple higher order social and territorial associations. Such groups included merchant organizations and regional administrative councils, as well as various affiliations of low-status craft producers and agriculturalists (e.g., the right-hand and left-hand castes of Tamil Nadu).

The scale of Vijayanagara was far larger than that of any of the states that preceded it. Even the most expansive of the earlier polities were predominantly based within a single linguistic zone and in a more or less unitary ecological regime. The exception to this, the ninth- to thirteenth-century Chola empire of Tamil Nadu, did at times extend its rule over larger territories, but these did not approach the scale of Vijayanagara. As Vijayanagara territories expanded, through a program of military conquest and incorporation, the empire's rulers faced enormous challenges in consolidating their power and forging their state. In this paper, I employ architectural evidence and information on the Vijayanagara urban plan to explore one aspect of the construction of a Vijayanagara imperial identity – the acknowledgment and use of the past, and its denial. The relevant pasts that Vijayanagara's rulers remembered included both the deep past of the ancient Hindu epics and the more recent pasts of the states and empires that preceded Vijayanagara's ascendancy.

My focus for this exercise is largely on the imperial center and on imperial constructions, rather than on the peripheries of, or acts of resistance to, the empire. This is not because I do not think the latter are important or interesting: quite the contrary. But given the nature of present archaeological evidence, which comes primarily from the Vijayanagara capital and its immediate hinterland, and the elite-centered historiography of South India, it is difficult at this point to consider such issues (though see Morrison 2001 for an important exception). In some sense then, this paper is more about elite manipulation of historical knowledge, rather than about social responses to elite actions that may have been shaped by collective, or selective, memory. Nonetheless, the reasons that these manipulations were successful (at least for a time and among some of the empire's diverse communities) no doubt lie in the fact that the relevant memories that elites called upon had, or could be made to have, broad resonance among numerous South Indian communities. An additional factor, I would argue, for their success, lay in the fact that multiple, indeed contradictory, claims concerning Vijayanagara legitimacy often co-existed, in ways that allowed Vijayanagara's rulers to stake different positions in different contexts and to appeal to a broad array of social groups and political actors.

As I will elaborate upon below, Vijayanagara's elites creatively employed the sacred, mythic past associated with the region where their first capital lay, as well as sources of legitimacy derived from prior South Indian states, particularly the Chola empire of the productive riverine and coastal zones of the southeast peninsula. Yet simultaneously, in political and military domains, Vijayanagara practices were based on different, upland political traditions, and on creative borrowing and transformations of beliefs and practices of the Deccani Sultanates to their north (states that emerged in the wake of the withdrawal of the Delhi Sultanate). After I discuss the balance between remembered and new sources of legitimacy during the Vijayanagara period, I turn to the period following Vijayanagara's collapse, when the empire itself became an object of memory – representing past grandeur, a source of political legitimacy, and more recently, a focus of nationalist discourses.

Vijayanagara and Historical Memory

The Vijayanagara empire has often been viewed by scholars as marking a significant break from earlier political and cultural traditions of South India (e.g., Nilakanta Sastri 1966; Stein 1985) – and certainly this interpretation has considerable merit. Vijayanagara's armies employed new forms of cavalry-based warfare to build South India's largest expansionist polity; and the Vijayanagara period was a time of significant political and economic restructuring. More recent scholarship, however, has sought to explore both changes and continuities in a more nuanced way – to consider Vijayanagara state-building as both acknowledging the past and creatively transforming its present. Here, I want to consider under what contexts these two processes co-occurred in processes of state-building and imperial legitimation. Both of these patterns are evident in the architecture and layout of the imperial capital.

The Vijayanagara imperial capital

The city of Vijayanagara, the empire's first and longest-lived capital, is located on the southern banks of the Tungabhadra River in the modern state of Karnataka. This semi-arid region was comparatively densely settled during the much earlier South Indian Neolithic (third millennium BC) and early historic (ca. 500 BC–300 AD) periods, and pre-Vijayanagara temples and forts of the tenth–thirteenth centuries AD to the north of the river attest to some occupation in that period.

We do not at present have good estimates for local population densities immediately prior to the founding of Vijayanagara, but ten thousand people is not an unreasonable upper limit. With the formation of the empire, populations grew rapidly and dramatically, as individuals and entire communities flowed into the capital from throughout peninsular India. By the early 1400s, the city had approximately 100,000 inhabitants; by the early 1500s, the population had likely reached well over a quarter million and the city core extended over nearly 30 square kilometers (see figure 2.1). The fortified suburban zone of the capital covered more than 600 square kilometers during the sixteenth century, and it contained numerous settlements and a range of other features amid areas of agricultural and craft production (see Morrison 1995; Sinopoli and Morrison in press).

Shortly after reaching its greatest extent, Vijayanagara was abruptly abandoned. In 1565 AD, the combined forces of three of the northern sultanates defeated Vijayanagara's armies. The city's inhabitants fled and the site was briefly occupied by the

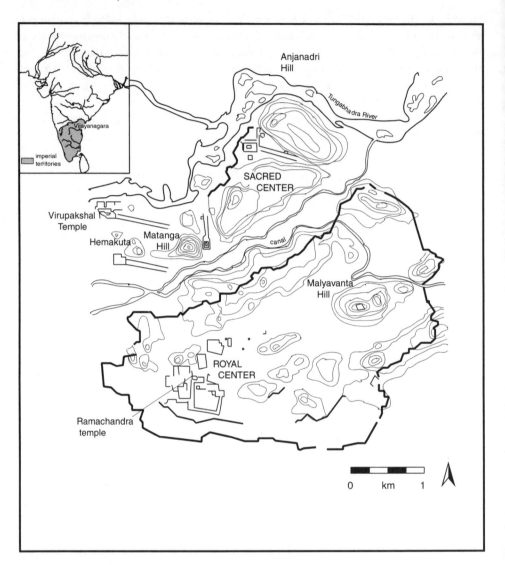

Map 2.1   Vijayanagara urban core and key locations in the region's sacred geography

victorious forces, as the Vijayanagara court shifted successively southwards – to Penukonda, Chandragiri, and finally to Vellore. Here I focus primarily on the empire's first and largest capital.

Sacred geographies

No doubt a range of factors contributed to the location of the first Vijayanagara capital. These included the fact that as the Vijayanagara state was forming in the 1330s and 1340s, this area was, to a significant extent, a political "no-man's land," not under the protection of any strong polity. Further, a bend in the Tungabhadra River provided a small arable zone in this otherwise semi-arid and rugged landscape (Morrison 1995). The region was also highly defensible; the high granitic outcrops of the southern extent of the Deccan Plateau both impeded movement and provided abundant raw materials for the construction of massive fortifications.

Along with the above-mentioned strategic reasons, it is also significant that the sparsely populated locale where Vijayanagara was founded was a place sacred to worshippers of both Shiva and Vishnu. These sacred associations were written on the landscape of the Vijayanagara region, inscribed in holy hills, the river, and other natural and constructed features, the latter including a Neolithic ash mound of the third millennium BC (believed to be the cremation ground of Vali, see below) and pre-Vijayanagara temples. These features provided a powerful source of memory and legitimation with which Vijayanagara's Sangama and subsequent kings sought to affiliate themselves.

As noted earlier, several small pre-Vijayanagara temples existed in the region where Vijayanagara was later founded. Most important of these was a complex of shrines dedicated to Virupaksha, a manifestation of the major Hindu deity Shiva. The earliest documented temple to Virupaksha, the "lord of Hemakuta," dates to the ninth–tenth centuries. Later shrines were added in the twelfth century AD, by which time the male Virupaksha was already linked with the goddess Pampa. The Virupaksha temple was expanded throughout the subsequent Vijayanagara period and remains today a major center of worship and pilgrimage.

By the Vijayanagara period, Virupaksha had become far more important in local religious traditions than his consort. Yet Pampa is the oldest documented deity of the area. The earliest inscriptional references to Pampa can be traced to the seventh century AD, and she was likely important long before then. Pampa appears to have been a local, aquatic goddess, associated with the Tungabhadra River, and with the power of a particular eponymous place on the river (modern Hampi). Verghese (1995:16–17) argues that this local, perhaps even "pre-Hindu," folk goddess, became Sanskritized, or brought into Hindu orthodoxy, during the pre-Vijayanagara period through her marriage to Shiva (Virupaksha). Following this, her stature diminished as Virupaksha's rose, but (and I will return to this below), Pampa nonetheless remained important in local beliefs.

The second major sacred association of the Vijayanagara region lay with Vishnu, the other major deity of orthodox Hinduism, in his form (avatar) as the god-king Rama, whose adventures are recounted in the Ramayana epic. The relevant portion of this tale concerns Rama's exploits and travels as he tried to rescue his wife Sita, who had been kidnapped by the ten-headed demon Ravana and taken to (Sri) Lanka. In his quest, Rama and his brother Lakshmana came to Kishkinda, kingdom of the monkey deities. On top of a hill called Matanga he encountered Sugriva, the dispossessed lord of the monkey kingdom. Through his valor, Rama helped Sugriva to overthrow his rebellious brother Vali. After Sugriva's enthronement, his liege Hanuman traveled to Lanka and rescued Sita while Rama awaited her return atop Malyavanta Hill.

The recognition of the Vijayanagara region as Kishkinda is not as ancient as its association with the river goddess Pampa. Nor are there any pre-Vijayanagara period Ramayana temples or images at the site. However, Verghese (1995) has suggested that a small number of textual sources indicate that the Ramayana association had begun as early as the eleventh century. Nonetheless, it is not until the late fourteenth- early fifteenth-century Vijayanagara "building boom" in the region that these associations were made materially manifest and were mapped onto the landscape through the construction of temples and countless sacred images, as well as in urban plan. Key structures, routes of movement, and urban layout were linked with features of the sacred landscape, including Matanga Hill, Malyavanta Hill, Anjanadri (Hanuman's birthplace), and other sites linked with Ramayana events (Fritz 1986, 1992; Fritz and Michell 1989; see figure 2.1).

Most striking of the structures associated with the Ramayana is an early fifteenth-century temple dedicated to Rama. This temple lies due south of Matanga Hill in the heart of the royal administrative and palace zone of the capital, which Fritz, Michell, and Nagaraja Rao (1985) have termed the "Royal Center" (see figure 2.1). The Ramachandra temple was constructed relatively early in the empire's history, during the reign of a king of the first, Sangama, dynasty (the temple does not have a foundation inscription, but is believed to date to the reign of Devaraya I, 1406–1422 AD; Michell 1992a:17–20). It is a comparatively small temple complex, consisting of a walled enclosure containing the central temple, as well as subsidiary shrines, wells, and columned pavilions. The events of the Ramayana are depicted in a series of narrative friezes on the structure's exterior and on the interior compound wall (see plate 2.1).

It is important to point out that the kings who were responsible for the construction of this temple were not primarily devotees of Rama. Instead, their tutelary deity was the Shaivite deity Virupaksha, discussed above. Even before the Sangamas sponsored the construction of a Rama temple, they had constructed a temple to Virupaksha in the Vijayanagara royal center. So why build a temple to Rama at all? And why place it at such a critical location in the city – at the nexus of key administrative and royal structures and the focus of multiple transport and processional routes?

As noted, no foundational inscription occurs on the temple. However, a fascinating, albeit brief, inscription on its principal shrine helps to date the shrine and to link the temple with the non-Ramayana dimensions of the sacred landscape. The Sanskrit inscription reads

> As Vani blesses king Bhoka, Tripuramba king Vatsaraja, and Kali king Vikramarka, so does Pampa now bless Devaraya. (trans. Rajasekhara 1992:27)

In this text, the Vijayanagara king Devaraya is explicitly linked with three great kings of the distant past, each of whom was protected by a powerful goddess. Like those earlier rulers, Devaraya has a protector – Pampa, the ancient goddess of this place.

The Shaivite affiliations of the Sangama kings were well established. Through affiliating themselves with the expanding Rama cult, the Sangama rulers broadened their ties to encompass the powerful Vaishnava sects of the period, and associated

Plate 2.1   The Ramachandra temple

themselves with a particular god – one linked with the land and with potent values concerning kingship and royal authority. However, by building a temple to Rama the Sangama kings did not disavow their prior loyalties. Indeed, the reference to Pampa in the above mentioned inscription demonstrates that these ties continued to be emphasized even as Vijayanagara's rulers added a new strand in their web of connections to the landscape, to the people they sought to rule, and to the sacred past. Construction of the Rama temple was an act of addition rather than replacement.

(a)
(b)

Plate 2.2 a and b Hanuman sculpture in Vijayanagara metropolitan region. Image 2.2a is a finely wrought image, while 2.2b is a more folksy representation, with distorted proportions (the pigment is recent, indicating that this Vijayanagara period image is currently in worship)

The increasing importance of the Ramayana and the expanded recognition of the Vijayanagara area as Kishkinda were not restricted to the political elite. Instead, this appears to have been a widespread phenomenon of the period. From the fourteenth through sixteenth centuries, hundreds (probably thousands) of images of Hanuman were carved on boulders and stone slabs throughout the Vijayanagara urban and sub-urban landscape. Representations of Hanuman significantly outnumber those of any other single deity at Vijayanagara and in its metropolitan region. Hanuman images occur in a broad array of contexts – along roads, near wells and agricultural features, and in countless small shrines in towns, villages, and rural settlements. These images vary considerably in artistic quality from finely wrought sculptures that follow classical conventions and proportions (e.g., plate 2.2a) to more "folksy" images carved by less skilled artisans (e.g., plate 2.2b). The extent to which the Vijayanagara kings encouraged the expansion of the Kishkinda cult in the capital is unknown, but it does seem clear that the explicit linking of the ruler with Rama, through the construction of the Ramachandra temple, was a deliberate act that had important consequences in legitimating their rule.

Temple architecture

The sacred geographies of the Vijayanagara region discussed above served to assert connections between the Vijayanagara throne, the imperial capital, and the territories of the gods. In this section, I continue my focus on the religious realm, but from a somewhat different perspective. Rather than consider the *content* of Vijayanagara temples in terms of the deities worshipped, I address the *form* of temples, and how Vijayanagara sacred architecture provided an important context for the recognition and reconfiguration of the past through the creation of a distinctive imperial architectural style.

As noted earlier, a number of small temples in the Vijayanagara region date to the pre-imperial period, from the ninth–tenth through early fourteenth centuries. These temples are typically relatively small and simple, with pyramidal stone towers and simple unadorned exteriors. In form and construction, they belong to local architectural traditions of the inland and upland areas of the peninsula. The earliest Vijayanagara temples of the mid- to late fourteenth century also adhere to this tradition. No radical changes in temple architecture corresponded with the initial founding of the city and empire; instead, architectural referents continued to be to local antecedents and traditions.

As Vijayanagara hegemony and claims to imperial status expanded beyond their upland core in the late fourteenth and early fifteenth centuries, a marked change occurred in both the scale and the style of temples. The result was a new and distinctive form of sacred architecture that spread across the empire and became increasingly elaborated over time. Architectural historian George Michell (1994:188) has described Vijayanagara imperial temple architecture as "revivalist," specifically, as imitating the architecture of the Chola empire, whose heartland lay in the fertile river valleys of the southeast coast. The Ramachandra temple (plate 2.1, and above) is among the earliest of the revivalist temples at Vijayanagara and its construction likely involved the importation of architects and master builders from Tamil-speaking regions to the imperial capital (Michell 1994:192). Over the next century, this revivalist style spread across imperial territories, producing a uniform and recognizable Vijayanagara temple style. Vijayanagara temples also increased in physical scale over time. By the sixteenth century, temple gateways, or *gopura*, towered over surrounding settlements, creating a distinctive and highly visible feature that marked the presence of the gods and their royal benefactors (see plate 2.3).

Over the last decade, several historians of Vijayanagara (e.g., Stein 1989; Talbot n.d.) have argued that Vijayanagara political and economic forms are best understood as having evolved out of upland Telugu and Kannada traditions of state organization. This perspective stands in marked contrast to traditional understandings of Vijayanagara, which sought Chola roots for Vijayanagara practices (e.g., Nilakanta Sastri 1966; Stein 1980). If these more recent arguments are correct, and I believe they are, why then did temple architecture in particular draw on a distant southern tradition that lay hundreds of kilometers and several centuries removed from Vijayanagara, especially as other forms of complex and sculpturally elaborate temple architecture lay somewhat nearer to hand in Kannada- and Telugu-speaking zones that comprised the core of the empire?

Michell views the development of Vijayanagara revivalist temple style as the result of a deliberate strategy by the imperial rulers to make imperial claims. This was accomplished in two ways. First, adopting the style of an earlier empire allowed Vijayanagara's kings to call upon memories of past (Chola) grandeur to portray a

Plate 2.3   Sixteenth century temple gopuram (Kalahasti, Tamil Nadu)

message of continuity and legitimacy. Second, the style adopted was that of a physically *distant* empire in preference to more proximate available alternatives. Given the
wide-ranging polity that the Sangama kings were attempting to form, this emphasis
on distance may have been part of a deliberate attempt to make a claim to universal
status as rulers of the entire south. The result was a "temple style that would give
expression to their imperial ambitions" (Michell 1994:195). In the sacred realm, then,
the new Vijayanagara architectural style was grounded in the past.

New architectural forms and new forms of power

Reference to the Hindu and South Indian past was, however, not the only architectural mode through which Vijayanagara's rulers expressed their visions of empire.
While temple architecture drew on historical knowledge and contexts, Vijayanagara
administrative or "courtly" architecture expressed very different kinds of relations and
political ideologies, based in the present rather than in memory. And while temple
architecture involved the relations of political authority to sacred authority, Vijayanagara courtly architecture was mainly about the political; it was as Michell (1992b:168)
described, "a means of defining the king's world."

The world of a Vijayanagara ruler was a large one. It included the polities and
peoples of the south who had been variously incorporated into the empire. It also

included other South Asian states and empires: particularly the five Deccani Sultanates to Vijayanagara's north and the large Hindu Gajapati state in Orissa, to its northeast. These polities were Vijayanagara's major enemies, and also its peers, and the relations among these states included warfare, trade, and diplomacy. Vijayanagara was also part of an international world; maritime commerce linked South India with East and Southeast Asia, the Middle East, and by the sixteenth century, directly with Europe.

Like temple architecture, Vijayanagara courtly architecture also entailed borrowing from other traditions. But here the references were not to the distant past, but to the newly configured political landscape and to new conceptions of kingship and authority that had emerged in the wake of the withdrawal of the Delhi Sultanate from the peninsula. As a result, the Vijayanagara king was a participant in a much broader political sphere than rulers of prior South Indian states. This had a dramatic impact on Vijayanagara political ideologies and political practices, with changes manifest in the emergence of new royal rituals, such as the "Robes of Honor" ceremony that was reported on by Portuguese visitors to the capital (Gordon 1996), as well as the adoption of new royal titles including the wonderfully multivalent "Sultan of the Hindu kings" (Wagoner 1996).

The new concept of kingly authority and royal ritual that emerged in South India during the Vijayanagara period drew creatively upon the political traditions and material forms of northern Muslim states. A distinctive Vijayanagara courtly architecture developed in the fifteenth and sixteenth centuries, and perhaps earlier (Michell, personal communications). It was restricted to public or royal structures, was found only at major imperial cities, and had clear associations with the architecture of the Deccani Sultanates (Michell and Zebrowski 1999). As such, Vijayanagara courtly architecture merged features from within and beyond imperial territories in the creation of an imperial style of public architecture.

Vijayanagara courtly architecture was distinctive in its building technologies as well as in external form. Structures in this category were built of small crudely cut stone blocks set in thick mortar and covered in plaster (Michell 1995:129), a marked contrast to the dry stone masonry technologies that characterized Vijayanagara temple and defensive architecture. Stylistic features derived from the north include domes, arches, and building layouts structured as a "geometric manipulation of one or more domed and vaulted chambers" (Michell 1992c:48). Features drawn from within the empire include stepped temple-like roofs, plaster decoration, and elaborately carved multi-tiered stone foundations. One of the best examples of this style at the capital is a structure in the royal center that is popularly referred to as the Lotus Mahal, which likely functioned as a reception hall (see plate 2.4). This structure combines ornate Islamic style arches decorated with incised plaster motifs with a temple-like sculpted basement and tiered roof. Other structures of this distinctive style found at Vijayanagara and the later capitals of Chandragiri, Penukonda, and Vellore include palaces, watchtowers, baths or water-tanks, and administrative buildings.

It is important to stress that Vijayanagara courtly structures did not simply mimic northern styles; instead, this was something new and distinctive, expressing very different kinds of identities and relations than are evident in contemporaneous temple architecture. It is also important to emphasize that the kinds of transformations evident

Plate 2.4   Vijayanagara courtly architecture: Pavilion in the Royal Center

in courtly architecture are also evident in several other cultural spheres. These include military and administrative organization, as well as the patterns of royal dress and royal titles noted earlier, all of which also manifest an awareness of and participation in a political landscape extending far behind the bounds of the Vijayanagara empire. It is perhaps in this transformed political and ideological landscape where we see the most radical breaks with the past, and the creation of new and different memory communities. That these new alliances occur at the same time that very different communities and connections are being expressed through sacred architecture and in literary texts attests to the simultaneity of multiple constructions of Vijayanagara imperial identities and the multiple audiences for those constructions.

Discussion

The discussion presented above paints a picture of a state very much in control of its "message," consciously manipulating existing beliefs, as well as new geopolitical situations, to meet specific ends. This is, to a large extent, a false picture. Certainly some of the processes described above, particularly the links made by Sangama kings to the God Rama, appear to have been the result of deliberate, conscious, political strategies by Vijayanagara elites. Other trends, such as changing elite clothing fashions and the emergence of new forms of Vijayanagara courtly architecture were likely far less deliberate, and emerged instead as a more gradual outgrowth of Vijayanagara's participation in an expanded and transformed political universe.

Vijayanagara as Memory

I noted earlier that the Deccani Sultanates were both peers and foes of Vijayanagara. In 1565, the foes won out. A major battle occurred to the north of the Vijayanagara capital that pitted Vijayanagara's armies against a confederation of three sultanates. Vijayanagara was defeated and its first capital was hastily abandoned. Over the course of the next century, Vijayanagara's rulers shifted ever further south to the cities of Penukonda, Chandragiri, and Vellore. Although each of these successive capitals was given the name Vijayanagara to link it to the former site of imperial grandeur, with each shift the empire became smaller and its authority weakened. As Vijayanagara declined (beginning even before the 1565 defeat), numerous smaller states rose to prominence across the empire's former territories. By the early seventeenth century (and even earlier in some areas), numerous large and small polities had emerged, with the largest and most effective of the successor states based in the southern and eastern parts of the former Vijayanagara territories. The rulers of these new "*nayaka*" states were the descendants of regional rulers or *nayakas*. The nayakas were military leaders, often from upland Telugu-speaking regions (modern Andhra Pradesh), who had risen to prominence as regional rulers in the Tamil-speaking south in the sixteenth century. From the beginning, many of these rulers had sought independence from the empire and nayaka political ideologies from the sixteenth century on thus involved a complex dynamic that both acknowledged Vijayanagara authority and legitimated resistance to it. The decline of the empire following the 1565 battle provided the opportunity for that resistance to take hold and for the nayaka states to declare themselves as autonomous polities.

However, even as the empire was fragmenting, Vijayanagara as memory and source of authority became extraordinarily important. We see this most strongly in the courtly literature and temple architecture of the nayaka states of the seventeenth and eighteenth centuries. In a recent book on the period, the central paradox of nayaka kingship has been defined as "the tension between inflated claims, and the limited scale" of their polities (Narayana Rao, Shulman, and Subrahmanyam 1992:xi). These were small states compared to their predecessor and many were fragile and short-lived. Yet, their rhetoric of kingship was vast, entailing, in many cases, claims to the mantle of Vijayanagara's legitimacy.

This pattern is evident in the origin stories of several nayaka states. For example, the origin story of the Madurai nayaka state (which is preserved in several versions) involves a complex recounting of interactions between the archetypal great emperor of Vijayanagara, Krisnadevaraya (1509–1529 AD) and the first ruler of Madurai and his eldest son. Extant versions of this complicated story probably date to the early eighteenth century, 200 years after Krisnadevaraya's death, and involve murder, rebellion, and threats of patricide. The Madurai story recounts the tale of the warrior Nagama, a powerful nayaka who recaptured the Madurai region for Vijayanagara, but then refused to hand it over. Nagama's son Visvanatha remained loyal to the emperor and turned against his father to regain the land for Krisnadevaraya. Following his victory, Nagama brought his defeated father to stand judgment before the emperor. The ruler acknowledged the heroism of the son by releasing the father to his custody. And then, moved by the heroism and loyalty of Visvanatha, Krisnadevaraya told his courtiers that Visvanatha "deserves a throne equal to our own" (Narayana Rao, Shulman, and Subrahmanyam 1992:49). Thus, he offered Visvanatha kingship of the South, saying (as the story goes):

> You have saved my throne . . . Moreover, we have said that we would create a kingdom for you equal to ours . . . If you don't take control of the southern country, the situation won't be good. If it weren't for you the country would be without a king, and we would have to be reborn ourselves to struggle with those *palegallu*. You had best hurry south to be king. (Narayana Rao, Shulman, and Subrahmanyam 1992:51)

The "reluctant" Visvanatha agrees. However, to properly begin his rule, Visvanatha requests and is granted a gift from the king: the "protective goddess of Vijayanagara Durgamahalakshmi," who he installs in his capital of Madurai (Narayana Rao, Shulman, and Subrahmanyam 1992:51). As the Vijayanagara imperial center to the north declines and is abandoned, Madurai rises to glory, bearing the mantle of Vijayanagara's greatness.

This tale contains elements found in many origin stories associated with the nayaka kingdoms. These include accounts of the self-made nature of the nayakas, whose success is due to their heroic acts rather than to their lineage (which was, in fact, often undistinguished). Also present in these tales, though not discussed here, are references to the wealth and territory that these heroes' efforts yielded. A further critical component is the establishment of connections to higher sources of authority: most often to Vijayanagara. These linkages were not transferred through heredity, but through acts of personal loyalty, and through the transfer of the symbols and rights of legitimate rule from a past ruler to his successor.

Like the references to the Chola period found in Vijayanagara temple architecture, the nayaka historical references are restricted to a particular time and place in history. The place is the first city of Vijayanagara and the time is the reign of Krisnadevaraya, arguably the most effective, and certainly the most remembered of Vijayanagara kings. Krisnadevaraya's rule marked the political apogee of the empire, when it reached its greatest geographic extent and greatest unity and wealth. Thus, an important Telugu royal text of the early 1600s, the *Rayavacakamu* or "Tidings of the King," was composed as if it had been written in the court of Krisnadevaraya, despite the fact that Krisnadevaraya had been dead for nearly 80 years by the time it was composed (Wagoner 1993). For the nayaka states, Vijayanagara had become the model and memory on which to build a state.

Nayaka architecture

Nayaka temple and administrative architecture also provides evidence for references to the Vijayanagara past, and for the exaggerated claims to power that dominated the period. Vijayanagara architectural forms continue, but become greatly elaborated in scale and ornateness. Many nayaka period constructions entailed expansions of existing temple complexes, either Vijayanagara or Chola constructions (or both). Often this involved fully enclosing the existing structures within new and elaborate enclosure walls or temple structures, so that the earlier structures were completely hidden from view. The past remained at the core of these structures, but the outward veneer was entirely of the present. In particular, the most visible part of temple complexes, the *gopura* or towered temple gateways of the nayaka period, were enormous; for example, the *gopuram* of the Tiruvannamalai temple (Tamil Nadu) built by the Thanjavur nayaka rulers reached a height of 66 meters (Michell 1995:91).

Sculptural elements also became greatly elaborated in scale and ornateness during the nayaka period. And it was during this time that portraiture – of rulers, their consorts, and elite temple donors – became well established. There are a small number of portrait sculptures from the Vijayanagara period, but most Vijayanagara depictions of rulers are highly stylized and do not make reference to specific individuals (that is, most often kings are depicted as small seated figures beneath a parasol, often shown as the endpoints of large processional scenes). By the seventeenth century, detailed, individualized, life-sized stone and bronze sculptural portraits had become widespread. Rulers and their queens were depicted in elaborate costume and with distinctive facial features. This new emphasis on portraiture is in keeping with the depictions of nayaka kings as "self-made" heroic leaders evident in the origin stories discussed above, and also with the enormous claims to royal authority and power that characterize the period as a whole.

It is important to emphasize that all of the elaboration typical of the post-Vijayanagara period – in royal rhetoric, architectural forms, and artistic representation – occurs at precisely the time when state authority was at its weakest. As noted, while the polities that many nayaka kings ruled were small compared to Vijayanagara, their claims to universal rule and legitimacy were not. And many of these claims were based in the past, as nayaka kings traced their ascendancy to their service to the deceased emperors of Vijayanagara. This is, at the very least, a cautionary tale for archaeologists: the most monumental constructions of a state may refer as much to memories of power as to its actual presence.

Conclusions

This paper has addressed the deployment of the past and the constructions of new pasts during two periods in South Indian history. For the most part, my emphasis has been on acts of rulers and their courts and the creation of messages of state authority (see also Papalexandrou, this volume). The forms and content of messages created by political elites extended far beyond those considered in this paper. Music, theater, political ceremonies, and temple rituals, among others, all no doubt played important roles in creating and presenting images of imperial power. Here, I have focused on the material construction and (re)presentation of memory by examining landscape and urban layout, and temple and administrative architecture – dimensions that structured and constituted the spaces inhabited and experienced by Vijayanagara's residents. I have explored how Vijayanagara authority was linked to the sacred, mythic past of the region (see also Meskell and Prent, this volume), incorporating South India's two major Hindu traditions, Vaisnavism and Saivism. This was a sacred landscape prior to Vijayanagara ascendancy, and Vijayanagara's rulers emphasized and expanded upon these sacred associations in support of their own legitimacy.

Vijayanagara temple architecture drew on the more recent memories of Chola imperial grandeur and architectural tradition, much as nayaka sacred architecture drew on those of Vijayanagara. In both of these cases, the past was used in claims of universality and legitimacy, and these claims were expressed in the universalizing idiom of the sacred domain. In administrative or "courtly" architecture, Vijayanagara's kings did not make claims on the past, but instead, with their northern neighbors, were involved in the creation of a very new architectural form. I have suggested that these forms were directed outward, toward the global political milieu in which Vijayanagara participated, and that they were part of broader political, economic, and ideological changes that affected all of peninsular India during the fourteenth through seventeenth centuries.

For the most part, I have not considered in detail who the audiences were for these various imperial constructions and messages, nor how they responded. Certainly, the audiences were diverse – rulers and elites of neighboring states, subject elites, powerful religious leaders and communities, and the many linguistic, ethnic, and caste communities that populated the empire. At Vijayanagara, there is considerable evidence that the association of the city with the sacred landscape of Ramayana was widely accepted. However, we do not know the extent to which the diverse non-elite worshippers of Rama drew the associations between the god and the Vijayanagara king that the court clearly intended. While we have various monumental and textual routes to considering elite responses, much more archaeological research needs to be done beyond the bounds of the imperial capital to examine the multiple non-elites of the Vijayanagara period.

As I noted at the start of this paper, memories of Vijayanagara continue to be important today in India, where they are deployed in various ways in national and regional political discourse. As in the past, these memories are multivocal and at times competing – involving diverse religious communities, multiple linguistic and ethnic communities (i.e., both Kannada and Telugu speakers lay claim to the empire), and the state, all with somewhat different claims to the memory of empire.

References Cited

Fritz, J. M. 1986: Vijayanagara: authority and meaning of a south Indian imperial capital. *American Anthropologist* 88, pp. 44–55.

Fritz, J. M. 1992: Urban context. In *The Ramachandra Temple at Vijayanagara*, by A. L. Dallapiccola, J. M. Fritz, G. Michell and S. Rajasekhara. New Delhi: Manohar, pp. 1–14.

Fritz, J. M. and Michell, G. A. 1989: Interpreting the plan of a medieval Hindu capital: Vijayanagara. *World Archaeology* 19, pp. 105–29.

Fritz, J. M., Michell, G. A. and Nagaraja Rao, M. S. 1985: *Where Kings and Gods Meet: The Royal Center at Vijayanagara*. Tucson: University of Arizona Press.

Gordon, S. 1996: "Robes of honour:" A "transactional" kingly ceremony. *The Indian Economic and Social History Review* 33, pp. 227–42.

Michell, G. 1992a: Historical context. In *The Ramachandra Temple at Vijayanagara*, by A. L. Dallapiccola, J. M. Fritz, G. Michell and S. Rajasekhara. New Delhi: Manohar, pp. 17–23.

Michell, G. 1992b: Royal architecture and imperial style at Vijayanagara. In *The Powers of Art: Patronage in Indian Culture*, ed. B. S. Miller. Delhi: Oxford University Press, pp. 168–79.

Michell, G. 1992c: *The Vijayanagara Courtly Style*. New Delhi: Manohar.

Michell, G. 1994: Revivalism as the imperial mode: Religious architecture during the Vijayanagara period." In *Perceptions of South Asia's Visible Past*, ed. C. B. Asher and T. R. Metcalf. Delhi: Oxford and IBH, pp. 187–98.

Michell, G. 1995: *Architecture and Art of Southern India: Vijayanagara and the Successor States. The New Cambridge History of India* I:6. Cambridge: Cambridge University Press.

Michell, G. and Zebrowski, M. 1999: *Architecture and Art of the Deccan Sultanates. The New Cambridge History of India* I:7. Cambridge: Cambridge University Press.

Morrison, K. D. 1995: *Fields of Victory: Vijayanagara and the Course of Intensification*. Berkeley: Contribution 52, Archaeological Research Facility, University of California, Berkeley.

Morrison, K. D. 2001: Coercion, resistance, and hierarchy: local processes and imperial strategies in the Vijayanagara empire. In *Empires: Perspectives from Archaeology and History*, ed. S. E. Alcock, T. N. D'Altroy, K. D. Morrison and C. M. Sinopoli. Cambridge: Cambridge University Press, pp. 252–78.

Narayana Rao, V., Shulman, D. and Subrahmanyam, S. 1992: *Symbols of Substance: Court and State in Nayaka Period Tamil Nadu*. Delhi: Oxford University Press.

Nilakanta Sastri, K. A. 1966: *A History of South India from Prehistoric Times to Vijayanagar*. Madras: Oxford University Press.

Rajasekhara, S. 1992: Inscriptions. In *The Ramachandra Temple at Vijayanagara*, by A. L. Dallapiccola, J. M. Fritz, G. Michell and S. Rajasekhara. New Delhi: Manohar, pp. 27–30.

Sinopoli, C. M. and Morrison, K. D. in press: The regional landscapes of the imperial city of Vijayanagara: Report on the Vijayanagara Metropolitan Survey Project. *South Asian Archaeology 1999*, ed. K. R. van Kooij and E. Raven. Groningen: Egbert Forsten Publishing.

Stein, B. 1980: *Peasant State and Society in Medieval South India*. Dehli: Oxford University Press.

Stein, B. 1985: Vijayanagara and the transition to patrimonial systems. In *Vijayanagara: City and Empire*, ed. A. L. Dallapiccola and M. Z. Ave-Lallement. Weisbaden: Franz Steiner Verlag, pp. 73–87.

Stein, B. 1989: *Vijayanagara. The New Cambridge History of India* I:2. Cambridge: Cambridge University Press.

Stein, B. 1998: *A History of India*. Oxford: Blackwell.

Talbot, C. n.d.: *The Nayakas of Vijayanagara Andhra: A Preliminary Prosopography*. Unpublished ms. in possession of author.

Verghese, A. 1995: *Religious Traditions at Vijayanagara as Viewed through its Monuments*. New Delhi: Manohar.

Wagoner, P. B. 1993: *Tidings of the King: A Translation and Ethnohistorical Analysis of the Rayāvacakamu*. Honolulu: University of Hawaii Press.

Wagoner, P. B. 1996: "Sultan among Hindu kings:" Dress, titles, and the Islamicization of Hindu culture at Vijayanagara. *Journal of Asian Studies* 55, pp. 851–80.

3
Memory's Materiality: Ancestral Presence, Commemorative Practice and Disjunctive Locales

Lynn Meskell

Introduction

Archaeological materials operate in *thirdspace*, a dialectical position that recursively shapes individuals and is concurrently shaped by us (Soja 2000). But such materials can be desired, reified and performed in very different ways according to the complex needs of different communities through time. Outlining these negotiations within the Egyptian landscape, we might effectively disentangle instances of commemorative practice (short term memory and performance) from what has been marked as cultural memory (long term memorialization), positing additional or altogether different valences – even disjunctive associations through changing temporalities and cultural hybridity. The following topoanalysis (Bachelard 1994) examines two culturally diverse moments in time, both set within the same geographic locale centered on Deir el Medina in the Theban West Bank (see Map 3.1). The first focuses on the New Kingdom (ca. 1539–1075 BC, Eighteenth–Twentieth Dynasties) village known as the "Place of Truth" and its specific material culture devoted to ancestor veneration. The second relates to the afterlife of the village and the revisioning of the site by later occupants and travelers to the West Bank.

Deir el Medina today is remarkably well preserved. It includes some 68 houses within an enclosure wall and approximately 400 tombs surrounding the village. The tombs were largely constructed in the New Kingdom but contained material from many centuries afterwards, since the site was continually reused for mortuary purposes. The first settlement was probably constructed at the outset of the Eighteenth Dynasty (ca. 1539–1295 BC). It was expanded during the Nineteenth and Twentieth Dynasties (ca. 1295–1185 BC and 1185–1075 BC, respectively) when the team of workmen was increased as the scale of the royal tombs grew more and more ambi-

I would like to thank Gay Robins for reading an early draft of the paper and to the editors for their close reading of the text. My thanks also to Richard Parkinson and Tania Watkins from the British Museum for assistance with the photographs and to Scott Kremkau for helping prepare the manuscript.

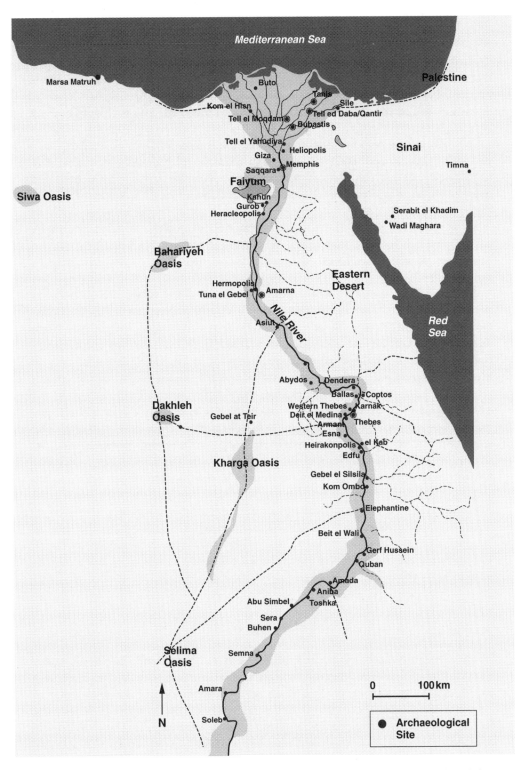

Map 3.1 Map of New Kingdom Egypt, showing location of Deir el Medina in the Theban West Bank

tious. The official role of the village came to an end during the reign of Ramesses XI, when civil unrest led to the site's abandonment. More information has been gleaned from this community than from any other in pharaonic history. Its highly literate occupants left a wealth of documentary data, and the favorable desertic conditions have preserved both houses and tombs. Whilst the textual data have received much scholarly attention, the material remains of Deir el Medina have only recently been analyzed systematically (Meskell 1997, 1999b).

New Kingdom commemorative practices, evidenced at Deir el Medina, were associated with remembering deceased individuals, as part of a belief system that engendered ongoing recursive gestures which were embedded within a social and physical landscape that conjoined living and dead communities. The reality of the past resides in the artifacts of its representation (see Foucault 1972). Focusing on the lived memories housed in intimate spaces the material expression of memory can be accessed through ancestor busts, stelae, and household features (Meskell 1998), whereas its immaterial aspects are often preserved in textual references to funerary practices and festivals.

After the New Kingdom, the preserved remains of the village and its adjacent cemeteries took on new meanings for the surrounding communities in Ptolemaic (332–30 BC) and Roman times (30 BC–395 AD). The residues of the past were inescapable in daily life and often monumentalized, as evidenced by the re-envisioned landscape around the West Bank, known collectively as the Memnonia. Deir el Medina's materiality remained directly available, visually and sensually, to later groups, yet the inhering cultural specificities were dramatically altered. From a "past in the past" perspective, I contend that the site became a numinous locale, without any recognition of its utilitarian purpose or, indeed, its past residents. From a hermeneutic standpoint, the specificities of memory can only endure within sustained contexts (Halbwachs 1992 [1950]). Memory cannot be transmitted without continual revision and refashioning. This entails diverse moments of modification, reuse, ignoring and forgetting (see Küchler 1993), and investing with new meanings. Thus the socio-spatial disjunctures at Deir el Medina are not surprising, but they are potent reminders of the erasure of memory and the ontological difficulties in assuming coherence of meaning over the long term. What may superficially appear to reflect continuity and memorialization might instead represent a palimpsest of meanings and a protean attitude to locality.

Collectivizing Memory

Places of memory anchor the past in the present and, alternately, the present in the past. The long, interleaved history of Egyptian monuments and cultural landscapes would imply a fruitful context for the analysis of memory and the re-working of memory. One might expect that the influential works of Aries, Bachelard, Halbwachs, Hobsbawm or Connerton could be applied to the Egyptian data, yet theoretical developments in this field have been negligible. The concept of memory has only recently attracted scholarly attention in Egyptological research (Baines and Lacovara 2002;

McDowell 1992, 1999; Richards 1999), but the degree to which long-term social memory was a pervasive theme is debatable. From texts and iconography one can demonstrate that the villagers at Deir el Medina had a very limited sense of the past and could remember scarcely more than two generations back in regard to their own commemorative family practices. There are very few written references to events even as recent as 20 years in the past (McDowell 1992). Yet popular in the cultic life of the village were the deified royals, Amenhotep I and his mother Ahmose Nefertari (see Cerny 1927), who were probably regarded as the founders of the village. They were the divinized patrons of the community whose images were the objects of devotion and supplication (Friedman 1994:111). Memory of them seems to have extended back many generations to the beginning of the Eighteenth Dynasty. Many statues, stelae, offering tables, and wall paintings attest their ongoing popularity. They were depicted in numerous tomb paintings dating to the much later reigns of Ramesside pharaohs such as those evidenced in the tombs of Khabekhenet (tomb 2), Ken (tomb 4), Neferabet (tomb 5), Ramose (tomb 7), Penbuy (tomb 10), Raweben (tomb 210), Neferhotep (tomb 216), Nebenmaat (tomb 219), Ramose (tomb 250), Inherkhau (tomb 299), and Nakhtamun (tomb 335). Scenes in Khabekhenet's tomb suggest that the image of Amenhotep was carried in procession during festival time, and festivals dedicated to the royal couple were the most numerous and diverse within Deir el Medina (Valbelle 1985:322–5). Perhaps the statue now in the Turin museum represents this type of performative cult statue (Plate 3.1). Processions depicting these images also appear in other media such as limestone stela. Cultic images and objects were the focus of dedication in the house and in the chapel areas, and were important foci within the tombs, suggesting some form of collective memory was operative.

Amenhotep I had another history within the village, as an oracle in statue form, a sort of afterlife for his divine image on earth. This statue of the dead king performed its oracular functions. Archaeologically, the remains of such activity might be located within Chapel D in the north of the site. This represents one of the major buildings devoted to Amenhotep I and Ahmose Nefertari, since it yielded more statuary than any other structure within the necropolis. Bruyère pointed out that tomb 1244 ran underneath this chapel and its roof formed a slab that could be opened to reveal the tomb and the statue underneath (Bomann 1991:72–3). It has been suggested that the cult statue would have been taken from its naos shrine, transported across the necropolis and set outside the tomb of Kaha (360). The pronouncements of the oracle were taken very seriously. In one recorded case the oracle ordered the policeman Amenkha to pay for a donkey belonging to Hormin the draughtsman, with serious repercussions if he failed to comply (McDowell 1999: 174):

> The god ordered the policeman Amenkha [to pay] 9 deben.
>
> First month of winter, day 10. He reported him again and he ordered him to pay yet again, for the third time. He made him take an oath of the lord, saying, "If I renege and dispute again, I will get 100 blows of a stick, and the donkey will be counted against me double."

Aside from the more performative oracular functions, there were more frequent, mundane activities associated with the cult of Amenhotep I, specifically devotion to

Plate 3.1   Statue of Amenhotep I, Turin Museum

his image in statue form. Texts from the site reveal that there were at least three daily rituals at dawn, midday and in the evening. Most significant were the morning rituals which served to awaken the god's image, and to wash, dress and feed it at the start of a new day (McDowell 1999). In this way the statue literally became Amenhotep I, and moved from being an object to being the deity himself (see below). There were also festivals dedicated to the deified pharaoh, perhaps the most public displays of commemoration involving whole communities such as Deir el Medina, which involved preparation of food, drink, and floral bouquets (McDowell 1999:96):

> *Year 7, third month of winter, day 29. The Great Festival of King Amenophis, the Lord of the Village was being held. The gang rejoiced before him for 4 solid days of drinking together with their children and their wives. There were 60 of inside (the village) and 60 of outside.*

This set of practices fits nicely with Connerton's (1989:7) view of recollection as operating in two distinct arenas of social activity: *commemorative ceremonies* and *bodily practices*. Festivals certainly constitute commemorative ceremonies, while the ritual devotions directed toward the cult statue constitute a set of bodily practices, for both the participants and the recipient.

Egyptian culture embodied a strong "sense" of the past; they were surrounded by its materiality, but it did not always evoke feelings of reverence. At Deir el Medina, the villagers incorporated older funerary monuments into new constructions and regularly robbed tombs in the process of burial preparations. In the vital area of the world of the dead, they inhabited and inspired to inhabit a doubly dead landscape in which the funerary monuments around them provided a model of achievement, even in their decayed form, as well as a physical environment into which they awkwardly inserted their current passage to a deceased status through destruction, usurpation, and reuse (Baines and Lacovara 2002). In Egyptian culture, death was not considered as the end of one's existence nor of one's effectiveness on earth. The dead were powerful beings who could intervene in the world of the living in both benevolent and malevolent ways. Ancestor busts and stelae are testament to this interplay since they provided a focus for these spheres of interaction and attest to the dead's willingness to intercede in the terrestrial. It is often said that the dead kept the living in line. But it is important in this contextual setting not to conflate social memory, which suggests the long-term, with commemoration, which refers to short-term practices operating only over a few generations.

While prior studies and observations are salient to the present work, it is noteworthy that Egyptologists have exerted most energy on mortuary analysis rather than on examining the role of memory in a lived context. The aim of the first part of this paper is thus to undertake an intimate study of dwelling and remembering. One of the most compelling studies that fuses memory, phenomenology and domestic space was conducted by Gaston Bachelard almost fifty years ago, although it has received little attention from archaeologists. His biographical and experiential approach to interior places, termed a *topoanalysis*, converges on the sites of our intimate lives (1994:8). Since memories are motionless, their spatialization transforms them into something more tangible, localizing a memory in time. The house embodies a community of memories in every room and corner, within its fixtures and features. As he famously remarked, the house is lived and an entire past come to dwell there. Its materiality constitutes a body of images that confer a sense of stability, specifically when one considers the sorts of social and ritual practices that ensured ancestral presence in the New Kingdom. This materialization of memory might form part of the dynamic rivalry between house and universe to which Bachelard refers. It is not simply a day to day existence with a narrative thread, but a co-penetrating series of memories about dwelling, about episodes, people and things.

My current work focuses on the households at Deir el Medina, the workmen's community that was responsible for the construction of the royal tombs on the Theban West Bank. The sixty-eight houses at Deir el Medina were divided and partitioned into a number of rooms ranging from three to ten, the most common number being between four and six. These strip houses had total residential areas ranging between 40 to 120 sq.m, the average being 72 sq.m (Valbelle 1985:117). The first room of the house was between 8 and 24 sq.m, whereas the second room was larger, somewhere between 14 and 26 sq.m. That second room was usually at a higher elevation, allowing light to filter through window grilles high in the upper walls. A series of smaller rooms lay toward the back of the house, between 3 and 6 sq.m in area. These have been designated as cooking and processing areas because of their archaeological emplacements: ovens, grinders, basins, and querns. It was in this area of the house that almost all of the staircases which allowed for roof access were located (Meskell 1998:234–7). For the purposes of this paper, the first two rooms are the most salient, specifically the second room where it is most likely that ancestor busts and stelae were situated.

Housing Memories and Material Biographies

The Deir el Medina houses were recorded in some detail in the 1930s by Bernard Bruyère (1939) and offer substantive evidence for ritual life. The majority of wall paintings and fixtures were located in the first and second rooms. This first room was notionally female-oriented space, with imagery and fixtures that centered around elite, married, sexually potent, fertile females of the household. As a space, it was laden with what we would describe as sexual and ritual images. Yet this room may also have been used for sleeping, eating and general domestic duties for many hours of the day. This space is usually designated the room of the enclosed bed, or *lit clos*. The majority of the houses have conclusive evidence of this bed-like structure. Its dimensions were roughly 1.7 m long, 80 cm wide, and 75 cm above floor level (Friedman 1994:97). The enclosed bed was associated with an amalgam of features: white walls, paintings, moldings, niches, Bes decorations, cultic cupboards, shrines and so on. In house SE5, for example, the *lit clos* was plastered, with molded and painted figures of Bes, a male deity associated with women, sexuality, fertility, music and magic. House C5 has a *lit clos* with an associated Bes painting, and in house SW6, where a woman named Iyneferty lived, there are also Bes decorations.

However, it is unlikely in the extreme that the structure actually functioned as a bed, or birthing bed, and such interpretations have been extensively critiqued. Yet many of the associated representations do deal with the theme of birth, and one could argue that these images and features housed and mnemonically activated memory: the memories of successive births and generations of family. Recently, additional archaeological evidence from individual houses at Deir el Medina and Amarna has been marshaled to suggest a more general link between cultic practices and the *lit clos* (Robins 1996:29–30). At Deir el Medina, and presumably at other sites, these fixtures had numerous social and religious associations (Meskell 1998). In house NE15 and in Iyneferty's house (SW6), the *lit clos* is built with an associated cultic cupboard. These shrine-like constructions or niches were the repository of ritual stelae, statues of deities such as Meretseger or Hathor, or ancestor busts. As Bachelard hints (1994:79), every cupboard and niche has a history, and a mute tumult of memories returns throughout temporal interactions with those fixtures. In many daily scenarios the mundane element of household spaces and features would be prevalent, whereas at moments of ritual or commemorative significance time and materiality would conjoin to animate such spaces. Yet evidence also posits more domestic utilization since troughs and mortars were found in the front rooms of houses NE14 and SW1. This should not be surprising given that Egyptian households were the sites of multi-functional room usage. We lack information about the specific rituals or practices that were employed to transform space, if indeed this was deemed necessary. Sacred and mundane are inherently Western taxonomies and such rigid separation of the spheres in a domestic contexts was not in accord with New Kingdom culture (Meskell 2001:199–201).

The second room, or divan room, possessed the highest frequency of ritual finds and revolved around the socio-ritual lives of the elite men of the household. These divans tend to be constructed in brick, are sometimes stone-lined, and always abut a major wall. The central focus within the elite male sphere would be the divan itself, which has a long history in later Egypt and the Middle East as a symbol of male activity, status, power relations and hospitality amongst other elite males. Just as Room 1 with the *lit clos* has a constellation of associated features signifying its ritual focus, the divan room has its own specific markers. In NE12 it is a cultic cupboard, in SE6 an altar, and more frequently we see false doors, painted red and yellow, embedded in the walls. Nebamentet, the house owner of SE7, had a false door and a wall painting; Nebamun, next door in SE8, had a divan bordered by stone with two pilasters against the western wall, plus red false doors with a central yellow band (Bruyère 1930:275). In mainstream mortuary practice, false doors were niched structures through which one's spirit could move back and forth freely, between this world and the other, to receive offerings. They were common throughout Egyptian history, dating back to the beginning of the Dynastic period, though they are not generally considered part of the domestic repertoire. In many cultures the door is a multivalent signifier, since it embodies both material and immaterial aspects:

> How concrete everything becomes in the world of the spirit when an object, a mere door, can give images of hesitation, temptation, desire, security, welcome and respect. If one were to give an account of all the doors one would like to re-open, one would have to tell the story of one's entire life. But is he who opens a door and he who closes it the same being? The gestures that make us conscious of security or freedom are rooted in a profound depth of being. Indeed, it is because of this "depth" that they become so normally symbolical. (Bachelard 1994:224)

In a household context false doors provided a portal between the world of the living and the dead and were an ever-present reminder of the deceased's eternal presence. Iconographic motifs present on the stelae are similar to those shown on inscribed false doors where the deceased is the recipient of food offerings (Friedman 1985). False doors facilitated contact with the spirits of ancestors, a view reinforced by the frequency of ancestor-related artifacts such as busts, statues and stelae that have been found in this room. We have to remember that Egyptian art fixed an event or individual in the memory, and thus formed a true memorial.

In order to apprehend the Egyptian material, we have to divorce ourselves from Western notions of art as a specific discursive category. While not eschewing the power of aesthetics, Egyptian representations were not solely "to be looked at." In Egypt, the term for sculptor was "he who keeps alive," which underscores the significance of the image as a living materiality. In pharaonic, Graeco-Roman and Late Antique times there was little distinction between the statue of a deity and the deity itself. Artemidorus, in his *Interpretation of Dreams*, argued that it made no difference whether one saw a statue of a goddess or the deity herself in the flesh, since a divine numen was present in both. Spirit animated the statue and thus one could actively petition it (Belting 1994:37), harking back to the pharaonic idea that the cult statue was equivalent to, and should be treated like, the divine body of the deity. Statues were provided with clean clothes each day, in addition to food and drink offerings in an ongoing daily routine of verbal and material sustenance. Altars piled high with provisions were set up, incense burned and libations poured. These are all actions which would have been familiar to the villagers at Deir el Medina, particularly in their veneration of Amenhotep III and his mother. Moreover, once the mouth of an image had been touched, that image could house the spiritual elements, thus providing the material entity for eternal life (Forman and Quirke 1996:32). Images were thus called upon to play active roles and fill gaps in the social fabric of daily life. As Belting (1994:45) contends, "many religions are concerned to make visible an object of veneration, to protect it and to approach it with the same piety that they would lavish on the higher being; symbolic acts toward the image thus reveal one's inner attitude." From an anthropological perspective, a statue in a temple was believed to be the body of the divinity, and also a spirit-medium, that likewise provides the divinity with a temporary body. Both are treated as theoretically on a par, despite the fact that the former is an artifact and the latter is a living deity (Gell 1998:7). Whereas this was possible for deified or royal personages, it did not always extend to the representations of the rest of society. In the Ramesside Period that availability was extended to ordinary people and could encompass the veneration of ancestral images.

The villagers of Deir el Medina called upon the deceased members of their own families, now in the realm of effective spirits and known as the *Akh ikr n Re*, "effective spirits of Re." We know this from the stelae they inscribed and erected in their houses and chapels. These practices probably occurred in the second room or divan room since most ritual finds emanate from there, as do the ritual fixtures and niches into which the stelae were placed. Examples have been found in houses C6 (those naming the individuals Baki and Mose); in SW5 (Khamuy and Pennub); and in SW2 (Khonsu, and for the woman, Sherire; see Plate 3.2). They are small round-topped limestone stelae, generally less than 25 cm high. They date from the end of the Eighteenth Dynasty, Nineteenth and Twentieth Dynasties with a preponderance in the Nineteenth Dynasty (Demarée 1983:283). They were dedicated to one, two or three individuals, usually without mention of their relations: in only a few cases do wives or children occur as offerants or dedicators (Demarée 1983:174). Some individuals had more than one stela devoted to them, suggesting that they were especially remembered or venerated within the community. The *Akh ikr n Re* were human beings who had been admitted to the afterworld, but more immediately they were deceased relatives who could be called upon in times of need. Their effectiveness was sustained by the ongoing practices of their descendants in the family cult. The materiality of the stela acted as a conduit for transactions between this world and the next,

Plate 3.2 Stela of Khonsu, Nineteenth Dynasty, from Deir el Medina (see Demarée 1983:106–9)

establishing contact with family members past and present. The fact that more men are named as dedicants and deified ancestors fits well with the location of these objects in the divan room, the area of greatest male potency.

The *dedicators* are not always depicted or named, but they could also include women (Friedman 1994:112). In most instances a seated man is depicted, smelling a lotus – which had associations of breath, rebirth and cyclicality – held in one hand. The other hand is either outstretched toward a table of offerings or holds the ankh sign, symbolizing life. These objects span the Eighteenth to Twentieth Dynasties and additional examples have been discovered at sites such as Amarna and Gurob. Others come from the palace of Merenptah at Memphis, the mortuary temple of Ramesses III, various West Bank Theban temples and Aniba in Nubia. Cultic activities surrounding these images were enacted in houses, chapels, tomb environs, and temples. Stela size and portability facilitated movement from and around a number of contexts. Find spots of the stelae in the Deir el Medina dwellings, in proximity to wall niches in the first and second rooms, suggest that their placement was in ritual recesses such as these.

Related finds are the so-called ancestor busts, which were painted limestone or sandstone anthropomorphic votives, often depicted with floral collars around the neck. They were activated in much the same manner as the stelae, through offerings and invocations. Ancestor busts have been discovered in various locations – domestic, mortuary and temple – from the Delta to the Third Cataract along the Nile. Approximately half of the extant 150 examples come from Deir el Medina, while the rest come from 14 other sites including the Faiyum, Gurob, Abydos, Karnak, Sesebi, Saqqara and Sedment (Keith-Bennett 1988:45; Friedman 1994:114). Another limestone bust of uncertain gender has recently been found in the excavations of the New Kingdom houses at Memphis (Giddy 1999:43). The fact that several unfinished examples were found at Deir el Medina verifies that they were made locally, perhaps when times of need were greatest. Such objects gather the universe in and around themselves: a past that goes back generations inheres in the material world and is redolent of power and fate (Bachelard 1994:84). They were tangible sites of embodied memory that simultaneously operated as a conduit between worlds. Moreover, they were not *art objects* or even *objects* in our sense, but were considered social agents themselves (Gell 1998:5). Persons or social agents, in contexts such as these, could be substituted by what Western interpreters would classify as art objects.

Ancestor busts, like stelae, were probably placed in niches, given the number discovered in domestic contexts. It has been suggested that their similarity to images in *Books of the Dead* (BD) and *Books of the Netherworld* would imply an additional funerary role (Keith-Bennett 1988:50). They are largely uninscribed, lacking names or titles, yet most scholars assume they are male due to the presence of red paint which characterizes male skin coloring. Yet red was also a magical color with potent associations, commonly found in the decoration of the first two rooms in the village houses, and also common on female figurines. Given the ritual potency of the name in Egyptian ritual practice, however, what might it signify that most busts were uninscribed or unnamed? One interpretation might be that the busts were generic figures and could evince or manifest any male relative who could be called upon. Perhaps multiple memories could reside in their material form. Their lack of specificity might also designate them as objects of forgetting, material places where fixed memory was deemed unnecessary. This potentially would make them very different from ancestor stelae.

Florence Friedman (1985:97) has argued that ancestor busts are an abbreviated form of the statue of the kneeling man presenting a stela that we witness in so many niched pyramidia at Deir el Medina. They could be moved about the village from houses to chapels and required offerings of food and recitations, in the same manner as other images and statues of the deceased. One spell in the Book of the Dead states: *as for him who knows this spell, he will be an effective spirit and he will not die again in the realm of the dead* (Faulkner 1985:175). Other spells, such as BD 100 and 101, allowed the spirit to travel on the solar barque of Re in the company of the other gods. Such spells, spoken by the living, assisted the deceased in the netherworld, and the rewards of their homage would hopefully filter back to those same individuals in an ultimate circle of reciprocity. The efficacy of spells was literally magnified by contemplation of the bust. The desire was to facilitate the progress from a deceased state, transforming the individual into an active and powerful being in the realm of the divine.

On one stela a man is shown worshipping in front of an ancestor bust, so we can assume that such practices of active supplication were indeed undertaken (Demarée 1983). We have entered a domain where "objects" merge with "people" by virtue of the existence of social relations between persons and things (Gell 1998:12), and between persons and persons *via* things. Anthropologists such as Gell have theorized how objects migrate across categories, having a certain agency that inheres in their materiality:

> Agency is attributable to those persons (and things) who/which are seen as initiating causal sequences of a particular type, that is, events caused by acts of mind or will or intention, rather than the mere concatenation of physical events. An agent is one who "causes events to happen" in their vicinity. As a result of this exercise of agency, certain events transpire (not necessarily the specific events which were "intended" by the agent). Whereas chains of physical/material cause-and-effect consist of "happenings" which can be explained by physical laws which ultimately govern the universe as a whole, agents initiate "actions" which are "caused" by themselves, by their intentions, not by the physical laws of the cosmos. An agent is the source, the origin, of causal events, independently of the state of the physical universe. (Gell 1998:16)

Other influential studies, like those conducted for medieval icons, have highlighted the relationship between the holy image and memory: images are imbued with moments from a narrative, although they are not narratives themselves (Belting 1994:10). Just as the portrait claims a certain power through its historicity, the image of the ancestor also performs as the receptacle of a certain life history. They have both a *presence* and a *history*. I would add, that in the Egyptian context, such objects were perceived as agents in themselves with appreciable timelines and active trajectories. Ancestral images acted as a mnemonic to reactivate the presence of a known individual and to capitalize on the ascendancy of the "effective spirit." Just as the mummified body formed the material substance that anchored the ethereal components of the deceased, ancestral images also constitute the material repository for the immaterial being. In the Egyptian cultic sphere it was not the *art* of memory, but the *content* of memory that was salient. And it operated between dual poles, being both retrospective and prospective simultaneously (Belting 1994:10). In this manner cultic objects were similar to an entire genre of writing, called "letters to the dead," that called upon deceased family members to intercede in the world of the living. In O. Louvre 698 we read one such letter from the Deir el Medina scribe Butehamun who petitioned his dead wife, Ikhtay, to speak favorably to the gods on his behalf (McDowell 1999:106):

If one can hear me
(in) the place where you are,
tell the Lords of Eternity,
"Let (me) petition for my brother,"
so that I may make [. . .] in [their] hearts,
whether they are great or small.
It is you who will speak with a good speech in the necropolis.
Indeed, I did not commit an abomination against you
while you were on earth,
and I hold to my behavior.
Swear to god in every manner,
saying "What I have said will be done!"
I will not oppose your will in any utterance
until I reach you.
[May you act] for me (in) every good manner,
if one can hear.

Other letters were more transparently self-serving. For example, sometime in the Nineteenth Dynasty a man wrote to his dead wife, Ankhiry, believing that she was maliciously interfering in his life. He writes: *What have I done against you wrongfully for you to get into this evil disposition in which you are? What have I done against you? As for what you have done, it is your laying hands on me even though I committed no wrong against you* (Wente 1990:216). He then vigorously states his loyalty, the fact that he did not divorce her, or cheat on her, how much he tried to please her and so on. To conclude, he implores that even three years after her death, he had not entered into a relationship with another woman or become involved with various women in his own household. It is the *materiality* of the letter itself – and its undoubted placement near the tomb – which marks its efficacy.

Ancestor busts or stelae similarly evoked a sense of the deceased and invoked their presence and potency to intervene in contemporary affairs. Ritual practice inheres in place. The position of the image, within the house or chapel, localized within the community itself, was crucial to the salience of the devotion and its desired results. Stelae or ancestor busts placed in the house were in the image of the deceased while representations of the deceased in statue form were traditionally situated at the tomb chapel. Both received offerings and were associated with a deceased individual, and thus were concurrently part of domestic and funerary cults. Once again, the individuals depicted on stelae were recently deceased members of the community who were being implored or appeased. Rather than the long dead, these were the fathers, sons, brothers, and husbands of the villagers who were part of living memory. The effective spirit could retain human form but could miraculously commune with deities such as Re and Osiris in the netherworld (Friedman 1994:114). Dedicants would have been keen to propitiate the deceased, since their perceived actions could impact on the living positively or negatively. When the image was venerated, a ritual memory exercise was accomplished. When this was coupled with larger festive offerings and performances, the effect must have been heightened: festivals were just such performances. At their core, festivals were fundamentally acts of commemoration and remembrance.

Festive Practice Remembered

Festivals provided occasions for a variety of pursuits: ritual, religious, social, sexual, sensory, visceral and so on. All these domains coexisted as overlapping spheres integrating both the living and the dead. Jan Assmann (1989:7) has offered one interpretation, influenced by Bakhtin's (1984) writing on European carnivals, through his textual analysis of Rabelais, and the social functionalism of Luhmann. He describes Egyptian festivals as highly stylized events, where everyday life is transformed into art. Following diverse scholarship on *carnivale* he argues that festivals forged social links, as one can imagine for any community. Assmann posits that society was less divided in antiquity, and that spheres of life – between households, between work and leisure, between public and private – were less distinct than in modern contexts. As such, festivals acted to produce difference. They had codes, moral values, and norms significantly different to those governing actions in other situations; they entailed a break with formal decorum. In festival time one could legitimately *follow your heart*, whereas social decorum would traditionally promote keeping the heart under control (Meskell 2002).

Cross-culturally, festivals take place in a supranormal time and space in which people experience themselves differently for the period of celebration, whether it be ecstatic encounter or sensual/sexual activity. Employing Bakhtin's (1984) insights in an Egyptian context proves even more illuminating than Assmann has indicated. The feast is always related to time: cosmic, biological, or historic. Festivals were linked to moments of crisis, the breaking points in the natural cycle or in the life of human society. Death and revival constituted such moments, as did change and renewal, leading to a more festive perception of the world. Whether organized by the state or more informally, such festivals did not create an alternative existential order; rather, they reinforced the existing one. People were released from the mundane and utilitarian, providing a taste of utopian possibilities. Yet festivals cannot be separated from bodily life, the earth, nature and the cosmos, which also entails a dialogue with death and existential reflections on being.

Rituals and commemorative ceremonies act as mnemonic devices that share two key features, formalism and performativity. Commemorative ceremonies such as festivals are distinguished from other rituals by explicit reference to prototypical historical or mythological persons and events, and by their use of ritual re-enactment. The latter is crucial to the constitution and shaping of communal memory (Connerton 1989:61). Religious festivals were not simply social celebrations – they actualized belief in a multiplicity of related spheres. One commonly overlooked was the possibility of communing with deceased ancestors. We have already seen the potency and popularity of the cult of the dead through ancestor veneration and through interconnected fear and affection for the deceased. In the New Kingdom there were festivals of the gods, of the king, and of the dead. The Beautiful Festival of the Wadi is a key example of a festival of the dead, which took place between the harvest and the Nile flood. In it, the divine boat of the god Amun traveled from the Karnak temple to the necropolis of Western Thebes. A large procession followed, and living and dead were thought to commune near the graves, which became *houses of the joy of the heart* on that occasion. It is likely that the images of deceased individuals were carried along in the procession and then returned to the grave. On a smaller scale, a family festival also took place as part of wider celebrations in which the deceased again took part (Bleeker 1967:137). In this way a link was forged between celebrating the gods and the dead in a single, all-encompassing event.

Festivals involved the entire community at Deir el Medina. Such groups "provide individuals with frameworks within which their memories are localised by a kind of mapping. We situate what we recollect within the mental spaces provided by the group" (Connerton 1989:37). Following Halbwachs, these mental spaces always have material referents and refer back to the material spaces that particular social groups occupy. Since physical objects change so little, particularly at the pre-industrial village level, they offer a sense of permanence and stability, or an illusion of rediscovering the past in the present, that is crucial at festival time. Those embodied moments were commemorative ceremonies that significantly shaped communal memory, as Connerton (1989:50) articulates:

> Carnival is here seen as an act in which "the people" organise themselves "in their own way" as a collectivity in which the individual members become an inseparable part of the human mass, such that "the people" become aware of their sensual–material bodily unity. By enabling such a collective body to coalesce, popular-festive forms may then be said to provide the people with a symbolic representation not of present categories but of utopia, the image of a future state in which there occurs the "victory of all the people's material abundance, freedom, equality, brotherhood." The rites of the carnival represent and foreshadow the rights of the people.

In theory, during festival times people were freed from the tedium of daily life, yet they were not entirely disengaged from the spheres of living and dead. Past, present and future fused at these conjunctures. People escaped into a sensual, intoxicating realm and could be transported into a state of elation (Bataille 1993:90). Festive events constituted the highlights and crises in the rhythm of the religious life of both community and individual (Bleeker 1967:24), as they were inflected with narratives of the life course: sowing and harvesting, seasonal festivals, calendrical dates, family festivals, religious events, festivals honoring divine figures, and the commemoration of individuals and happenings. The word for festival – *ḥb* – was written with the determinative for a hut and a dish or bowl. The former was a primitive "tabernacle" or simple temple; the latter was used in purification or libation ceremonies (Bleeker 1967:27). In depictions of festivals, such as the Opet festival shown in the Luxor temple, small, temporary huts are sometimes shown covered in leaves and associated with jars presumably containing beer or wine. Festivals were predominantly the domain of the goddess Hathor, also known by the epithet, Lady of Drunkenness. In principle, the consumption of alcoholic beverages provided a medium through which ancestors and deities could be vividly recalled and approached. Remembering entails evoking a concrete image within the mind, fostered by the imagination: memory and imagination are to some degree interchangeable. Unlike the materiality of the ancestor busts and stelae, festivals were inherently social occasions, where memory was enhanced by immaterial external stimuli: singing, dancing, drinking, and other sensory pleasures. Festivals such as these were inherently performative and embodied spheres, although this aspect of social memory – what Connerton has specifically referred to as *bodily social memory* – has long been neglected.

In the Egyptian context, the phenomenological experience of festivals and funerals had much in common, and the ritual practices of the two may have been comparable. Festivals and funerals were both powerful episodes in the Egyptian lifecycle, sharing many of the same symbols, practices, rituals, and paraphernalia. Tomb scenes such as those of Paheri at el Kab probably parallel the activities enjoyed at festivals, demonstrating an overlap in iconographies. At festivals, drinks were raised and participants were exhorted *for your ka, drink the good intoxicating drink, celebrate a beautiful day* (Tylor and Griffith 1894). The phrase "celebrate a beautiful day" probably links to the presence of Hathor at the festival, bestowing benevolence and joy upon the dead. Both festivals and funerals were transitional moments that served many functions: emotional expression and remembering, feasting, social interaction, religious observance, and communing with the gods. Key to each was the reinstatement of dead individuals, through commemorating their lives and their continued presence among the living. The entire notion of personhood, situated temporally and spatially, is a component of innumerable cultural institutions and practices. Egyptian conceptions of self traversed life and death, since both worlds were porous, and both contexts of existence possessed a shared substrate. Ancestral shrines, tombs, memorials, and sacred sites and so on, are all associated with the extension of personhood beyond the confines of biological life (Gell 1998:223).

Disjunctive Memories: the Memnonia

The Theban West Bank was invested with meaning because of its mortuary associations, its vast temples, and its ritual festivals which continued on a yearly schedule. It remained important through time because it contained the sites of sacred events like the Festival of the Wadi. Such places were invested with cosmological and mythic significance, enacted by humans, making reference to symbolically potent features of the natural topography. This was a dynamic locale, and memories of mythic, cosmological, ritual, and funerary significance fused together to create a set of shared memories and experiences for the people of pharaonic Egypt. It was a sacred geography, known as the "Memnonia."

The "Memnonia" was a fluid toponym that could be used interchangeably to mean the administrative district with its southern border somewhere south of Medinet Habu and the northern between Deir el Medina and the Dra abu'l Nagga; the town of Djeme which grew up around Medinet Habu; or a collective term for the whole Western necropolis, including Deir el Medina (Montserrat and Meskell 1997:182). While names create locales, these taxonomies can be permeable and overlapping. At Deir el Medina, the impact of the desert setting, its views across to the monuments of the East Bank, its proximity to other religious sites, its vestiges of hundreds of tombs, chapels and pyramidia, and the ritual associations of its temple all suggest an enigmatic quality that could draw people to the site. The presence of rock graffiti dating to Roman times suggests that travelers passed through Deir el Medina on their way to visit the popular tourist destination of the Valley of the Kings. A characteristic of Graeco-Roman culture was the "allure of the peripheral" where the visitor might experience firsthand the exotic, true and most ancient (Frankfurter 1998a:19). Specific individuals were so overcome by the awe-inspiring landscape and the monumental remains at Deir el Medina that they were impelled to record their experience of the place by making an obeisance (or *proskynema*). *Proskynemata* may be seen as expressions of awe and piety, a way of propitiating the dangerous aspects of local deities to obtain a sort of safe-conduct through their domain. At Deir el Medina and its environs, Roman travelers made *proskynemata in the presence of the great gods in the holy mountain* (Montserrat and Meskell 1997:183). Those who witnessed the standing architectural remains at the site and the adjacent temple were emotionally moved. They failed to realize that they were surveying the remnants of a workmen's village that did not constitute holy ground. In this sense they were not performing acts of cultural memory, but were constituting new, hybrid forms of commemorative practice.

Here we confront an historically layered landscape, imbued with visible remnants from the past, inspiring an ongoing system of activities; that milieu and those activities are linked by rules as to what is expected and appropriate (Frankfurter 1998b). Rutherford (2000) has similarly demonstrated the interleaved and multiple reinterpretations of the monuments at Abydos, although with less disjuncture than we see at Deir el Medina. Diachronically, this mutual interaction between people and landscape changed drastically, despite the explicit religiosity, so that most travelers in later times had no real, cultural point of contact – although they certainly experienced embodied responses. Visitors assumed that Deir el Medina constituted sacred ground, yet they could not comprehend fully the pharaonic mechanisms by which it was activated. Hundreds of years had passed, and whilst the practices of ritual and commemoration may seem superficially analogous, the discursive reasons for their enactments were very different. From my perspective, this is not social memory, in the sense of a continuous body of knowledge passed on between generations or other social groups. However, if one relied exclusively on material responses, lacking the textual documentation, we might conclude that this represented long-term memorial practice. Thus it affords us a cautionary tale in the ascription and conflation of meaning and cultural continuity.

Different cultural groups mark and organize space differently. Space and time can act together to reinforce one another, leading to greater overall effect. Even in an established mortuary locale such as Deir el Medina, this can be clearly seen after the departure of the original New Kingdom occupants. Spatial organization and identity retained importance, although their parameters shifted. If one looks at the long-term choreography of the site, one can also see that real cultural difference was operative. Hundreds of years after the site's abandonment, in Ptolemaic times, the site attracted other, more regular visitors who performed more mundane activities. The tombs of the Western cemetery were re-opened and used by an organized group of funerary workers, called choachytes. These were the libation-pourers of Djeme who were responsible for maintaining the mortuary cult of those buried in the necropolis of Djeme. Their role was cultic and performative, bringing the necessary food and water offerings to the tombs (Vleeming 1995). The tombs in question were not generally newly constructed mausolea; rather, they were usurped monuments from much earlier periods such as those at Deir el Medina. In the Ptolemaic period numerous bodies were deposited in tombs 1126, 1233, 1346, and in later times into 1126, 1140, 1153, 1154, 1155 (Bruyère 1929:39–43). The extensive archives of the choachytes, in Demotic and Greek, outline their economic activities in some detail and show them to have been a cohesive, endogamous group closely identified with the West Bank (Montserrat and Meskell 1997:182). This social group regularly visited tombs which the owners had entrusted to them, and tombs – particularly older ones without owners – which they had simply occupied (Pestman 1993:8). Their involvement was not limited to depositing bodies and to enacting cultic practices; they also stored their equipment and documents at the site, and used it as a temporary storage facility for mummies awaiting burial. One text mentions a large tomb in which 17 related individuals were deposited in 124 BC (Pestman 1993:450). This has tentatively been identified as TT5 at Deir el Medina (El-Amir 1959:13). Moreover, the choachytes participated in local religious festivals such as the journey of the cult image of Amun during the Festival of the Wadi (Montserrat and Meskell 1997:183).

The cemetery landscape of Deir el Medina was still potent, but without the same concatenation of meanings that it once held in the New Kingdom. This reinforces the nexus of four salient dimensions of cultural landscape: time, space, meaning, and communication. Without understanding of this specific historical and cultural situation, one might conclude that only time had changed, whereas I would posit that meaning and communication had also been irreversibly changed. Artifacts and past places "surrender their claim to evoke substantive meanings out of the past" while the "inner life of those who fashioned culture in the past remains hidden and inaccessible" (Hutton 1993:21). Perhaps we need to question the notion that memory is inherently authentic, which is undoubtedly a fiction based on the notion of total recovery of the past and the erasure of subjectivity and imaginings. The waning, renewal, and revisioning of memory might prove potentially even more compelling.

To graphically illustrate this disjuncture, I turn to an elite Roman family burial at Deir el Medina interred within the cellar of an ordinary village house. A purposeful and expensive burial, it is unlikely that those responsible for the burial actually recognized this as a non-sacred context. Given an adjacent cemetery of pyramid-topped tombs, why would one choose a rather unimpressive household cellar? I have argued that at post-New Kingdom Deir el Medina, the significance of the burial context gradually decreased in importance through time (Meskell 1999a). Concern for the material structure and even the immediate surroundings of the place of burial vanished. The materiality of death, as well as its attendant material culture, virtually disappeared, and objectification of the body and bodily treatments took its place. Other explanations might posit that a domestic context was less obvious and thus more secure or, more plausibly, that the specific character of the structure was simply unknown. It is the only such post-New Kingdom burial within the village enclosure. It is axiomatic that the boundaries between mortuary and domestic are selectively permeable, varying over time, thus allowing people to cross these borders and enter spatial domains at different times. The people who buried Pebos and his family, some nine individuals spanning two generations, certainly crossed that boundary.

The exceptionally wealthy burials and elaborate bodily treatments in this case are striking. From the epigraphy, we know this was a local family of national prominence who came to live in Alexandria. Their names relate to local Theban cults, suggesting a close affiliation with the Theban area (Montserrat and Meskell 1997:190). Memory and locality conjoin in this instance and gather force in the return to a past lived landscape for a meaningful burial: yet the specific funerary context is disjunctive – offering two levels of mnemonic association. It must have been vital that the family members were laid to rest in their local area and, yet, despite their obvious rank and station in life, they were buried in the cellar of a workman's house. This was a fact probably unknown to them, but it stresses that although the landscape was imbued with a sense of sanctity, the family members had no real knowledge as to why this was the case. Perhaps the entire region now had a valency irrespective of its histori-cal specificities, a sort of counter-memory where cultural memories had been re-worked or irrevocably lost (see Foucault 1977). Hybrid groups like people living in Roman Egypt certainly had a knowledge and interest in their particular Egyptian setting, and they developed traditions not seen in native Roman culture. Yet this is not social memory, this is a conflation of mortuary images like pyramids, which were extremely familiar, with evocative local settings with powerful, but perhaps lost asso-ciations. One could argue that there is a fairly rapid change of meanings within a somewhat static natural and material landscape and, as such, we cannot assume an implicit continuity on the basis of a similarity of forms.

Influenced by the seminal work of Halbwachs, Hutton (1993:78) has formulated an eloquent assessment of the contingency of memory which is instructive for archaeologists, given our preoccupation with both temporal and spatial dimensions of the past:

> In remembering, we locate, or localize, images of the past in specific places. In and of themselves, the images of memory are always fragmentary and provisional. They have no whole or coherent meaning until we project them into concrete settings. Such settings provide us with our places of memory. Remembering, therefore, might be characterized as a process of imaginative reconstruction, in which we integrate specific images for-mulated in the present into particular contexts identified with the past.

Deir el Medina, originally a workman's village, in later times became the site of a Christian monastery from which the site derived its modern name. This rather modest site, with its explicitly pagan associations, became another holy place within a new set of cultural parameters, thus removing meaning still further from its original context. This prompts us to question the historical status of memory. Would we really conflate pharaonic religion with Greek, Roman, or Christian ideologies – because the archaeological data might suggest that there was considerable overlap – despite the fact that from the culturally specific, historical perspective we can construct a very different picture? The entire West Bank leaves us with a very ambiguous and multivalent picture of the landscape and impels us to question the degree to which social memory can be continuously examined in the long term. Today the West Bank continues to serve as a vast canvas of memory and imagination. Recent events highlight, albeit violently, its powerful contemporary presence in national modernity (Meskell 2000). Given the interpretive climate of current scholarship, the Place of Truth must now be cast as the place of many Truths.

References Cited

Assmann, J. 1989: Der schöne Tag. In *Sinnlickkeit und Vergänglichkeit im altägyptichen Fest. Das Fest*, ed. W. Haug and R. Warning. Munich: Wilhelm Fink, pp. 3–28.

Bachelard, G. 1994: *The Poetics of Space: The Classic Look at How We Experience Intimate Places.* Boston: Beacon Press.

Baines, J. and Lacovara P. 2002: Burial and the dead in ancient Egyptian society: respect, formalism, neglect. *Journal of Social Archaeology* 1(2), pp. 5–35.

Bakhtin, M. 1984: *Rabelais and His World.* Bloomington: Indiana University Press.

Bataille, G. 1993: *The Accursed Share: Volumes II and III.* New York: Zone Books.

Belting, H. 1994: *Likeness and Presence: A History of the Image before the Era of Art.* Chicago: University of Chicago Press.

Bleeker, C. J. 1967: *Egyptian Festivals: Enactments of Religious Renewal.* Leiden: E. J. Brill.

Bomann, A. H. 1991: *The Private Chapel in Ancient Egypt.* London and New York: Kegan Paul International.

Bruyère, B. 1929: *Rapport sur les Fouilles de Deir el Médineh (1928), Deuxième Partie.* Cairo: Imprimerie de l'Institut Français d'Archéologie Orientale.

Bruyère, B. 1930: *Rapport sur les Fouilles de Deir el Médineh (1929), Deuxième Partie.* Cairo: Imprimerie de l'Institut Français d'Archéologie Orientale.

Bruyère, B. 1939: *Rapport sur les Fouilles de Deir el Médineh (1934–1935), Troisième Partie FIFAO 16.* Cairo: Imprimerie de l'Institut Français d'Archéologie Orientale.

Cerny, J. 1927: Culte d'Amenophis I chez les ouvriers de la nécropole Thébaine. *Bulletin de l'Institut Français d'Archéologie Orientale* 27, pp. 159–203.

Connerton, P. 1989: *How Societies Remember.* Cambridge: Cambridge University Press.

Demarée, R. J. 1983: *The 3h Ikr n Rˁ-Stelae: On Ancestor Worship in Ancient Egypt.* Leiden: Nederlands Instituut voor het Nabije Oosten te Leiden.

El-Amir, M. 1959: *A Family Archive from Thebes: Demotic Papyri in the Philadelphia and Cairo Museums from the Ptolemaic Period.* Cairo: General Organisation for Government Printing Offices.

Faulkner, R. O. 1985: *The Ancient Egyptian Book of the Dead.* London: British Museum Press.

Forman, W. and Quirke, S. 1996: *Hieroglyphs and the Afterlife in Ancient Egypt.* London: British Museum Press.

Foucault, M. 1972: *The Archaeology of Knowledge.* London: Routledge.

Foucault, M. 1977: Nietzsche, genealogy and history. In *Language, Counter-Memory, Practice*, ed. D. Bouchard. Ithaca: Cornell University Press, pp. 139–64.

Frankfurter, D. 1998a: Introduction. In *Pilgrimage and Holy Space in Late Antique Egypt*, ed. D. Frankfurter. Leiden: E. J. Brill, pp. 3–48.

Frankfurter, D. (ed.) 1998b: *Pilgrimage and Holy Space in Late Antique Egypt*. Leiden: E. J. Brill.

Friedman, F. 1985: On the meaning of some anthropoid busts from Deir el Medina. *Journal of Egyptian Archaeology* 71, pp. 82–92.

Friedman, F. 1994: Aspects of domestic life and religion. In *Pharaoh's Workers. The Villagers of Deir el Medina*, ed. L. H. Lesko. New York: Cornell University Press, pp. 95–117.

Gell, A. 1998: *Art and Agency: An Anthropological Theory*. Oxford: Oxford University Press.

Giddy, L. 1999: *The Survey of Memphis II. Kom Rabi'a: The New Kingdom and Post-New Kingdom Objects*. London: Egypt Exploration Society.

Halbwachs, M. 1992 [1950]: *On Collective Memory*, ed. and trans. L. A. Coser. Chicago: University of Chicago Press.

Hutton, P. H. 1993: *History as an Art of Memory*. Hanover: University of Vermont.

Keith-Bennett, J. L. 1988: Anthropoid busts II: not from Deir el Medineh alone. *Bulletin of the Egyptological Seminar* 3, pp. 43–72.

Küchler, S. 1993: Landscape as memory: the mapping of process and its representation in a Melanesian society. In *Landscape: Politics and Perspectives*, ed. B. Bender. London: Berg, pp. 85–106.

McDowell, A. G. 1992: Awareness of the past in Deir el-Medina. In *Village Voices*, ed. R. J. Demarée and A. Egberts. Leiden: Centre of Non-Western Studies, pp. 95–109.

McDowell, A. G. 1999: *Village Life in Ancient Egypt: Laundry Lists and Love Songs*. Oxford: Oxford University Press.

Meskell, L. M. 1997: *Egyptian Social Dynamics: The Evidence of Age, Sex and Class in Domestic and Mortuary Contexts*. Ph.D. thesis. Cambridge: Cambridge University.

Meskell, L. M. 1998: An archaeology of social relations in an Egyptian village. *Journal of Archaeological Method and Theory* 5, pp. 209–43.

Meskell, L. M. 1999a: Archaeologies of Life and Death. *American Journal of Archaeology* 103, pp. 181–99.

Meskell, L. M. 1999b: *Archaeologies of Social Life: Age, Sex, Class etc. in Ancient Egypt*. Oxford: Blackwell.

Meskell, L. M. 2000: Sites of violence: terrorism, tourism and heritage in the archaeological present. Presented at American Anthropological Association, San Francisco.

Meskell, L. M. 2001: Archaeologies of identity. In *Archaeological Theory: Breaking the Boundaries*, ed. I. Hodder. Cambridge: Polity.

Meskell, L. M. 2002: *Private Life in New Kingdom Egypt*. Princeton: Princeton University Press.

Montserrat, D. and Meskell, L. M. 1997: Mortuary archaeology and religious landscape at Graeco-Roman Deir el Medina. *Journal of Egyptian Archaeology* 84, pp. 179–98.

Pestman, P. W. 1993: *The Archive of the Theban Choachytes (Second century B.C.): A Survey of the Demotic and Greek Papyri*. Leuven: Peeters.

Richards, J. 1999: Conceptual landscapes in the Egyptian Nile valley. In *Archaeologies of Landscape*, ed. W. Ashmore and A. B. Knapp. Oxford: Blackwell, pp. 83–100.

Robins, G. 1996: Dress, undress, and the representation of fertility and potency in New Kingdom Egyptian Art. In *Sexuality in Ancient Art*, ed. N. B. Kampen. Cambridge: Cambridge University Press, pp. 27–40.

Rutherford, I. 2000: Pilgrimage in Graeco-Roman Egypt: new perspectives on graffiti from the Memnonion at Abydos. Presented at Encounters with Ancient Egypt Conference, University College London.

Soja, E. W. 2000: *Postmetropolis: Critical Studies of Cities and Regions*. Oxford: Blackwell.

Tylor, J. J. and Griffith, F. L. (eds.) 1894: *The Tomb of Paheri at El Kab*. London: Egypt Exploration Fund.

Valbelle, D. 1985: Les Ouvriers de la Tombe. *Deir el Médineh à l'époque ramesside, BdE 96*. Cairo: Institut Français d'Archéologie Orientale.

Vleeming, S. P. 1995: The office of a choachyte in the Theban area. In *Hundred-Gated Thebes*, ed. P. W. Pestman and S. P. Vleeming. Leiden: E. J. Brill, pp. 241–55.

Wente, E. 1990: *Letters from Ancient Egypt*. Atlanta: Scholars Press.

4

Memory Tattered and Torn: Spolia in the Heartland of Byzantine Hellenism

Amy Papalexandrou

The facades of medieval buildings can tell us much about the thought-worlds of their contemporary builders, patrons, and viewers. In the region of central Greece, the walls of many Byzantine (fourth to fifteenth centuries AD) churches are a particularly out-spoken indicator of a complex attitude toward the past. This is often seen in the pur-poseful inclusion and, at times, careful arrangement of ancient building material, or spolia, within the medieval building fabric. It was an activity at once subversive and constructive; whether or not its perpetrators were conscious of it, the use of spolia cunningly enabled (then as now) both the suppression and endorsement of past memories while simultaneously re-ordering them into a fresh "memory network" (Carruthers 1998) of altered meanings.

Despite its striking potential to shed light on greater issues of communal and in-dividual memory for the Byzantine East, the phenomenon of spoliated masonry has not generated the attention it deserves within this specific context. This is due, I think, on the one hand to the negative press that has often befallen these facades. The overall visual effect of their appearance has traditionally been deemed rude and rustic, the product of tasteless pilfering by less sophisticated masons operating within a depleted economy. Such a dim view cannot help but color modern interpretations and may be partly responsible for the overwhelming tendency to think of immured spolia in terms of firmly imbedded "superstitions" (Maguire 1994; Mango 1963) rather than the poten-tially nuanced "memories" of those who built and regarded these monuments.

On the other hand, the omission of memory from discussions of spolia may be the result of the tendency to take the notion of commemoration for granted, espe-

I wish to thank Susan Alcock and Ruth Van Dyke for including me in the Mediterranean Memories session in early 2001 and for subsequent advice and constructive criticism regarding some of the issues discussed here. I am also grateful to Robert Nelson, Walter Kaegi, Matt Canepa and Galina Tirnanič for lively discussion and valuable insights at the Late Antique and Byzan-tine Studies Workshop at the University of Chicago, where an earlier version of this text was presented in March of 2001. My husband, with his usual erudition, enlightened many aspects of my approach to the material. All errors, and any lapses of memory, remain my own.

cially since it is deeply implicit in nearly every aspect of the society and material culture that Byzantinists study. We need only think of the overwhelming extent to which the memory of Attic culture (in the form of *mimesis*) permeated most scholarly, religious, and artistic activity in the Middle Ages, at least among the influential elite in their conscious imitation of the "high" style of ancient literature and art; or the monastic enterprise of copying which, it is generally believed, required rote memorization as the primary tool of its scribes; or the use of certain church plan types to prompt the recollection of specific holy places, most notably Christ's tomb in Jerusalem; or the tremendous attention given, at all times and within all ranks, to the written or inscribed preservation of a patron's eternal memory in the face of the inevitable dangers of time, envy and oblivion. Perhaps it is, indeed, this overwhelmingly constant, if quiet, presence of *mneme* that has obviated a systematic analysis of its place in Byzantium. No matter what the reason, *The Book of Memory* has yet to be written for the Byzantine Middle Ages as it has for the Latin West (Carruthers 1990). I offer this paper as a brief inquiry into the potential for one aspect of Byzantine building practice to raise larger questions of meaning, intention, and reception within a complex web of memory associations, specifically those encountered on the Greek mainland after the supposed "end" of antiquity (i.e., after the seventh century AD). Alternative readings of the phenomena of fragmentation and reuse here take into account shifting notions and attitudes toward the historical and mythological past, appropriations of the local landscape, the perpetuation of a patron's self-image, and the possibility of viewer response to the material "display" of constructed walls, each set within the many-layered framework of the church as the arena of commemoration *par excellence* in Late Antiquity and the Middle Ages.

Spoliated Masonry and Modern Interpretation

The Mediterranean basin is saturated with spoliated monuments (map 4.1). They are in evidence from the late antique period to the present century, the motley appearance of their walls often the result of a random placement of nondescript materials. Their abundance defies enumeration; they dot the countryside and line the streets of villages and cities from Spain to Syria. As common as it is, however, this type of construction reached a crescendo of expression in a few choice buildings of the Byzantine period (especially from the ninth to thirteenth centuries AD) in areas with a surfeit of ancient sites and, by extension, of readily accessible building material. I feel it necessary to state at the outset – and temporarily to placate those who will always privilege the notion of utilitarian necessity over that of ideological investment – that economy was certainly a factor in this activity. Stone was no longer quarried with abandon, and suitable construction material was naturally sought closer to hand. The process of despoliation was convenient and cheap, and the medieval mason was nothing if not practical.

   At the same time, however, the buildings examined here suggest a sophistication of organization that belies purely pragmatic explanations for their form and appearance. The so-called "Little Metropolis" in Athens is the classic example, where more

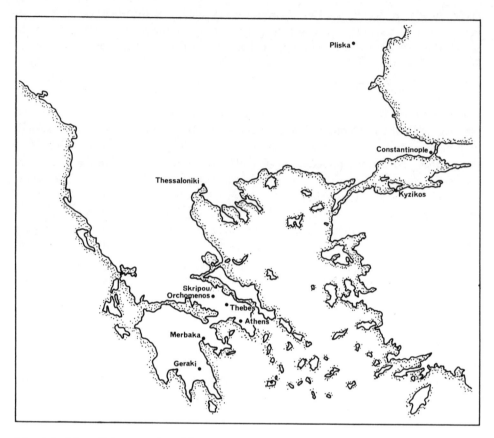

Map 4.1   Map of sites mentioned in text

than ninety spolia were gathered from various monuments (in this case medieval as well as ancient) and re-configured within its thirteenth-century walls (plate 4.1). Unlike those of most Byzantine monuments its masons completely avoided the use of brick, even for the filling of joints or the construction of arched window openings. Brick stringcourses, a standard device employed to distinguish or isolate features or sections of wall, were avoided altogether. Instead, every square inch of the facade, from foundation to cornice, was tightly packed with blocks of dressed stone, pieces of architectural members, carved sculptures, tombstones (or *stelai*), and inscriptions (Michel and Struck 1906). Perhaps most noticeable is the series of large panels that form a frieze-like band above the level of the door openings (visible in plate 4.1). This frieze completely envelops the structure and may be understood to comprise its visual focus. Whether it holds the key to our understanding of the overall iconographic schema or not (Maguire 1994), the inclusion and accentuation of such an array of antiquities was clearly of fundamental importance, certainly during construction and probably even from the initial laying out or "design" (whatever this

Plate 4.1   The "Little Metropolis," Athens. General view from northwest (photo by permission of the Deutsches Archäologisches Institut-Athen)

means for the Middle Ages) of the building. Only this can explain the consistent height at which the panels were immured and the care taken to ensure their unbroken flow across all four facades.

From our modern, archaeological point of view, this building is a virtual "museum" of artifacts, many of which were salvaged from the city's collection of famous, by then derelict, ancient monuments. The medieval viewer certainly did not regard it in the same way. Indeed, the practice of "collecting" *per se* was not in evidence for Byzantium after the seventh century AD, at least not in the terms we are accustomed to recognizing it (Guberti Bassett 2000). Still, one cannot help but notice the diligence with which certain spolia were positioned in highly visible or symbolically significant locations. A sculpted figure (perhaps Selene) was placed at the pinnacle of the building's east gable, arguably the most prominent (and perhaps triumphal) setting for a figure that commanded a forceful presence over the eastern, most sacred, realm of the building. Moreover, a section of Doric frieze from the sanctuary of the Athenian Eleusinion was conspicuously immured above the south doorway, while a calendar frieze representing the Athenian months was cut to size, re-ordered and re-positioned above the main, west entrance (seen in plate 4.1). This is not to suggest that the "find spots" of these sculptures had any relevance to the medieval builders, but simply that certain pieces were singled out for emphasis. They were highlighted by the symmetricality of their placement, not to mention their frank presence at

Plate 4.2   Church of the Virgin at Merbaka. Detail of north facade (photo by the author)

critical points of convocation and transition from the external, profane world to its sacred antithesis within. In the case of the calendar frieze, it is even apparent that the medieval builders took stock of the original content, (re-)arranging the depicted signs of the zodiac in good order so that the sequence moved from spring, on the left, to winter on the right (Simon 1983:7). Mention should also be made of the matching Corinthian capitals that neatly flanked the calendar frieze and demarcated the north and south corners of the facade; the symmetrical placement around window openings of chancel panels and ancient coffering; and the paired sculptures studiously placed as pendants to one another on the east facade. One has the impression that the medieval builders, if not also the beholders, were attentive to how these objects were immured in the walls before them.

Another important church, this one in the Argolid peninsula of the Peloponnese, displayed a similar "taste" for the antique (plate 4.2). Constructed probably in the thirteenth century AD and known today as the church of the Virgin at Merbaka, its walls similarly incorporate a substantial amount of spolia in a remarkable way (Coulson 2002; Struck 1909). While conforming to the usual Byzantine tendency to employ brick in the masonry, most notably in the form of decorative stringcourses, large blocks of plain dressed stone from ancient monuments were used exclusively at the corners and in the lower tracts of the walls. The latter were neatly arranged two to three courses high and were separated from the remaining wall surface by the aforementioned stringcourses. Spolia were also used in the creation of a two-step pedestal upon which the vertical walls rest, perhaps recalling the base (*crepis*) of an ancient temple. The overall impression was one of stability and strength, the worked stones visually equipping the building with a sense of powerful rustication. The dressed blocks were doubtless taken from the temple of Hera at the nearby site of Argos, and in fact a marble cornice immured in the central apse can easily be traced to this source. Two ancient, sculpted *stelai* were showcased near the east end of the building on the north and south facades. Male and female figures, clad in classical garb and now faceless, peer out from within the sculpted architectural frames of the grave-stones (plate 4.2). They offer a suitably direct reminder of the local, ancient resources that were tapped for the building's construction. As with the Little Metropolis, the inclusion of all these antiquities was clearly not an ad hoc affair, but an organized project that required forethought and purpose. The size, conspicuous placement, precise juxtaposition to one another and splendid isolation of the *stelai* neatly under-score this point.

Several interpretations of the practice of spoliation and reuse in the Byzantine period have been advanced by a number of scholars. Economics aside (and always, at a very basic level, assumed), one of the most fundamental, yet until recently over-looked, explanations concerns aesthetics. As rightly emphasized by Saradi-Mendelovici (1990:52–3), antiquities could be incorporated simply because they enlivened the surface of a building. They endowed it with variety (*poikilia*), the prerequisite of any building of high repute in Byzantium. Surfaces should glitter and walls should gleam, and an embroidery-like texture in facades was always a primary goal. Ancient spolia enriched and often enabled this aesthetic aspiration, even in the most humble of country churches.

There is also the widely accepted contention that spolia, especially those exhibit-ing pagan reliefs, were assigned a new, Christian re-interpretation and/or apotropaic value appropriate to their new post-antique context. This was most forcefully argued by Mango in 1963 and was followed (with much textual reinforcement intended to shed light on the arrangement of sculptures at the Little Metropolis) by Maguire in 1994. The theory holds that the average Byzantine viewer largely distrusted, if not feared, ancient statuary. As the receptacles *par excellence* of residual demons from the pagan past, antiquities were dangerous and so required special measures to neutralize their (mostly evil) powers. Indeed many written sources, especially saints' *Lives*, expose commonly held beliefs and perceptions that fully justify this explanation. In line with this approach, the addition of crosses to the ancient "artifact" was thus thought to counteract any remaining evil spirits. This, according to the theory, would explain the frequent addition of carved crosses on several of the sculpted reliefs immured in the Little Metropolis.

While a strictly Christian reinterpretation may seem the most logical explanation, I know of few instances where the evidence in its favor is absolutely explicit. They do exist, though; for example, in an unpublished *stele* from the archaeological museum in Thebes, a relief inscription was carefully carved into the space surrounding a clas-sical male figure. As at the Little Metropolis, the usual generic crosses are present, but here it is the inscription itself that guarantees the transformation of a pagan gentle-man into a Christian saint, in this case St. Stephanos. We are left to assume such interpretations, however, for most of the ancient, figural sculpture immured in the walls of churches. The explanation of apotropaic safeguarding, such as the wrapping of the Little Metropolis with a "cage of crosses" (Maguire 1994), seems a more measured approach, although the presence of crosses in Byzantium (sculpted, inscribed, painted) was often considered a necessary prophylactic in construction regardless of the presence of antiquities (Čurčić 1992:17–20). And we are still at a loss to explain the immured sculptures for which the cleansing power of the cross was not required at all. What, for example, are we to infer about the two *stelai* at Merbaka which are entirely devoid of such protective devices? Indeed, here the figural statuary play a celebrated rather than diminished role within the overall decorative and iconographic program of the main facades.

Liz James' more nuanced interpretation of ancient statuary in Byzantine contexts (1996), although not directed specifically to the issue of immured spolia, has much to recommend it given her consideration of notions of reception and contextualization. The force of her argument lies in the determination to look beyond the legends and lore typically associated with ancient statues, while simultaneously re-evaluating contemporary versus modern perceptions of the nature and value of the material. She rightly points out that the power of an ancient object was often viewed in positive rather than disparaging terms, and so begins to expose the ambiguous nature of pagan and Christian themes and images, especially in terms of how these objects were "read" and "misread" by the medieval beholder. What remains to be addressed is the specific role of *memory* in this process of appropriation and transformation of the past in some Byzantine buildings. What, for example, do the choice and arrangement of spolia tell us about acts of intentional or non-intentional remembering and forgetting? And was their placement more compelling in contexts that were themselves already rich in memory associations?

Recalling the two supreme examples of the Little Metropolis and Merbaka, it would seem that buildings in which ancient material is incorporated in so distinctive a manner belong to a particular class of monuments whose patrons were attempting to confront the past as represented through its physical remains. I want to suggest that a multitude of messages may be encoded in spoliated masonry, among them an appreciation – if not admiration – for antiquities as a visual link to a very great past, the memory of which became increasingly pronounced in the Middle Byzantine period. This appears to be true of a ninth-century AD foundation in Boeotia, known as the church of the Virgin "of Skripou," that I include as my primary case study. The building is significant for our purposes because of the substantial amount of spolia used in its construction, the manner in which this was incorporated, the proximity and looming presence of a renowned ancient site, and especially because of the testimony of its patron. Unlike the "classic" examples of Merbaka and the Little Metropolis where, despite their antiquarian spirit, we have no definitive patrons, dates, or textual sources that might illuminate the circumstances of construction, the church of Skripou is not anonymous. On the contrary, its founder "speaks" to us through the medium of contemporary inscriptions, thereby equipping us with a sufficient body of evidence with which to decipher his intentions.

Skripou: Patron and Monument in a Landscape of Memory

The church of the Virgin "of Skripou" (hereafter Skripou) is located in the heart of central Greece. It occupies the site of ancient Orchomenos, one of the famed, wealthy cities of the Greek mainland that thrived and prospered from the Mycenean period onward. Significant remains, among them the so-called "Treasury of Minyas" (actually a Mycenean tholos tomb) are visible today (Schliemann 1881). They offer impressive and enduring reminders of the earliest history of the site. Also "on view" is a Hellenistic theater and its auxiliary buildings; a temple allegedly of Asclepius; Mycenaean schist tombs; Archaic statue bases (their figural counterparts long since removed); copious springs of mythological affiliation; and a fortified acropolis that dominates the vast, surrounding plain (Lauffer 1989:492–4). The medieval church takes its place within this local landscape of antiquity as a vivid reminder of the continued presence of human activity well into the Middle Ages and beyond. At the same time its walls, as we will see, offer an inextricable link to an extensive "memory network" of the ancient site that was, according to many modern interpreters, pulled apart in order to facilitate the creation of its post-antique successor. This is an important point in the case of Skripou/Orchomenos, for scholars have seen to it that the ancient and medieval components are considered in complete isolation from one another despite the opportunities that a more mutually inclusive investigation might hold for determining the longevity of cultural memory as it exists and endures within a particular site (Papalexandrou 2001b).

Skripou is most often referred to as one of the primary monuments marking the end of the so-called "Dark Ages" (seventh to early ninth centuries AD) while also signaling the initial flowering of art and culture of the "Middle Byzantine" period (ninth to early thirteenth centuries AD). It is assigned a prominent role in the history of Byzantine architecture in part because of the firm date for its construction – 873/4 AD – a welcome if unusual inscriptional gift of chronological precision that offers a perfect correspondence to the period of intense revival of arts and culture during the reign of the Byzantine emperor Basil I (867–86 AD). The building is impressive on several counts: it is large, in fact one of the largest Byzantine churches in Greece (roughly 29 m × 31 m); its interior space is covered with high, stone vaulting; a series of elaborate, contemporary inscriptions elucidate the circumstances of construction; and it was outfitted with a nearly unprecedented program of decorative sculpture, both inside and out. The general sense is that of an important and lavishly appointed foundation of the late ninth century on the rustic plains of the Byzantine periphery (Papalexandrou 1998).

Of the building's patron we learn much from the aforementioned series of monumental inscriptions, immured one per facade in the lower reaches of the building fabric. They tell us the name of the patron – Leo – and his high rank of *protospatharios* within the imperial administration. We surmise that he came from Constantinople to central Greece, unquestionably a backwater at this time, in his old age, and that he constructed a church and monastery where he could (perhaps) retire and (certainly) be buried and remembered in perpetuity. The latter is made clear in his supplicatory inscriptions, where intercession in the afterlife is sought from the Virgin and saints on his behalf. His burial within the church may in fact be confirmed by the recent discovery of what appears to be a tomb in the narthex, perhaps the patron's own. The inherent funerary function of the building adheres to the common formula of the period in which monasteries, along with a community of monks to perform the requisite rituals, assumed the primary role of commemoration. This fundamental notion – that an attendant monk, priest or any reader of the patron's inscriptions becomes the "performer" of his memorial – must lie at the heart of any analysis of the form, appearance and meaning of the building (Papalexandrou 2001a:279).

In order to properly contextualize the building, we must also look deeper into the issue of its immediate surroundings. Although a richly fertile region for agricultural production, then as now, the more subliminal reputation of the Boeotian plain was likely recognized as well. Ancient Orchomenos was still known to the (educated) Byzantines as the home of the Graces. The goddesses are explicitly affiliated with the site in late antique literature and with epigrams that were still being read, or perhaps read anew, in the ninth and tenth centuries. Contemporary writers also made the connection between deities and site, sometimes with expansive erudition (Papalexandrou 1998:314). The ancient musical and theatrical festivals of the Graces, known as the *Charitesia*, had been celebrated in Orchomenos and are preserved in the literary sources that preoccupied a small circle of *literati* in the capital. Scholia on Pindar's *Olympian* and *Pythian Odes* and the epics of Homer make the best case for this interest, but the marginal remarks in Theocritus' poem to the Graces demonstrate it equally well (Boeckh 1811:291–6, 423; Wendel 1914:330–1). For the educated reader, these mythological figures and historical events may have lent the site a reputation imbued with poetic and musical energy, a potential counterpoint to the widely accepted charges of discontinuity with the classical past as allegedly experienced by the average Byzantine (Mango 1981:54–6). Furthermore, knowledge concerning the historical battles waged and the famous oracles and wealthy cities situated upon the plains of central Greece was probably not entirely overlooked in the process of its textual dissemination through Byzantine scriptoria (Papalexandrou 1998:317). The exotic flora and fauna of Lake Copais, on whose shores the church was built, were still known and regarded as natural wonders, and the illustrious Muses continued to haunt nearby Mount Helicon in the writings of the Byzantine patriarch and scholar Photius (Henry 1971). Indeed, even in the realm of so-called "low-level" saints' *Lives*, the central Greek city of Thebes retained its heroic "seven-gated" designation in the ninth century (Paschalides 1991:178). It is within this mytho-historical landscape – a landscape charged with the memory of antiquity – that our patron conceived his foundation.

The reality of the material evidence at Skripou exposes the practical side of this impulse wherein Leo's builders despoiled a Hellenistic cemetery, the (now excavated) theater across the road, and an anonymous columnar building. The latter has frequently been identified as the famed Temple of the Graces, a completely fictitious notion of the early travelers which has, however, proved enduring because of its local memory associations. What we see in the walls of Skripou are a preponderance of column

Plate 4.3   Church of the Virgin of Skripou. Detail of south facade (photo by the author)

drums, Hellenistic funerary *stelai* with inscriptions, a series of tripod and statue bases, several inscribed "Victor Lists" (that is, the protracted inventories of victorious competitors in the ancient musical contests), a single sculpted *stele* strategically immured inside the building at the main entrance into the nave, and a plethora of otherwise standard, unadorned building material (see plate 4.3). The only medieval intruders into this otherwise uniformly ancient assemblage are the large, contemporary inscriptions of the founder, three of which contain his prayers for salvation. These are neatly fitted into the "collage" of antiquities but are strictly confined to the eastern, most sacred, area of the sanctuary walls.

A reconstruction of the south facade (figure 4.1) offers an impression of the building's original appearance as determined by the archaeological record. A narrow string-course (roughly 2.5 m above ground level) effectively divides the building horizontally into two zones, the upper ledge of its brick band projecting significantly outward while its lower edge lies flush with the surface of the wall. Spolia immured above this line of demarcation were evidently concealed by a layer of plaster (Papalexandrou 1998:252). Those embedded below, by contrast, were left completely exposed. In other words, the worked blocks bearing the written word, whether old or new, were immured within the lowest, most visible tracts of masonry.

Of this general aspect, moreover, we should note that what we see today at Skripou differs markedly from what its builders initially intended. The present state of the walls testifies to more than 1100 years of weathering and repair, and all surfaces (rather than

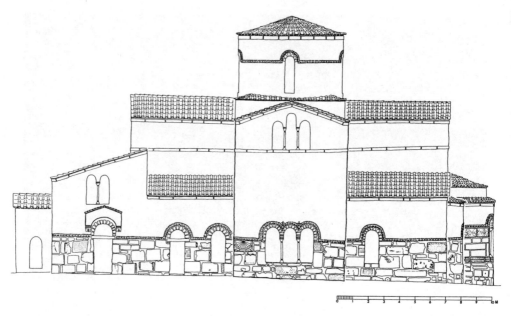

Figure 4.1   Church of the Virgin of Skripou. Reconstruction of south facade (drawing from photo taken by the author)

just the lowest courses) are now in full view. The inclination among scholars is to label this masonry an awkward conglomeration. We must remember, however, that the contemporary viewer did not necessarily share our own value judgments (of which more will be said below), and that the incorporation and display of spolia in the lower walls likely enabled the requisite dose of variety in the building fabric. More to the point is the possibility that the immured fragments offered visual cues for stimulating memory on a number of different levels. The most obvious involves the construction of identity, especially on the part of a patron of high social status who had the means to appropriate and re-integrate the local past for its beneficial associations.

The crucial piece of evidence at Skripou that illuminates the effect of its external walls is a dedicatory inscription immured in the west facade. Here, far from the supplicatory inscriptions of the sanctuary walls, we encounter a patron who is released from his more usual, spiritual obligations of pious humility. We see instead a worldly act of commemoration, one that places a degree of emphasis on the ancient site while simultaneously articulating the patron's place within the continuum of its history. The inscription is a secular panegyric, a poem addressed directly to Leo in the most flattering of terms. Composed in metered verse, it was probably intended to be performed on important occasions such as the dedication of the building and, ultimately, at the death and memorial services of the patron (Papalexandrou 1998:141–51, 2001a: 277–9). The first section of the 12-line text rather predictably assures Leo that his works will not be forgotten, and that in fact his memory will endure precisely because of the construction of the church we see before us:

> Neither envy nor time eternal will obscure the works
> of your efforts, most wonderful one, in the vast depths of oblivion;
> Because your works roar out, even though they are mute
> and you have brought to completion this famous precinct
> of the Virgin Mother, of the Mighty Goddess (*Iphianassa*) who
> received God,
> which is a delightful thing, gleaming on all sides with lovely radiance;
> And on either side of Christ stood both the apostles,
> the hallowed dust of whom a clump of Roman earth covers . . .

The text of the inscription then takes an interesting turn in its final four lines. Here the patron is effectively propelled into a context of timeless abundance while the historical reputation of the ancient site is evoked as a means to anchor this romantic image within a more immediate, even palpable, context of local memory and topography. It is important to imagine the epigram being read aloud, before the building and amidst the nearby ruins, in order to gain a clear sense of the contextual arena for its performance. The conclusion runs as follows:

> Among the bountiful creatures through the endless cycles of time,
> O highly praised Leo the great protospatharios,
> rejoicing in your property and in your most excellent offspring,
> as you command the area of the legendary Orchomenos.
>   (Papalexandrou 2001a:279)

In these verses Leo has not only appropriated some essence of the past, but in owning and consuming the bounty of the site, he has fully vanquished the heroic city of his (pagan) predecessors. He has become its new, overtly Christian commander-in-chief, a most appropriate accomplishment for a man who was at once a literary connoisseur (or so he would have us believe) and a high-ranking military officer of the imperial court. I would point out that the inscription is written in epic hexameters, that it is inscribed in the ancient manner (unlike the other contemporary inscriptions which are carved in low relief) and that it is replete with classical allusion and metaphor, including a reference to the Virgin as *Iphianassa*, the Homeric Iphigeneia. In other words, the west facade inscription departs dramatically from the others on the building through its imitation of the literary form, diction, and appearance of an ancient inscription, as well as through its celebratory, subcelestial content. In this epigram Leo has enshrined his *own* memory (his *kleos*, or fame) for the future by fusing it with a well-chosen memory of the past. I suggest that the conspicuous inclusion of an unprecedented amount of ancient spolia was but the material equivalent of his verbal expression of fame. The fragmented antiquities have, in effect, become participants in the panegyric to the founder.

Spolia and their Readers

At this point I wish to shift the discussion away from the traditionally conspicuous domain of patrons to that of beholders and especially to a more intensive evaluation of the perceptions of spolia within the context of memory. Here I work under the assumption that the anonymity or reticence of patrons, as for example at the Little Metropolis and Merbaka, is not necessarily a hindrance but rather a provocative challenge, one that can also be applied to Skripou as we move beyond the "official" to the "unofficial" realm. It warrants the question of how the minutiae of archaeological evidence, as accessed through a detailed visual analysis of standing remains, can aid us not only in dissecting messages of intention, but also of contemporary reception in the visual consumption of spolia–bearing walls. I will focus on two broad issues. How, precisely, might the act of despoliation and reuse have facilitated memory? And why might it have been important to remember in this particular way? Of the former question, I want to explore further the notion, as suggested by Carruthers (1998:52–57), that ancient, fragmented material in second use held tremendous potential as a mnemonic device for the viewer. Then, as now, such fragments could function as visual stimuli – cues for remembering, albeit perhaps in an oblique and not always intentional way. I hope to demonstrate that spolia bearing ancient inscriptions furnish a particularly interesting case for analysis, one that has been largely neglected but which can generate a series of stimulating questions concerning medieval perceptions of, and relationships to, the past, and present, as triggered through the visible presence of the ancient written word. I will concentrate on the three buildings already discussed, where the placement and, in the case of Skripou, proliferation of inscribed stones suggest the perceived importance of the embedded material.

The inscribed word in Byzantium, as in antiquity, was a remarkably powerful medium of communication and commemoration. Its force was understood at the psychological as well as the intellectual level, and the symbolic import of its visual form was likely felt by all (Thomas 1992:80). The dedicatory inscriptions at Skripou provide one very good and pertinent example of the careful attention paid to the inscribed messages of contemporary founders (Papalexandrou 2001a). Although no comprehensive study has been devoted to the issue, the rich stock of surviving inscriptions and epigrams from the Byzantine period suggests the continued emphasis placed upon them as permanent articulations that were integral to communicative life at all periods and at all levels of society.

But what can we say about the inscribed word that was itself understood or perceived to belong to a past era? And here it is safe, I think, to assume that an "old" inscription would have been recognizable as such, certainly by members of the educated elite and perhaps even by those who were only functionally literate. Contemporary letterforms, for example, were expressly different from those employed in antiquity, and it is clear that some Byzantines at least were looking at and often reading the content of ancient inscriptions. This is attested from as early as the sixth century but with increased frequency from the Middle Byzantine period on (Dagron 1983). Yet the questions remain. Did visibly "old" inscriptions hold greater, or less, significance than contemporary writing? Can we assume that all texts in stone, whether new or old, held an innate symbolic significance? Or did the appearance of greater antiquity lend a more venerable quality to the word? And could such inscriptions have generated the type of responses (verbal, aural, tactile, emotional) from the viewer that contemporary inscriptions likely did? While I do not wish to (and indeed cannot) answer all these questions here, they form a fresh backdrop against which to consider the material. It is with this in mind that I tentatively offer a few interpretations.

Concerning the issue of a potential mnemonic function there is much to be said. The outer walls of a building such as Skripou, in that they comprise a great pastiche of fragments locally derived and re-fashioned within a new Christian context, neatly recall Mary Carruthers' scenario of "crowding" and "relocation" (Carruthers 1998: 53–6). This is a means of manipulating social memory by appropriating visually re-cognizable material remains and re-installing them into a new "web" of associations, thereby recharging them with new meaning. In the material she examines, however, (she is looking specifically at the late antique use of spolia) it is the primary purpose of "forgetting" rather than remembering that is at stake, this within a world still hostile to the pagan past. There are several theories at work here. One holds that too many images lead to confusion and subsequently to a canceling out of the original meaning. Another has to do with displacement (sometimes erasure) and its tendency to pro-mote, rather than destroy, memory. In Carruthers' view, the negative connotations of antiquity in places like Rome and Antioch could be "forgotten" not through anni-hilation but through the kind of "intentional mnemonic replacement" we see in spo-liated masonry.

While the spoils in the masonry of Skripou are indeed crowded and relocated, it seems to me that the mentality, to the extent that it can be traced in the founders' inscription, is quite different and perfectly in accordance with shifting attitudes toward antiquity in the Middle Byzantine period (Saradi-Mendelovici 1990:58–60). As we have seen, Leo does not wish to displace the memory of ancient Orchomenos. Rather, he affirms its existence within his own personal "web" of associations and predicates it as a place in which both he and the venerable site are neatly accommodated, without any violent interruption of the "endless cycles of time" of his inscription. The physical remains – the spoils – with their direct visual impact and evocative capacity as frequently inscribed reminders of the past, are as found objects, crowded into a newly constructed memory place without necessarily blocking their alliance with the greater memory landscape. The crowded facade full of fragments seems less the result of determined forgetfulness than of organized recollection, and in fact calls to mind the Byzantine world view of the ninth and tenth centuries known as *ency-clopedism*. The heroic attempts to collect and classify nearly everything, from laws and imperial ceremonial to literature to agricultural lore, reflect nothing so much as the impulse to fight memory loss (Hunger 1986:515–16; Lemerle 1986:309–46).

Regarding more specifically the appearance of ancient inscriptions, the mnemonic possibilities of "old writing" seem strong. This is not to imply that the ancient inscrip-tions reused on Byzantine facades were always read with comprehension. In those instances where an inscription is turned upside-down or sideways, for example, it is generally presumed that reading comprehension was not the goal. Here it is certainly reasonable to postulate a degree of subversiveness on the part of builders, perhaps with the aim of negating the authority of the past. It would be easy to rush to such a conclusion at Skripou, where the vast majority of inscribed *stelai* are turned on their sides.

On the other hand, I suggest the possibility that certain easily-recognizable words within an ancient inscription, even when turned sideways, might have attracted the attention of a patron or beholder. After all, in our own day, a tilted inscription does not preclude the perusal of its content. Again, I do not mean to imply a careful reading of the inscription in all cases. But as Dale Kinney (1996) has pointed out for several inscribed columns reused in the medieval churches of Rome, an ancient text could be at least partially read, and misread, and ultimately utilized by its readers to "generate local histories." In other words, certain easily distinguishable words or phrases within an inscription might have suggested an immediate, site-specific association that would have been understandable either by itself or in tandem with a topical legend that helped to clarify it.

In this context, inscriptions of considerable length – the lists, treaties, and edicts of antiquity – immured in a great many Byzantine churches throughout central Greece acquired added significance, especially since they were nearly always immured right-side up and at eye level or below. In the village of Geraki, in the Peloponnese, the small church of St. John features four impressive sections of Diocletian's famous Price Edict (*Inscriptiones Laconiae et Messeniae* V[1]:1115A–D; *Corpus Inscriptionum Latinarum* III[2]:816–19) placed so as to completely frame the main entrance in the form of door-jambs and lintel. A long list of competitors in the *Musaea* (the games in honor of the Muses, *Inscriptiones Megaridis et Boeotiae* VII:1776) was incorporated within a church at the foot of Mount Helicon. At the Little Metropolis two ancient, inscribed cornices (*Inscriptiones Atticae aetatis Romanae* III:1736) referring to the Athenian suburban areas of Kifissia and Flua were carefully positioned in pendant locations on the north and south walls of the western vestibule. Might these inscriptions, like those on the reused columns in the churches at Rome, have recalled a past age, one in which the local inscribed site occupied a distinctive place? They are almost always immured in prominent locations such as doorways. Perhaps more importantly, they were positioned upright so as to be visible *and* legible. Two of the original four such inscriptions survive *in situ* at Skripou (*Inscriptiones Megaridis et Boeotiae* VII:3195, 3196). Both are positioned as doorjambs and list the victors in the *Charitesia* of ancient Orchomenos. Bearing this in mind, and remembering Kinney's "local histories" as enhanced by inscriptions, it seems possible that portions, at least, of their content were known, if only partially understood. The evocative quality of certain words, such as "Orchomenos," *rapsodos* ("singer"), *auletes* ("flautist"), and *kitharistes* ("guitarist"), may have helped to create or define a mystique attached to local topographies and mythologies. Indeed, it hardly seems coincidental that the poet of Leo's dedicatory inscription chose the Homeric word *panaoidemos* ("famous in the singing of songs") to describe his ninth-century foundation.

As a parallel case, I note the later example of Merbaka, where a decree in Latin (*Corpus Inscriptionum Latinarum* III[1]:531) was placed upright in the lowest course of orthostates on the west facade. The large, clearly lettered words of the inscription make reference to an *imperator* of *Italicum* who was also *negotiator* with the people of Argos in the heyday of the Roman empire. I should think that its prominent placement could be seen as a means of careful appropriation of the past in order to forge a link, not only to the memory of the ancient city, but also to the culture and history of a non-Greek dedicant of the Roman period. The antiquarian interests of the alleged founder of the church, William of Moerbeke, are well-known, as are his Flemish ethnicity and appointment as Latin archbishop to the region in the thirteenth century (Wilson 1996:226–7). Perhaps the inscription reverberated with the scholar-patron who was, himself, a western foreigner in the Greece of his own day.

It is worth reiterating that Byzantine men of letters clearly did observe, and some-times read, ancient inscriptions at all periods and in areas where they survived in great numbers. This is amply demonstrated during the later Byzantine period (thirteenth to fifteenth centuries AD), at a time when we might expect to see antiquarian inter-est due to the influence of the Italian Renaissance (Saradi 1995:46). But the mental-ity existed earlier as well. In the eleventh century, Michael Psellos puzzled over an old inscribed stone in Constantinople at the behest of the emperor Constantine Doukas, who was intent on understanding its meaning (Dagron 1983:118–19). Theodore, Bishop of Kyzikos in Asia Minor, noticed many broken inscriptions strewn about that ancient site in the tenth century. "On account of the letters" and their size, he was able to deduce the existence of a once prosperous civilization (Saradi-Mendelovici 1990:59). The tenth-century compilations of epigrams that ultimately became known as the "Greek Anthology" derived in part from first-hand recordings of ancient inscriptions. An apparently extensive journey is believed to have been undertaken in the tenth century by one Gregorios Magistros of Kampsa during which this visitor read and copied epigrams directly from the tombs and sarcophagi on which they were inscribed (Wilson 1996:138). In the eighth century we detect something surprisingly akin to an "archaeological tour" of Constantinople aided by inscriptions in the anonymous *Parastaseis Syntomoi Chronikai* ("Brief historical notes"). In one instance, the author enjoins us to "research accurately the inscriptions of the Forum," promising that we will be "really amazed" at what we learn about the city's history (Cameron and Herrin 1984:103). Admittedly, those readers who might accept such a challenge were certainly few in number, the majority of the population presumably lacking the interest as well as the ability for such epigraphical pursuits.

How then might the appearance of this writing, on a more symbolic level, have affected the "average beholder" in Byzantium? For the sake of argument we will assume such a beholder to be semi- or non-literate, although as Mullett has empha-sized (1990:156–63), the surviving evidence for the nature and extent of Byzantine literacy is far from conclusive and certainly varied from one century to the next. Conservative estimates favor a "functional literacy" (Mullett 1990:163), at least amongst the masses. We are probably safe, however, in assuming that letter forms became meaningful even when they could *not* be read. The beholder, for example, may have relied on intermediaries who could read and communicate the otherwise arcane knowledge of the inscriptions.

On the other hand, and I think this is more to the point, we should consider the extent to which words or individual letters might be perceived as objects rather than as writing *per se* – a role in which they may be especially pregnant with content and value. As one possible scenario I propose that viewing ancient inscriptions may have evoked a shared experience or sense of identity with one's ancestors or, to put it in terms often used when discussing the classical past of Byzantium, with one's "cultural heritage" (Jeffreys 1979:207). Assuming that a viewer spoke Greek, a commonality with the past would be immediately forged through the visual appearance of the Greek language, or script. This could have reinforced the sense that "this past before my eyes is my own." The non-Greek-speaking viewer, by contrast, would be effectively excluded from participation in this shared experience. Bierman (1998:36–43) offers a similar approach in her discussion of a series of mosaics from Early Christian cult buildings in Jerusalem, in which three similar and nearly contemporary pavements are distinguished from one another primarily by means of their Jewish, Christian, or Armenian inscriptions. She concludes that it is not the *content* of the inscribed text that determines its identification with a specific group of people so much as the mere *presence* of their own alphabet and the visual force of its script. In this context I note the example of the Bulgarian chieftain's palace at Pliska, built in the early ninth century following a series of spectacular victories over Byzantium. Here a series of spoliated columns bearing Greek inscriptions were incorporated into the ruler's newly constructed ceremonial pathway (Papalexandrou 2001a:280). Presumably the inscriptions were not understandable to the "average" Bulgarian beholder. But their very presence, in the language of the conquered and inscribed upon *spolia* pilfered from famous Greek cities and fortresses that bore the place-names of their origin, sent a powerful message. It reminded the indigenous viewer of the potential inferiority of a distinct cultural identity as demonstrated by the enslavement and reification of its script. The same may help to explain the decorative imitations of Arabic writing ("pseudo-Kufic") found on the facades of many Middle Byzantine churches of Greece.

In this context of "group-based" mentalities (Bierman 1998:36–43), the case of Skripou, with its overwhelming presence of Greek writing on the external walls, is noteworthy. The large and prominent Byzantine inscriptions contend with the numerous ancient names that are inscribed on *stelai* in the lower tracts of walls. Together they indicate a vast spectrum of history, and cultural continuity, as visually conveyed through the written record. I would note that the presence of invading Slavic tribes is well attested for central Greece from the seventh century onward, to the extent that the construction of the church has been viewed as a necessary statement of "Hellenizing" propaganda in an allegedly "barbarian" countryside (Megaw 1966:25). Perhaps an abundance of Greek words on all exterior facades, and especially in or near the crucial juncture of doorways, acted as a protrusive visual reminder of language, history, and culture. A modern analogy can be found in the fraternities and sororities on American college campuses. To the first year student who has not had any experience with the Greek alphabet, the "Sigma Phi Omega" on the building down the street may be more or less meaningless, except as the signpost of an exclusive organization. But to the student who is an initiated member, the foreign letters are a veritable memory bank, evoking an entire social, cultural, and even ancestral network to which he or she belongs. In the case of medieval monuments, a consideration of social context might likewise encourage us to think of the greater impli-

cations of this kind of writing on the walls, perhaps as a means of promoting a cog-
nizance of the past that could legitimate cultural identity.

As another avenue of inquiry, it is possible that ancient funerary inscriptions such
as those found at Skripou (plate 4.1) were immediately recognized as signifiers of
their original use as grave monuments – a notion that acquires added importance
considering the intended funerary function of the church. The forms and appearance
of ancient *stelai* were still remembered in the Middle Ages, as many pagan types and
forms had simply been adapted to Christian monuments. The seventh-century *Life* of
Alypius the Stylite provides a case in point, where the saint not only recognized an
ancient *stele* but initially even admired it (Saradi-Mendelovici 1990:55). Having taken
up residence in an ancient cemetery in northern Asia Minor, he focused upon one
clearly ancient monument incorporating a mythological creature (described as a *tau-
roleon* or "bull-lion") atop a column. According to the text, Alypius embraced the
stone and addressed it fondly as something "marvelous to look at . . . a precious stone
assigned for use as a funeral monument by those who built it" (Delehaye 1923:176).
One version has it that he then chose it as the spot for his own death. The anecdote
illuminates many important aspects of the experience and reception of antiquity in
the Middle Ages (Maguire 1999:191–2), but in the context of the present analysis it
invites consideration of a particular grave *stele* incorporated into the masonry at
Skripou. This gravestone was raised above the other inscribed blocks and was promi-
nently positioned so as to flank the northern entrance into the church's narthex (the
western vestibule where funeral services were held in the Byzantine period). Its
ancient inscription – "Aristea farewell" – contains nothing unusual in and of itself
(*Inscriptiones Megaridis et Boeotiae* VII:3269). What is intriguing is that we find an echo
of the name of the deceased (*Aristea*) in an epithet – *panaristos* ("most wonderful
one") – bestowed on the *protospatharios* Leo in his own panegyric inscription just
around the corner. A reading of the ancient *stele* may have reverberated in concert
with the versified memorial of the founder, especially given its location flanking a
point of access into his place of burial. An ancient grave monument, then, could have
been easily recognizable, and the sight of one may have triggered intellectual or emotional responses appropriate to a commemorative context.

It should be emphasized, however, that the Byzantines tended to remember selectively, a fact that likely enabled the inclusion of a great deal of otherwise "question-
able" *spolia*. Although classical antiquity was indeed their cultural heritage, the status
of that heritage was always ambivalent. It was both a blessing and a curse, and so we
assume a very general evocation of antiquity – the adoption of form but without the
pagan content. Spolia such as the statue of a goddess immured in the east gable of
the Little Metropolis, for example, was surely not understood as Selene in the thirteenth century AD. In literary texts such assumptions are rendered explicit, as has been
eloquently pointed out by Henry Maguire (1990). A tenth-century *ekphrasis* of a
church in Constantinople contains a panegyric to the emperor in which he is likened
to "a fruitful tree of the Muses and a shining plant of the Graces; not, of course, the
Muses of audacious Homer, but the undefiled virgin muses who . . . represent the
godly virtues." One might possess, through a kind of literary spoliation, the attributes

of pagan art and literature but without all the (morally hazardous) trappings of its subject matter (Maguire 1990:220).

The situation was clearly no different a century earlier, as a letter from the patriarch Photius to a high official in central Greece demonstrates. In it, the church official admonishes a *protospatharios* Leo (perhaps the very patron of Skripou?) for his devotion to military pursuits and classical literature at the expense of the "good lessons" (i.e., the Scriptures) – those "solemn, sweet odes" of the Christian faith. He urges this Leo to "give yourself over entirely to *our* noble Muses, who differ from the Greek Muses so much as free people differ in nature from slavish character, and truth from flattery" (Laourdas and Westerink 1984:109, translation and emphasis my own). This *protospatharios* had clearly been remembering too much, or had not forgotten enough, or was perhaps appropriating the memory of the ancient past for the wrong reasons. Regardless of the patriarch's own tendency to couch his reprisal in the ornamentation of classical metaphor, the message is nonetheless clear. One's memory must be selective, even within the seductive, spiritual landscape of antiquity as preserved in medieval Hellas.

As to the question previously asked: Why remember in this particular way? Why create these "museum-like" walls? The theories most frequently submitted hold that the fragmentation and re-arrangement of antiquity's physical remains be understood as a means of empowerment. This is the scenario discussed by James (1996) wherein builders as well as viewers emerge triumphant before walls in which pagan artifacts have been pressed into the service of the church. While this may indeed account for one current in the iconographic underpinnings of these monuments, we might consider other ways to explain the manipulation of antiquities for the storage and apprehension of memory. One possibility is that spoliated masonry could offer a kind of virtual alteration of the actual physical setting of a place, especially in underdeveloped areas far from the "civilizing" center of Constantinople. Put simply, the memory of past urbanity could help one to mentally re-order a predominantly rural setting. The discomfort of the countryside is often at issue in the letters of Byzantines who were either sent as official administrators or expelled as political exiles to the far-flung provinces (Mullett 1990:178). The situation seems to have been especially acute for those who found themselves in central Greece (Herrin 1973). In the case of Skripou/Orchomenos, the relics of a city famed for its wealth, military might, and high culture must have been extremely potent in a region that was now remote and, according to those in exile there, completely deprived. Perhaps the memory of the past evoked the aura of urban life and, consequently, the possibility of a momentary escape from the contemporary rhetoric of "harsh reality."

Closely aligned with this notion is the idea that the Byzantines in certain circles were becoming acutely aware of the grandeur of their past, and that the physical remains of antiquity provided a convenient means of engaging in a dialogue with it. There is no question that such an impulse existed in the late twelfth century in Athens. That city's famous cleric-historian Michael Choniates contrasted the glorious past of the ancient city, which he called "the nurse and mother of wisdom," with the barbaric rusticism of its modern inhabitants from whom, he complained, "the Muses have fled" (Thallon 1923:303). Indeed, his ardor for the city's former greatness often led him to mentally re-create it, imagining himself within a harmonious urban land-scape where he was happy enough to dance "as Alexander danced the Pyrrhic to the music of Timotheos's flutes" (Thallon 1923:299). And there are other, equally remark-able, instances whereby Byzantine writers appreciated classical antiquities not because they were given a Christian reinterpretation and not strictly on the merits of their artistic beauty, but because of the prosperous and esteemed civilization – the lost virtue (*arete*) – that they represented (Saradi-Mendelovici 1990:59). While this type of dia-logue with the past is paralleled in other cultures (Meskell, this volume), it is this issue of continuity – the accessibility and remembrance of the past even centuries later – that lends an extra measure of potency to the construction of social memory in Byzantium.

Fragmentation: The Interference of Modern Sensibilities

The question remains whether Byzantine intellectuals would have approved of the pastiche of antique fragments in churches like the Little Metropolis or Skripou, or whether the construction of their facades would have been viewed as an act of "barbarism" on the part of contemporary inhabitants. It is here that we must take into account medieval ideas and attitudes toward fragmentation, for they would seem to differ distinctly from our own and may help us overcome the often negative schol-arly view of the practice of spoliation. In our modern estimation, the fragment itself is insufficient. We are dissatisfied, uncomfortable, even troubled by it. The tendency, especially among archaeologists, has been to think of it primarily as a means to re-create a scientifically imagined original, so that the value of the fragment lies solely in its potential to complete the picture. Forster (1982:11–13) has singled out our techniques of archaeological reconstruction as a case in point: The tendency since the 1960s to connect fragments of figural statuary by means of metal bars, ostensibly to evoke a sense of completeness, in fact exacerbates our negative estimation as we are faced with a sense of distance and ruination effected through historical time. The frag-ment, in other words, emphatically enhances our perception of a great chasm sepa-rating us from a remote past. Even when Malraux declares the fragment of sculpture "freed" by means of modern photography, its isolation in space and time still marks it as a lamentable object to modern sensibilities (Bergstein 1992:476, 487). That the negative connotations of fragments, in general, still pervade our consciousness is suggested by the movie *Toy Story*, where the character Sid's dismantling and perverse re-configuration of the neighborhood toys is portrayed as a distinctly sinister act, and the spoliated results are intended to scare, even horrify, our children and us.

In the Byzantine Middle Ages it would seem that the fragment did not suffer the same ill repute, though here, again, a thorough study of the phenomenon in Byzantium would clarify matters as it has for the medieval West (Walker Bynum 1991). One need only think of the overwhelming affection for saintly relics which, as discrete objects, were assigned enormous value in and of themselves as powerful enablers of memory (Brown 1981). Indeed, on rare occasions even architectural spolia such as the well-head upon which Christ addressed the woman of Samaria could attain the rank of holy relic (Mango 1959:61). The general collection of building debris for use in church construction was not disparaged. In the tenth-century *Life* of St. Nikon of Sparta, the only stipulation for this action was that the end result be as beautiful as possible so as to win the favor of the saint (Sullivan 1987:119). In terms of an "aesthetic" of fragmentation there can be little question that medieval perceptions differed from our own. In the realm of imagery, as also in building practice, the wholesale borrowing and application of parts of compositions was fully acceptable (Nelson 1999:87), if not preferable, and the visual effects achieved in many facades suggest that complexity, rather than monumentality, was the primary means of expression.

We must imagine, moreover, an intimate kinship with antique fragments simply by virtue of their more tangible physical presence and greater abundance. As noted by Mango (1994:102), early images of the city of Athens (Stuart and Revett 1762–1830) may take us one step closer to the medieval situation, where Byzantine and post-Byzantine buildings rose cheek-by-jowl with the famous monuments of the ancient city. This may be usefully contrasted with our post-Renaissance treatment of sites, where we prefer to experience buildings isolated in space so that they are somehow more pure, or noble, and less adulterated by anachronistic context. The churches of Skripou and the Little Metropolis, for example, are now free on all sides and preceded by large public squares, the long lineup of portable antiquities formerly crowding the area before and within the buildings having long since been removed to museums. Less fortunate monuments were sacrificed *in toto* so as to salvage the ancient inscriptions embedded within their walls. Our modern interventions, therefore, have made it progressively more difficult for us to reconstruct the messy vitality in the overlap of ancient and later structures, or the medieval context in which the creation of new walls from ancient fragments was but a natural exponent of a greater sense of continuity with the past and its physical residue.

Conclusion

The foregoing discussion has, I hope, invited consideration of spoliated monuments in a slightly different way – in terms of each building's membership within a living and vibrant contextual milieu. I have argued that, within such environments, certain spolia may have been perceived as tangible vehicles for the transmission of social memory, primarily as mnemonic devices capable of operating at various societal levels. The case of Skripou is noteworthy, for the abundance of spolia in the walls seems to be in concert with the recorded words of its patron. Together they suggest a nostalgic impulse, one that could communicate at the level of the connoisseur (in the case of the founder's inscription) and perhaps also in visual terms accessible to the "average" beholder (who gazed at the mass of reused antiquities). While the motives of the former may be easily traced, a more in-depth examination is necessary to determine what constitutes the beholder's experience, and this has encouraged closer scrutiny of the material record as well as greater license in interpreting its evidence.

The results may ultimately reward, especially because of their potential to peel back some of the layers of meaning concealed beneath the "official" testimony of an elite patron.

The case of Skripou is also compelling when we consider the visual appearance of its walls together with the function of the building. It was constructed as a monument teeming with visible words, both ancient and contemporary, so that one has the sense of past and present conveyed together within the renewed context of the Christian Middle Ages. At the same time, the experience of this building involved movement, not only through (i.e., inside) but also *around* its walls. Only in this way could inscriptions have been read and antiquities noticed. We are thus led to understand what Connerton (1989) has called "embedded" memory through the existence of "bodily practices" – those involving gesture, ritual, or procession (i.e., all forms of commemoration): The building functions as a church (the storehouse *par excellence* of Christian memory), and the placement of inscribed spolia within its walls was a purposeful act which then required movement or effort in order to see and read them. Of equal significance, however, is the fact that the spolia were themselves written records. Skripou thus affords an interesting combination of both "embedded" and "inscribed" memory (see also Joyce, this volume.) But while Connerton assigns a secondary role to the latter, the situation at Skripou suggests that written ("inscribed") memory could in fact be an equally important component in the construction of a social awareness of the past.

I conclude by considering the overcrowded "display" of spoliated facades in a very basic way – as something inherently visual. This notion of visuality carries with it a great deal of intellectual baggage, much of which has been discussed by others for the period in question (Brubaker 1989:72; Nelson 2000:146–52). I wish simply to emphasize the close connection of sight to memory as cogently stated by the patriarch Photius in the ninth century, not long before the construction of Skripou: "Has the mind seen? Has it grasped? Has it visualized? Then it has effortlessly transmitted the forms to the memory" (Mango 1958:294). It is a simple theory of mnemonics, but it shows that intellectuals of the period understood the experiential process and the interconnectedness of sight and memory. While Photius was primarily interested in figural imagery and its ability to evoke the memory of a Christian past, we can only assume that, for the medieval beholder, *all* perceptual images were evocative, including non-figural commodities like buildings, or words, or the visible signs of antiquity. Sight could conjure up much, and churches such as Skripou, Merbaka and the Little Metropolis contained plenty of images with which to get "tuned in" (Carruthers 1998:57) to the powerful memory bank of associations that reverberated between monument, patron, viewer, and the contextual surroundings to which they all belonged.

References Cited

Bergstein, M. 1992: Lonely Aphrodites: on the documentary photography of sculpture. *Art Bulletin* 74(3), pp. 475–98.

Bierman, I. A. 1998: *Writing Signs: The Fatimid Public Text*. Berkeley: University of California Press.

Boeckh, A. 1811–1812: Scholia on Olympian 14 and Pythian 12. In *Editione Pindari*, vol. 2 part 1. Berlin.

Brown, P. 1981: *The Cult of Saints: Its Rise and Function in Latin Christianity*. Chicago: University of Chicago Press.

Brubaker, L. 1989: Byzantine art in the ninth century: theory, practice, and culture. *Byzantine and Modern Greek Studies* 13, pp. 23–93.

Cameron, A. and Herrin, J. 1984: *Constantinople in the Early Eighth Century: The Parastaseis Syntomoi Chronikai*. Leiden: Brill.

Carruthers, M. 1990: *The Book of Memory: A Study of Memory in Medieval Culture*. Cambridge: Cambridge University Press.

Carruthers, M. 1998: *The Craft of Thought: Meditation, Rhetoric, and the Making of Images, 400–1200*. Cambridge: Cambridge University Press.

Connerton, P. 1989: *How Societies Remember*. Cambridge: Cambridge University Press.

Coulson, M. L. 2002: Gothic in Greece: the architectural sculpture of Merbaka church. *Twentieth International Congress of Byzantine Studies* 3, p. 340.

Ćurčić, S. 1992: Design and structural innovation in Byzantine architecture before Hagia Sophia. In *Hagia Sophia from the Age of Justinian to the Present*, ed. R. Mark and A. S. Çakmak. Cambridge: Cambridge University Press, pp. 16–38.

Dagron, G. 1983: Psellos épigraphiste. In *Okeanos. Essays Presented to Ihor Ševčenko on his Sixtieth Birthday by his Colleagues and Students,* ed. C. Mango and O. Pritsak. Cambridge, Mass.: Ukrainian Research Institute, Harvard University, pp. 117–24.

Delehaye, H. 1923: *Les Saints Stylites*. Paris: A. Picard.

Forster, K. W. 1982: Monument/memory and the mortality of architecture. *Oppositions. A Journal for Ideas and Criticism in Architecture* 25, pp. 2–20.

Guberti Bassett, S. 2000: "Excellent offerings:" The Lausus collection in Constantinople. *The Art Bulletin* 82(1), pp. 6–25.

Henry, R. 1971: *Photius Bibliothèque*, vol. 3, codices 186–222. Paris: Société de l'Édition les Belles Lettres.

Herrin, J. 1973: Aspects of the process of Hellenization in the early Middle Ages. *Annual of the British School of Athens* 68, pp. 113–26.

Hunger, H. 1986: The reconstruction and conception of the past in literature. In *XVIIth International Byzantine Congress. Major Papers*. New York: Caratzas, pp. 505–22.

James, L. 1996: "Pray not to fall into temptation and be on your guard:" pagan statues in Christian Constantinople. *Gesta* 35(1), pp. 12–20.

Jeffreys, E. M. 1979: The attitudes of Byzantine chroniclers towards ancient history. *Byzantion* 49, pp. 199–238.

Kinney, D. 1996: Making mute stones speak: reading columns in S. Nicola in Carcere and S. Maria in Aracoeli. In *Architectural Studies in Memory of Richard Krautheimer*, ed. C. L. Striker. Mainz: P. von Zabern, pp. 83–6.

Laourdas, B. and Westerink, L. G. 1984: *Photii Patriarchae Constantinopolitani. Epistulae et Amphilochia*, vol. II. Leipzig: Teubner.

Lauffer, S. 1989: *Lexikon der Historischen Stätten von den Anfang bis zur Gegenwart*. Munich: Beck.

Lemerle, P. 1986: *Byzantine Humanism*. Canberra: Australian Association for Byzantine Studies.

Maguire, H. 1990: Style and ideology in Byzantine imperial art. *Gesta*, 28(2), pp. 217–31.

Maguire, H. 1994: The cage of crosses: ancient and medieval sculptures on the "Little Metropolis" in Athens. In *Thymiama: Studies in Memory of Laskarina Boura*. Athens: Benaki Museum, pp. 169–72.

Maguire, H. 1999: The profane aesthetic in Byzantine art and literature. *Dumbarton Oaks Papers* 53, pp. 189–205.

Mango, C. 1958: *The Homilies of Photius, Patriarch of Constantinople*. Washington, D.C.: Dumbarton Oaks Studies 3.

Mango, C. 1959: *The Brazen House*. Copenhagen: Royal Danish Academy of Sciences and Letters.

Mango, C. 1963: Antique statuary and the Byzantine beholder. *Dumbarton Oaks Papers* 17, pp. 55–77.

Mango, C. 1981: Discontinuity with the classical past in Byzantium. In *Byzantium and the Classical Tradition*, ed. M. Mullett and R. Scott. Birmingham: Centre for Byzantine Studies, University of Birmingham, pp. 48–57.

Mango, C. 1994: L'attitude byzantine à l'égard des antiquités gréco-romaines. In *Byzance et les Images*, ed. A. Guillou and J. Durand. Paris: La Documentation Française, pp. 95–120.

Megaw, A. H. S. 1966: The Skripou screen. *Annual of the British School at Athens* 61, pp. 1–32.

Michel, K. and Struck, A. 1906: Die Mittelbyzantinischen Kirchen Athens. *Mitteilungen des Deutschen Archäologischen Instituts, Athenische Abteilung* 31, pp. 279–324.

Mullett, M. 1990: Writing in early mediaeval Byzantium. In *The Uses of Literacy in Early Mediaeval Europe*, ed. R. McKitterick. Cambridge: Cambridge University Press, pp. 156–85.

Nelson, R. S. 1999: The Chora and the Great Church: intervisuality in fourteenth-century Constantinople. *Byzantine and Modern Greek Studies* 23, pp. 67–101.

Nelson, R. S. 2000: To say and to see: ekphrasis and vision in Byzantium. In *Visuality Before and Beyond the Renaissance*, ed. R. S. Nelson. Cambridge: Cambridge University Press, pp. 143–68.

Papalexandrou, A. 1998: *The church of the Virgin of Skripou: architecture, sculpture and inscriptions in ninth-century Byzantium*. Ph. D. dissertation, Princeton University.

Papalexandrou, A. 2001a: Text in context: eloquent monuments and the Byzantine beholder. *Word & Image* 17(3), pp. 259–83.

Papalexandrou, A. 2001b: Conversing Hellenism: the multiple voices of a Byzantine monument in Greece. *Journal of Modern Greek Studies* 19(2), pp. 237–54.

Paschalides, S. A. 1991: *The Life of the Holy Myrrh-bearing Theodora of Thessaloniki* (in modern Greek). Thessaloniki: Kentron hagiologikôn meletôn.

Saradi, H. 1995: The *kallos* of the Byzantine city: the development of a rhetorical *topos* and historical reality. *Gesta* 34(1), pp. 37–56.

Saradi-Mendelovici, H. 1990: Christian attitudes toward pagan monuments in late antiquity and their legacy in later Byzantine centuries. *Dumbarton Oaks Papers* 44, pp. 47–61.

Schliemann, H. 1881: *Orchomenos. Bericht über meine Ausgrabungen im Böotischen Orchomenos*. Leipzig: F. A. Brockhaus.

Simon, E. 1983: *Festivals of Attica: An Archaeological Commentary*. Madison: University of Wisconsin Press.

Struck, A. 1909: Vier Byzantinische Kirchen der Argolis. *Mitteilungen des Deutschen Archäologischen Instituts, Athenische Abteilung* 34, pp. 189–236.

Stuart, J. and Revett, N. 1762–1830: *The Antiquities of Athens, Measured and Delineated*. London: J. Haberkorn.

Sullivan, D. 1987: *The Life of Saint Nikon: Text, Translation, and Commentary*. Brookline, Mass.: Hellenic College Press.

Thallon, I. C. 1923: A mediaeval humanist: Michael Akominatos. *Vassar Mediaeval Studies*, ed. C. F. Fiske. New Haven: Yale University Press, pp. 275–314.

Thomas, R. 1992: *Literacy and Orality in Ancient Greece*. Cambridge: Cambridge University Press.

Walker Bynum, C. 1991: In praise of fragments: history in the comic mode. In *Fragmentation and Redemption. Essays on Gender and the Human Body in Medieval Religion*. New York: Zone Books, pp. 11–26.

Wendel, C. 1914: *Theocritus. Scholia*. Leipzig: Teubner.

Wilson, N. G. 1996: *Scholars of Byzantium*. Cambridge, Mass.: Medieval Academy of America.

5
Glories of the Past in the Past: Ritual Activities at Palatial Ruins in Early Iron Age Crete

Mieke Prent

Introduction

Crete is known for its splendid Bronze Age or "Minoan" civilization, named after the legendary king Minos. Minos was the son of Zeus and Europa, to whom ancient Greek authors, from Homer to Plato and Diodoros Siculus, ascribed great fame as lawgiver and mighty ruler of the seas (for an overview of ancient sources see Poland 1932). Archaeological research since the late nineteenth century has done much to underscore the pre-eminence of Minoan Crete. Excavation and survey have revealed a large number of sites, ranging from monumental palaces, villas and sanctuaries to smaller settlements, roads and harbors. During the middle and late phases of the Bronze Age (ca. 2000–1600 and 1600–1200 BC respectively) the island was densely populated and knew a highly organized and complex civilization, with the Minoan palaces as their administrative, political, and religious centers.

By the end of the thirteenth century BC, the majority of these Bronze Age centers were abandoned and left to decay. This happened in tandem with the widespread destruction and dislocation of people that affected large parts of the Mediterranean in this period, and which the contemporary Egyptian texts ascribe to the "Sea Peoples" (Sandars 1978). In Crete, changes included a movement of population from low-lying coastal areas to defensible sites inland (see esp. Nowicki 2000) and a concomitant shift in economy, which became more localized and less oriented towards seaborne trade.

The Early Iron Age in Crete is subdivided into the Protogeometric period (1000/970 BC–810 BC) and the Geometric period (810–700 BC). It is followed by the Orientalizing period (700–630 BC), the Archaic period (630–480 BC), the Classical period (480–330 BC), the Hellenistic (330–67 BC) and Roman (67 BC–330 AD)

Many thanks are due to the editors of this volume, for their constructive suggestions and remarks, and to Stuart MacVeagh Thorne, who patiently read and commented on several versions of this paper.

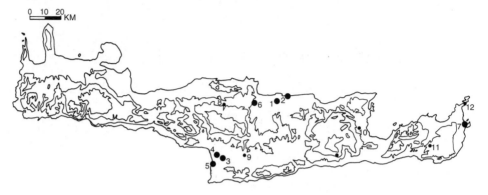

Map 5.1 Map of Crete, with sites mentioned in the text: (1) Knossos, (2) Amnisos, (3) Phaistos, (4) Ayia Triada, (5) Kommos, (6) Tylisos, (7) Palaikastro, (8) Axos, (9) Gortyn, (10) Lato, (11) Praisos, (12) Itanos

periods. Traces of activity at the old Cretan centers remain scarce until the Early Iron Age (the tenth to eighth centuries BC). In the course of this period, Crete, like most other regions in the Greek world, experienced a number of crucial and interrelated changes, eventually leading to the formation of the Greek city-states or *poleis*. The population began to grow, settlements increased in size and number, and the differentiation in tombs and votive assemblages at sanctuaries indicates the articulation of different social groups, including that of a leading group of aristocratic warriors. These demographic and socio-political changes were accompanied by an intensification of overseas contact both within the Aegean and with the Near East, a broad improvement in material standards, and the rediscovery of forgotten skills such as writing and specialized metal working. It was in this same, formative, period that the ruins of a number of the old Minoan sites – some two to three hundred years after their abandonment – were singled out as the foci for ritual activities. At present, seven instances of such Early Iron Age "ruin cults" are known: at the former palaces of Knossos and Phaistos; at Ayia Triada, Kommos, Amnisos, and Tylisos; and at Palaikastro in the far east of the island (map 5.1). Each of these sites has yielded evidence for the lasting visibility of monumental sections of the former palaces and associated building complexes. Such remains constitute potentially strong markers for the local remembrance of a glorious Bronze Age past, suggesting that their selection as a cult place in the Early Iron Age represents a deliberate choice. However, as will be explored below, the motives for these choices indicate the complexity of the phenomenon of memory, with different roles played by the social, historical, and religious components.

Cult Amidst the Ruins

One of the first excavators to observe the phenomenon of the prolonged visibility of Cretan Bronze Age monuments was Arthur Evans at Knossos. He described how

Plate 5.1   Amnisos. Part of the more than 44 m long Bronze Age wall (photo by the author)

fragments of a Minoan relief-fresco depicting a charging bull, in the Northern Entrance Passage to the palace, were found one meter higher than the Late Bronze Age strata, on a level which he associated with Geometric sherds found 20 m further to the north (Evans 1930:171). Imposing sections of the Minoan palace, including its decoration, clearly had remained visible during the Early Iron Age. This is also indicated by the discovery of a votive deposit of that date in the southwest corner of the palace's Central Court. Here, near the level of the Minoan paving, Evans encountered some terracotta figurines, one of which may have belonged to a clay cauldron, and drinking equipment consisting of a Geometric krater and tens of drinking cups ranging in date from the Protogeometric to the Hellenistic periods (Coldstream 2000:284–8; Evans 1928:5–7, 346 n.1). A possible Classical or Hellenistic cult building was erected between the ruined walls of the adjacent West Wing. Initially, however, cult activities would have taken place in the open air. The presence of a concentration of ash and bone (Evans 1899–1900:17) may indicate that the earliest rituals involved animal sacrifice and/or sacrificial dining.

Evidence for the lasting visibility of the architectural vestiges of the Bronze Age and their association with cult activities has since accumulated. At Amnisos, a Minoan harbor town which probably belonged to the territory of Knossos, an imposing Bronze Age ashlar wall, more than 44 meters in length, attracted cult activities from the later Protogeometric period (plate 5.1). A layer resting against it, more than 0.70 m thick, contained ash, animal bones, fragments of precious bronze tripods and bowls, bronze figurines, terracotta drinking cups, kraters, amphorai, and storage vessels –

Plate 5.2   Phaistos. Early Iron Age and later sanctuary at the foot of Bronze Age ashlar walls. (From Pernier and Banti [1951: Figure 83], reproduced by permission of the Libreria dello Stato – Istituto Poligrafico e Zecca dello Stato, Rome)

remnants of sacrificial refuse – ranging in date from the late ninth to the seventh century BC. Due to limited excavation, the original function of the Bronze Age building has not been determined, but the size and execution of the exposed wall point to a public character. Traces of seventh-century BC occupation were found in a Late Bronze Age house some 400 m west of the sanctuary, indicating that other buildings of the harbor town remained visible at this time (Schäfer 1992:350). While the surrounding settlement was never reoccupied at a large scale, the Early Iron Age sanctuary was frequented for cult purposes into Roman times. During the Classical period a cult building was erected, as implied by the discovery of architectural fragments of that date, and portions of the upper courses of the Bronze Age wall were rebuilt (Schäfer 1992:182–5).

At Phaistos, the second-largest Minoan palace site of Crete, there is comparable evidence for the lasting visibility of sections of the former palace and for Early Iron Age cult activities associated with the remains. The early excavators of Phaistos, in contrast to Evans, considered that later inhabitants used the Bronze Age ruins merely as a source for ashlar blocks (Pernier and Banti 1951:14). It now appears significant that a votive deposit of Early Iron Age bronze shields and bowls was found at the foot of the two well-preserved Bronze Age ashlar walls (ca. four meters high) which had retained the southwest section of the palace. These walls must then have been standing as they are today (plate 5.2), and they formed an impressive backdrop for the Early Iron Age open-air cult. In the seventh century BC a cult building was erected, which was subsequently enlarged in the Hellenistic period (Pernier 1907:262–4).

At Ayia Triada, only 3 km west of Phaistos, there is evidence that a monumental Bronze Age Stoa and adjacent paved court became the focus for cult activities during the late ninth century BC. In an illuminating restudy of the old excavation material, L. D'Agata (1998) concludes that in this period a small room was built against the northeast corner of the standing Stoa. While no votives were found inside the Stoa, numerous late ninth to early seventh-century anthropomorphic and animal figurines in both terracotta and bronze had been deposited along the exterior face of its north wall and on the steps of the monumental Minoan staircase to its east. A second concentration of votives of the same date came from the paved court and a stepped area to the south.

At Tylisos, a partially excavated Bronze Age site in the eastern foothills of the Ida mountains, an arrangement of Stoa and a paved court similar to that at Ayia Triada was discovered. As at the latter site, it was this monumental area that began to attract open-air cult activities in the Early Iron Age. A stone-built altar has been associated with bronze and terracotta figurines and with a probable fragment of a bronze tripod of Cypriot type. Most votives remain unpublished and can therefore be dated only broadly from Geometric to Hellenistic times. It is clear, however, that these were found in conjunction with the Bronze Age remains, only a few centimeters above the latest Bronze Age paving (Chatzidakis 1934:66–9, 109–10, pl. XIV).

The clearest picture is provided by Kommos, a site on the south coast of Central Crete, under excavation since 1976. The use of detailed, modern excavation techniques has made it possible to ascertain that numerous Bronze Age walls were visible until late in the eighth century BC. This applies both to the more modestly constructed Minoan houses on the slope and summit of the settlement hill – where a complete Protogeometric krater was found among the ruins (Shaw 1981:213, pl. 61d) – and to the monumental remains of ashlar complex P/T and its associated court at the bottom of the hill. This complex, for which the excavators propose a palatial or public function, attracted cult activities from ca. 1000 BC. At that time a first small cult building – Temple A – was erected, measuring ca. 5.5 × 6.7 m. Temple A actually incorporated part of one of the ashlar walls of the ruined Bronze Age building T, and both Temple A and its late ninth-century successor Temple B were founded on a heap of collapsed ashlar blocks from Building T. Visitors also reused some of the galleries of Building P, the roof of which may have been partially preserved (Shaw and Shaw 2000:8–16). Animal bones, drinking vessels, and plates are indicative of repeated sacrificial dining, while characteristic votives consist of life-size and miniature weaponry (including some bronze shields), large terracotta bull and horse figures, and small ones in terracotta and bronze (Shaw and Shaw 2000:691).

At Palaikastro, in the far east of the island, a portion of a large Bronze Age settlement was converted into a sanctuary for Diktaian Zeus during the Protogeometric or Geometric period (figure 5.1). Recently, Crowther (1988) has argued that the mention by the first-century author Diodoros Siculus of a city, founded by Zeus but still visible in ruined state during the author's day, refers in all likelihood to the Bronze Age town at Palaikastro. Re-study of the old excavation material, combined with

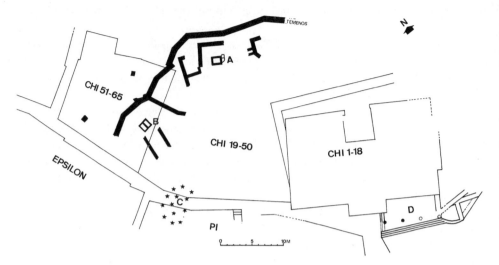

Figure 5.1   Plan of the sanctuary at Palaikastro: (A and B) architectural remains of the fifth century BC and later, (C) Early Iron Age ash altar, (D) stepped area

information from the new excavations, shows indeed that house and street walls were standing until long after the thirteenth-century abandonment of the settlement. More specifically, a stepped area (situated at the southeast limit of the excavated area and therefore only partially explored) may constitute a later addition to a partially ruined Bronze Age house. During the Early Iron Age, cult activities focused on the area of former house block Chi (figure 5.1). In this area an ash altar was found, and around it were fragments of bronze tripod-cauldrons, bronze bowls, decorated shields and armour, terracotta drinking cups, and other vessels (Hutchinson et al. 1939–40). Architectural fragments, ranging in date from the later sixth century BC to the Hellenistic period, indicate the existence of a series of cult buildings during the later life of the sanctuary (MacVeagh Thorne and Prent 2000).

The monumental character of the Bronze Age ashlar walls that were visible at these seven sanctuaries would have stood in sharp contrast to the modest, small-stone architecture of the Early Iron Age itself (e.g. Hayden 1981:139–41). It is not inconceivable that such massive ashlar walls inspired, besides admiration for the technical skills required to build them, stories of supernatural origin, in the same way that the megalithic walls of Tiryns on the Greek mainland were believed to have been built by giant, one-eyed Cyclopes under the direction of Zeus (Bacchylides, *Ode* 11.72–80). Confirmation for the idea that monumental walls had divine connotations during the Early Iron Age can be found in the Homeric epics – in the *Iliad* (7.445–52, 8.519) the city walls of Troy are said to have been built or founded by the gods. Nevertheless, it must be emphasized that Early Iron Age Cretans do not appear to have suffered from any vague, indiscriminate feelings of awe or respect towards ancient monuments. Outside the immediate areas of the sanctuaries, the reuse of Bronze Age structures for habitation and other profane purposes, and their destruction by the dismantling of walls and quarrying of ashlar blocks, is well-attested (e.g. Sackett 1992:1–2 for examples at Knossos). Even within areas dedicated to cult, there may be evidence for the quarrying of ashlar blocks, as revealed by the layer of stone chips around Temple B at Kommos (Shaw and Shaw 2000:24).

Instead of generalized feelings of awe for Bronze Age remains, more specific considerations seem to have led to the singling out of precisely these sites at which to worship. Not only are the chosen ruins of the finest ashlar masonry, they are part of complexes that had served palatial or related public functions during the Bronze Age. (The only exception is Palaikastro, although suggestions have been made that a palace is hidden in the unexcavated area immediately south of the sanctuary.) Rather than a random choice of monumental remains, this implies a relatively faithful preservation of the memory of the special character of these places. In some cases, the apparent avoidance of the surroundings of these sanctuaries for habitation strengthens this idea. The abandonment of Amnisos, Ayia Triada, Kommos, Palaikastro, and possibly Tylisos in the thirteenth century BC here needs no explanation beyond the widely attested changes in settlement pattern and economy that characterized the closing centuries of the Bronze Age. At a site like Knossos, on the other hand – which continued to be an important settlement center long after the Bronze Age – the absence of later habitation in the area of the palace is striking. Several scholars propose it was the result of conscious avoidance, or even a taboo placed on habitation (Coldstream 2000:296–8; Evans 1928:7). At Phaistos, one of the few other Cretan Bronze Age sites that was continuously inhabited into the Early Iron Age, the picture is unfortunately more fragmentary. The early excavators report the removal of a number of "later structures" from over the Bronze Age palace without giving precise dates. Both "Greco-Roman" and "Hellenic" occupation are mentioned, but it is uncertain if the latter term was meant to include the Geometric period. Well-preserved Early Iron Age houses have been recorded immediately west of the palace. From there occupation certainly extended west, up the slope, and southwards along the bottom of the palace hill, in a pattern broadly corresponding to that at Knossos (La Rosa 1992:240).

To recapitulate, at places such as Knossos, Amnisos, and Kommos, there is evidence for the lasting visibility of larger parts of the Bronze Age sites, including dwellings, which invited different kinds of reuse, from quarrying to re-habitation. There is, however, a distinct preference for monumental constructions as the location for Early Iron Age cult. Apparently, from the tenth century BC on, certain Cretans developed a special interest in the monuments that centuries earlier had served palatial or related functions. Their interest found expression in the dedication of sometimes precious votives and in rituals of sacrificial dining and drinking. The fact that cult was predominantly practised in the open air would have reinforced the dramatic effect of these gatherings amid the age-old ruins.

The Worshippers and their Motives

The composition of the votive assemblages associated with these Early Iron Age sanctuaries provides some indication as to who worshipped there. Although the assem-

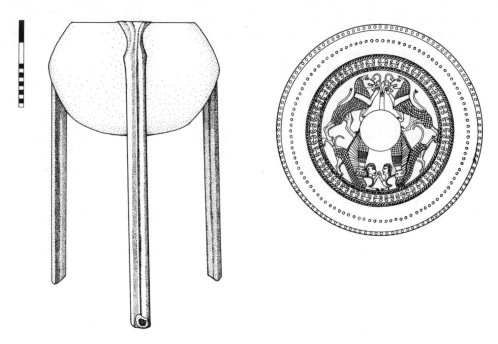

Figure 5.2   Bronze tripod-cauldron and decorated shield from Palaikastro

blages at first glance seem far from uniform, there are a number of recurrent features. One of these is the predominance of bronze objects at many of the sanctuaries. This, in a period when the overseas contacts to obtain the necessary metals were only gradually increasing and specialized skills of metalworking only recently regained, indicates a distinct wealth of votary. We can learn more about the social standing and aspirations of the dedicants by considering the nature and symbolic connotations of the attested types of votive in some detail.

At four of the seven sanctuaries – Amnisos, Phaistos, Kommos, and Palaikastro – votive assemblages are dominated by large bronzes, which take the form of tripod-cauldrons and shields (figure 5.2). Objects of this kind constituted the most precious and conspicuous dedications available in the early Greek world and define the stature of the votary. Their presence in large numbers is significant because it shows how much wealth people were prepared to consecrate (Snodgrass 1980:52–4).

The military–aristocratic connotations of the dedicated shields speak for themselves. The possession of this kind of armor, often elaborately decorated, was clearly the reserve of an elite. Bronze shields and other weaponry occur as grave offerings in rich Cretan tombs from the late ninth to the seventh century BC and would have articulated the deceased's role as warrior and leading member of the developing aristocracy. The dedication of such objects in sanctuaries would have had a similar function, but added an element of greater visibility and permanency. Precious votives could remain on display for generations, as attested by ancient authors such as Pausanias. He mentions seeing such votives and being told that these were of great antiquity and offered by famous rulers (e.g. Paus, III.2.8, III.3.8., V.19.6). Clearly, the religious dedication of precious objects implied special relations with higher powers. Like a claim to military prowess, this relationship enhanced a donor's position in the community and would have been considered as more than worth the expense.

The bronze tripod-cauldrons, though lacking the overt military connotations of the shields, were no less tied to the aristocratic ethos. An indication of their value may be gained from the Homeric epics, in which they constitute the most prestigious gift exchanged between fellow aristocrats. In a passage of the *Iliad* (23.703–5), a tripod is estimated to have a value of twelve oxen, whereas a skilled, female slave is considered to be worth only four. O. Murray (1983) has argued that the special meaning of bronze tripod-cauldrons in early Greek times derived from their use as cooking vessels at communal dining parties. Drawing on anthropological parallels and the Homeric epics, Murray describes these as competitive, ritualized affairs, in which the leading members of society would try to outdo each other in generosity, including the provision of vast quantities of food. Tripod-cauldrons would thus have developed into symbols of the owner's wealth and – no less importantly – of the ability to feed, sustain and organize a group of followers. As pointed out by W. Burkert, bronze cauldrons were also the ideal vessel in which to boil the parts of the sacrificial meat that were not roasted. Their frequent setting up in sanctuaries may have been a way of "giving permanence to the sacrificial act" (Burkert 1985:93).

Snodgrass (1980:55–64) and Morgan (1990) have discussed how in the Early Iron Age precious votives such as tripod-cauldrons and armor tended to accumulate at specific sanctuaries and how these sanctuaries played a key role in the formation of regional aristocratic and religious identities. Their analyses concentrate on famous mainland Greek sites such as Olympia and Delphi, whose location, far from contemporary settlement centers, contributed to their development as relatively neutral meeting places for the leading members of the hundreds of independent Greek communities. Here, people would gather, participate in a common cult, and engage in friendly exchange as well as in more competitive display of achievement and wealth – the latter materially reflected in the dedication of precious votives. In like manner, the accumulation of large bronzes at the sanctuaries of Amnisos, Kommos, Palaikastro, and Phaistos in Crete may point to their function as meeting places for the elite. The sanctuary at Phaistos, which was part of a thriving settlement, could have served prominent residents of the surrounding settlement, whereas the other three cult places – which were extra-urban in location – could have attracted worshippers from beyond the borders of the local community.

The elite connotations of the Cretan ruin cults are confirmed when two other recurrent features of their votive assemblages are taken into account. First, the abundant presence of animal bones and vessels for drinking and eating (figure 5.2) suggests that sacrificial dining was an important aspect of the rituals conducted at these sanctuaries. Recent literature shows how in early Greece ritualized forms of dining – particularly when centering around the consumption of meat and wine – became the prerogative of a male elite and eventually evolved into specific institutions such as the symposion ("drinking together") of Archaic times. There, as elsewhere, ritualized dining can be seen as a way of selective bonding, of creating a sense of unity between participants and, at the same time, defining the exclusiveness of the group in relation to other segments of society (Murray 1990; Schmitt-Pantel 1992). Second, it is noteworthy that the associated votive assemblages lack the vast numbers of simple, inexpensive terracotta votives that characterize the large community sanctuaries of this period. At sanctuaries of that kind at Axos, Gortyn, Lato, and Praisos, literally hundreds of clay anthropomorphic and animal figurines were dedicated from the eighth century BC on. Apparently, cultic association with vestiges of the Bronze Age was *not* used as a way of binding together different segments of the community with reference to a common past. Instead, the ruin cults appear to have been the exclusive domain of smaller and more restricted groups of worshippers, to whom association with the past would have been a mark of social distinction.

The status of these cults may also be expressed in the choice of deity. At Amnisos and Palaikastro there is later literary evidence for the worship of Zeus, who, as the *primus inter pares* (first among equals) of the gods, is already an object of identification for aristocratic warriors in the Homeric epics (Van Wees 1992:73–5, 142–6, 198). At Kommos the principal deity was probably Apollo, but a Hellenistic inscription also mentions Zeus and Athena (Shaw and Shaw 2000:692–3). These three divinities may have formed a cult triad, which is also known from elsewhere in the Greek world and which displays close connections with the political institutions of the poleis. For the sanctuaries at Phaistos and Knossos, the worship of Rhea, mother of Zeus and the other Olympian gods, has been proposed (Evans 1928:5–7; La Rosa 1992:240). Clearly, the attested deities come from the highest ranks of the Greek pantheon. Their worship would have assumed special relevance for those belonging to, or aspiring to belong to, the highest ranks of society.

Similar exclusive and aristocratic connotations seem to have been characteristic of cult activities at the remaining three sanctuaries – Knossos, Ayia Triada, and Tylisos – even though here an accumulation of large bronze votives is less apparent or not attested at all. To some extent this lack may be due to the vagaries of archaeological preservation and discovery – as for instance in the case of Tylisos, where too few finds were retrieved for us to be able to consider such matters further. It may also apply to Knossos, where the deposit of ceramic drinking equipment and figurines in the Central Court may have been the only one to escape later plundering and disturbance.

At Knossos, however, the drinking equipment found implies the involvement of a male elite, an idea which becomes more persuasive when considering the evidence from the North Cemetery (after ca. 1100 BC the central burial ground for the inhabitants of Knossos) and the formation of distinctly aristocratic burial styles in the same period. Coldstream has observed that this cemetery experienced a growing trend towards uniformity in the course of the tenth century BC, with cremation in rock-cut chamber tombs becoming the prevailing rite. The concurrent introduction of funerary meals or symposia, as indicated by the drinking sets in some tombs, is significant, in that it provides a link with the votive assemblage of the sanctuary at the former palace. The presence in the tombs of imported Attic drinking sets has been cited as an indication that gift-exchange with leading families on the Greek mainland led to the transmission of the custom of symposia (Coldstream and Catling 1996:715–7) – a result of the increased intercommunication between the rising elite groups in different parts of the Aegean.

Subsequently, in the second half of the ninth century BC, some Knossians began to use exceptionally large chamber tombs, which remained in use for several generations. These were among the richest in the cemetery and in plan and form are so similar to Late Bronze tombs that it is hard to tell whether they are indeed just thoroughly cleared-out earlier graves or simply very close imitations. Coldstream has convincingly interpreted this phenomenon as a conscious attempt of leading Knossian families to associate themselves more closely with the Bronze Age past, an interpretation which is further corroborated by his analysis of the associated pottery. While contemporary more modest cremations were placed in coarse pithoi, or in belly-shaped urns decorated in the older Protogeometric tradition, the straight-sided urns in the large chamber tombs seem to imitate a Bronze Age form (the pyxis of similar straight-sided shape) and are decorated in the new Protogeometric-B style, which drew part of its inspiration from Bronze Age motifs. That these motifs were easily found is indicated by the presence, in at least ten of the large chamber tombs, of fragments of Late Bronze Age clay larnakes: left-overs, apparently, of an earlier and interrupted use of the burial plot. Their decoration may well have inspired some of that observed on the straight-sided urns and of other pottery from the tombs, such as the bird-and-tree theme and the representation of female figures. Somewhat later, in the eighth century BC, there also is a short-lived revival of the Minoan octopus motif (Coldstream 1988, 1991:291–7).

The changes in burial rite and tomb-furnishings, as described by Coldstream, provide an insight into the outlook of these early Knossians, which may serve as a parallel to their attitude toward the still visible remains of the Bronze Age palace. This attitude may be described as one of interest and identification, which resulted in specific forms of "sanctified" reuse and imitation. It is important to note here the specifically Cretan character of this response. In other regions of the early Greek world the discovery of Bronze Age tombs often led to the installation of a cult (see Antonaccio 1995). The Cretan attitude certainly contrasts to that of an eighth-century grave digger in Attica who, upon the accidental discovery of a Middle Bronze Age burial, tried to reassemble the broken bones and left an oinochoe with it – as if to make up for the disturbance (Coldstream 1976:11). In Early Iron Age Crete, a certain pragmatism and purposefulness on the part of those pursuing the association with the Bronze Age past cannot be denied. Such an association provided instruments for the articulation and legitimization of the claims to power and authority of rising aristocratic groups. Further insight into the reasons and motives behind the installation of cults at the ruins of the most conspicuous Bronze Age monuments may be gained by considering the situation in the western Mesara, where at three sanctuaries Bronze Age remains existed in close proximity to one another.

Territory and Trade

At Ayia Triada no large bronzes such as tripod-cauldrons, shields, or other armor were found. We cannot, therefore, make the assumption that the sanctuary served as an exclusive meeting place for the aristocratic members of surrounding communities.

Nevertheless, the presence of dozens of bronze animal and anthropomorphic figurines suggests substantial investment of wealth. In addition, several classes of votive objects, such as the small terracotta shields, and bronze and clay wheels which presumably belonged to model chariots, carry military–aristocratic connotations comparable to those proposed for the large shields at other sanctuaries. Some kind of aristocratic involvement or concern, in other words, seems manifested.

D'Agata has called attention to similarities in the general composition of the assemblage from Ayia Triada with that of Artemis Orthia at Sparta, a sanctuary especially known for the rites of passage for young Spartan aristocrats (D'Agata 1998:23–4). Closer to home, Lebessi (1991:108–10) has pointed to the parallel occurrence of certain types of figurines at Ayia Triada and Syme, a sanctuary in the mountainous southeastern region of Crete that also may have specialized in male initiation rites. Common types include figurines of bovids, of a young man holding a cup, and of couples consisting of a mature and a younger male. For the votives from Syme, Lebessi has demonstrated a connection with the description by the fourth-century author Ephoros of an "old Cretan custom," which modern scholarship interprets as an initiation ritual for young, aristocratic men. This custom consisted of the staged abduction of an adolescent boy by an adult man. They would retreat to the countryside for an initiatory period of two months, a period which they spent hunting, feasting, and love making, and which came to a conclusion with a ceremony in which the initiate was presented with a warrior's attire, a wine cup (symbolizing his right to participate in the messes of the male citizens) and an ox, which was to be sacrificed to Zeus (Burkert 1985:261; Strabo X. 4.21). Key elements of the ritual described by Ephoros – which no doubt formed an elaborate and prestigious form of initiation – seem to be reflected in the categories of votives that are common to Syme and Ayia Triada. While it is difficult to say if the initiation rites at Ayia Triada correspond in detail to those Ephoros reports, it may be assumed that the sanctuary indeed played an active part in the articulation of the highest social class. Again, it may be significant that the worshipped deity was Zeus (Willetts 1962:250–1).

Ayia Triada is thus of interest for showing the variation in the forms of aristocratically-inspired cults at Cretan Bronze Age remains. While, at the sanctuaries discussed previously, the focus was primarily on established aristocrats and their relationship with one another, at Ayia Triada it seems to have been on the formation and education of the young men who were soon to join their ranks. By situating such initiation rituals near the visible remains of the older age, a tangible link with the past was forged, which would reinforce the idea that these warriors and rulers-to-be were also the privileged heirs of a more glorious or heroic age.

The sanctuary at Ayia Triada is of interest for other reasons as well. One of these is that the site knew an earlier period of cult activities during the twelfth and eleventh centuries BC, which seems to have ended some 150 years before the Early Iron Age cult was installed. A brief discussion of this earlier cult – which differs in some significant aspects from that of the Early Iron Age – may serve to illustrate two points: the rise of aristocratic concerns during the period of temporary abandonment of Ayia Triada as a cult place and the interrelationship of this site with the two nearby sanctuaries at the Bronze Age ruins of Kommos and Phaistos.

During the twelfth and eleventh centuries BC, cult activities at Ayia Triada concentrated on an area south of the Bronze Age Stoa. Votives primarily consisted of
large terracotta bovine and other animal figures and so-called Horns of Consecration,
stylized bulls' horns, a well-known cult symbol during the Minoan period. With the
relative absence of military connotations, L. Banti, who first published this votive
deposit, proposed that cult was principally aimed at the promotion of the fertility of
land and livestock (Banti 1941–43). One of the reasons for using Ayia Triada for a
sanctuary directly after the abandonment of the Bronze Age settlement may indeed
have been its proximity to the fertile valley to the north (see on this issue also De
Polignac 1992; Nixon 1990). Territorial claims would have been helped by association with the old town that controlled the area during the Bronze Age. The relationship of the twelfth–eleventh-century cult with the ruined buildings, however,
remained undefined and none of them seems to have been reused or incorporated
in the cult activities taking place. Whether the presence of the ruined Bronze Age
architecture was of primary importance to the location chosen for this early cult place
therefore remains unclear.

By contrast, when cult was resumed around 840 BC, its orientation and content
seem to have changed in the way discussed above. Given the dedication, also in this
later period, of small animal figurines in terracotta and bronze, it is possible that something of the older agricultural interest remained. Such interest, however, seems to have
been overshadowed by newly developed concerns of a stronger, military–aristocratic
character. By this time, the custom of dedicating Horns of Consecration and large
bovine figures had come to a halt. The reason for this can hardly have been that
votives of these types had gone out of vogue, since the large bull figures began to be
dedicated at the nearby coastal site of Kommos in the tenth century BC. D'Agata has
made the convincing suggestion that the tenth-century rise of the sanctuary at
Kommos initially was at the expense of Ayia Triada, causing cult at the latter site to
wane during that period. D'Agata adds that this shift may reflect a change in interest on the part of the community that controlled the territory (La Rosa and D'Agata
1984:181).

This suggestion leads us back to Phaistos, as this is the most likely candidate to
have exerted territorial claims in the western Mesara. Although Phaistos was not
the only Early Iron Age settlement in the area, it certainly was one of the largest
communities – and had been so since early in the Bronze Age. Particularly close ties
seem to have existed from early in their existence between Phaistos, Ayia Triada and
the harbor town at Kommos. A Bronze Age road, part of which has been traced at
Kommos, probably connected the latter with Phaistos, some two hours away on foot.
Ayia Triada, which is located close enough to Phaistos to have been called the latter's
"summer palace" by the early Italian excavators, seems to have been part of the same
administrative unit during most of the Late Bronze Age (La Rosa 1985). Considering the short distances between the three sites, this traditional relationship may well
have been preserved and rekindled in the Early Iron Age.

Although Kommos, like Ayia Triada, is located near valuable arable land, the reasons
for the tenth-century shift of interest to this site are probably to be sought largely in
its coastal position. Of great interest in this respect is the evidence for Phoenician

visitors at the sanctuary from the late tenth to the mid eighth century BC. This evidence consists of the fragments of Phoenician transport amphorae, faience figurines and vessels and, above all, of the architectural form and furnishings of the second cult building at the site, Temple B (Shaw and Shaw 2000:20–4). This cult building was erected around 800 BC and provided with a small tripillar shrine. The latter consisted of an ashlar base with three upright worked stones and is of a form foreign to Crete, but closely paralleled by Phoenician examples. Substantial foreign interest and attendance seems indicated, although the present lack of Phoenician material from the earliest levels of the sanctuary refutes the idea of a Phoenician foundation or colony (*contra* Negbi 1992:599–615). There is, on the other hand, a characteristic, continuous series of votives of local origin and manufacture extending from the beginning of the cult in the tenth down to the end of the seventh century BC. These votives (weaponry, horse and bull figures, vessels for drinking and eating) betray, as discussed above, clear aristocratic connotations. A more plausible conclusion is, therefore, that the foundation of the Early Iron Age sanctuary at Kommos – which indeed soon afterwards developed into a meeting place with merchants from overseas – was the initiative of leading residents from local communities, Phaistos at their head.

The transference of cult activities, from Ayia Triada to the ruins of a large Bronze Age town with a harbor, points to a worldly, practical objective: the establishment of a presence in an area which had been largely abandoned since the end of the Bronze Age, but which reassumed its importance when, in the tenth century BC, overseas communication began to increase. This presence would have been justified by an explicit association with the old Bronze Age building that itself had been the public center of an international harbor in the Late Bronze Age. At Kommos, the period of Phoenician attendance is followed by one for which imports point to contacts with various regions on the Greek mainland, the Aegean islands, East Greece and Egypt (Shaw and Shaw 2000:31–5). Kommos's function as an international meeting place from early in its history onward is therefore of the utmost relevance. As argued by De Polignac, the existence of such "international sanctuaries" in the Early Iron Age seems to have had a regulating effect (whether intended or not) on the – then still intermittent – contact with people from faraway places. Religious festivals would provide an excellent opportunity to meet and trade, but, if contact concentrated on such occasions, it may have become confined to specific places and people (De Polignac 1992:122–5). In this way, foreign contacts and the possession of foreign artifacts would become the monopoly of the controlling elite. At sanctuaries like Kommos, cult participants were able to kill three birds with one stone. While the dedication of precious votives testified to their special relationship both with the gods and with a glorious past, contact with people from overseas, in a time when long-distance traveling was far from common, would likewise have added to their prestige.

As with Phaistos and Kommos, Knossos may have made good use of the past in strengthening or reclaiming ties with her traditional harbor town at Amnisos. A close relationship between the two sites is attested by both archaeological and literary sources for different periods in their history. As at Kommos, parts of a possible Bronze Age road connecting Amnisos with Knossos were found. In the Linear B tablets discovered in the Bronze Age palace of Knossos, Amnisos is listed as part of that palace's territory. Homer (*Od.* 19.188) referred to the site as the (windy) harbor belonging to Minos (Schäfer 1992:46–9, 52, 323). It is likely that Knossos, one of the few sites in the area that remained inhabited after the Bronze Age, stayed in control of Amnisos during the Early Iron Age. Unfortunately, the limited excavations at Amnisos have not yielded the kind of detailed picture as do the storerooms and large numbers of imports at Kommos. For the later seventh or sixth century BC, contact with East Greece or the Levant is indicated by a series of imported faience vessels and figurines (Schäfer 1992:183, 251–2). These finds, and Amnisos's well-documented function as a harbor in earlier periods, strengthen the idea that the appeal of the Early Iron Age sanctuary was enhanced by similar maritime use.

Palaikastro was also the site of a Bronze Age harbor, but here concrete evidence for a resumption of its use as port during the Early Iron Age is altogether missing. Trade with people from overseas may have been less of a concern than at the other two coastal sanctuaries, simply because there were equally good harbors in much closer proximity to the contemporary settlements. The nearest Early Iron Age settlement was Itanos, some 8 km to the north and itself located on the sea. Even the inland community of Praisos – developing into the most important polis of eastern Crete and, according to written sources, in control of the sanctuary in Classical times – preferred other harbors, on the north and south coast, with which it was connected via more easily passable valleys (Spyridakis 1970:27–9).

Religious Continuity: The Case of Palaikastro

While harbor functions are not attested for the sanctuary at Palaikastro, the available evidence does allow – more so than in the cases of the other sanctuaries – an insight into quite different considerations at work in the decision to install a cult in the ruins of a Bronze Age site. At Palaikastro, archaeological and textual sources suggest a form of religious continuity – the local preservation of the memory of the site as the place of worship of an important Bronze Age god, in historical times known under the name of Diktaian Zeus or Zeus "of Dikte."

With Early Iron Age habitation concentrated in the mountainous hinterland, the area around Palaikastro seems to have been largely deserted. To understand the rise of the sanctuary here, it is important to note the specific way in which the settlement configuration in this part of Eastern Crete developed. Unlike Amnisos and Kommos, Palaikastro probably constituted an independent polity during much, if not all, of its history. The pattern of settlement abandonment at the close of the Bronze Age was more universal in East Crete and can be seen to have affected not only Palaikastro but every major Bronze Age site in the region. Most people seem to have withdrawn to the mountainous hinterland, where they regrouped in new communities (e.g. Nowicki 2000). Consequently, in East Crete there were no sites of the caliber of Knossos and Phaistos, which – continuously inhabited from the Bronze into the Early Iron Age – could boast traditional territorial ties with nearby coastal regions.

Palaikastro's remote setting, on ground which – at least in the Early Iron Age – would not have belonged to the territory of any specific community, encouraged its development into a sanctuary with regional functions. As such, it would have provided a neutral meeting place for emerging elites from the various surrounding mountain communities, whose attendance is attested to by the valuable and prestigious tripods, shields, and other weaponry found at the sanctuary. At this distant site leading aristocrats would gather to join in the worship of a god, who was already in antiquity recognized as being of peculiar and ancient origin. The identity of this god and the nature of his cult is illuminated by inscriptions and other written sources and by the remarkable recent find of a Bronze Age cult image not far from the site of the later sanctuary.

A Roman inscription, found in the southeast portion of the sanctuary, preserves the text of a hymn of sixth–fourth century BC date and confirms the identity of the god as Zeus "of Dikte" (Crowther 1988:37 n.3). Scholars agree in regarding this Zeus as an indigenous, Bronze Age god, and more specifically as a manifestation of the Cretan-born Zeus, well-known in ancient literary sources. The associated mythology centers on the story of his birth, the earliest preserved version of which can be found in Hesiod's *Theogony* (Thorne 2000). The Palaikastro hymn suggests that important elements of the god's Bronze Age iconography and identity were indeed preserved into historical times. It addresses the god as a youthful figure or "greatest Kouros," something which is in accordance with the portrayal of male gods in Minoan art but goes against the canonical Greek depiction of Zeus as a mature man with a beard. Among the many kinds of blessings asked from this Kouros are those concerning the fertility of fields and flocks. This, and the fact that the god is asked to come to Dikte "for the year," suggests an origin in the Minoan religious framework of annually dying and reborn vegetation deities (Nilsson 1950:546–66).

The location of "Dikte" or "Dikta" has long been disputed, both in antiquity and in modern times, but gradually a consensus has been reached which connects the toponym with eastern Crete. In a recent reappraisal of the ancient references, Crowther (1988) argues for a more specific identification of Dikta with the area of Palaikastro. Particularly important is his inclusion of epigraphic evidence from the large Bronze Age peak sanctuary of Petsofas, just south of Palaikastro. This peak sanctuary yielded four stone tables of offering with Linear A inscriptions reading "JA-DI-KI-TE-TE." Apart from one comparable inscription from Mount Jouktas near Knossos, this word is not attested elsewhere. Crowther therefore proposes to interpret it as the Minoan for "Dikta."

Petsofas is clearly visible from Palaikastro, and its summit is a walking distance of less than 30 minutes, suggesting a close relationship between the two sites. This is further corroborated by the recent discovery of the "Palaikastro Kouros," a chryselephantine statuette of fifteenth-century BC date which represents a young male deity with both arms bent and fists at the chest. This image, almost 0.50m in height, is made of ivory, with the upper part of the head and hair in black serpentine, eyes of rock crystal, and sheet gold for the sandals and sword sheath. The gesture of the bent arms with fists at the chest finds a parallel in numerous terracotta figurines from the Minoan peak sanctuary at Petsofas, but elsewhere in Crete the attitude is relatively rare, confirming the close cultic links between Palaikastro and Petsofas. Since the votives at the latter site are generally of an earlier date, the excavators propose that the focus of the worship of the youthful god shifted to the settlement in the course of the Late Bronze Age (MacGillivray and Driessen 1990:404). A terracotta figurine belonging to the last phase of Bronze Age habitation still displays the gesture of bent arms (MacGillivray, Sackett et al. 1991:132–3, fig. 9), suggesting that worship of the deity continued until the settlement was deserted.

There is a time gap of at least 300 years from the final abandonment of the Bronze Age settlement at Palaikastro to the dedication of the first Early Iron Age votives in the sanctuary of Diktaian Zeus. During this gap there is no proof of an active cult. However, the fact that in the hymn of historical times a god is again represented as "Kouros" and is asked to come to "Dikte" strengthens the idea of some form of religious continuity from the Bronze Age. This is not to say that the resumption of a cult in honor of the old Bronze Age god would not have entailed changes in form, audience, function, and associated beliefs. There can be no doubt that the radically different conditions of the Early Iron Age resulted in modifications and reinterpretation in all these aspects. For one thing, the numerous offerings of small terracotta images of the god during the Bronze Age are in sharp contrast with the unequivocally aristocratic tripods and shields of the Early Iron Age – indicating a shift from the active participation of a far larger proportion of the local population to monopolization by an elite group. As at Ayia Triada, the nature of the cult seems to have changed as well, with the rise of a warrior aristocracy resulting in a greater emphasis on military aspects. At Palaikastro too, the Early Iron Age rituals have been interpreted as relating primarily to the initiation of aristocratic men (Burkert 1985:262).

Despite these shifts, the sanctuary at Palaikastro presents a clear example of the potential strength of local cult traditions. It may therefore be tempting to suppose a similar kind of religious continuity at the other six sites as well. There are, however, reasons for caution, which are prompted by the differences in local circumstances surrounding the installation of the Cretan ruin cults. The situation in East Crete is extraordinary because the presence of later inscriptions, still in a pre-Greek language, and later Greek literary sources combine to indicate the survival of an autochthonous population (e.g. Od. 19.176; Her. VII.170–1; Strabo X.4.6.12). Hence, the idea that later generations went back to the settlements of their forefathers and founded cults that, at least in some respects, followed the old traditions gains in plausibility. In Central Crete, on the other hand, the centuries from the Late Bronze to the Early Iron Age show a more variegated development, with indications for the arrival of new people from the Greek mainland. Although it is notoriously difficult to assess the extent and effects of such new arrivals on the basis of archaeological evidence alone, the reality of migrations during the transition from the Bronze to the Early Iron Age is generally accepted. Thus, at Knossos, changes in the material culture, funerary customs and language have been related to the arrival of mainlanders, including groups of Dorian-Greek speaking people during the eleventh century BC (e.g. Coldstream 1984:317; Hood and Smyth 1981:14). This difference in historical development with eastern Crete may have been profound enough to have given the appreciation and reuse of Bronze Age monuments a different nuance. It may seem somewhat paradoxical that the majority of known ruin cults were installed in Central Crete, perhaps "by people who preserved no continuity of memory – and little enough of blood" (Coldstream 1976:10, quoting Cook). However, ethnic differences may have increased the contestability of claims to authority and power, making the need to seek legitimacy in *precedent* more immediate and urgent. The association with monuments of the Bronze Age past may, more so than in the east of the island, have taken the form of purposeful appropriation, with the higher ensuing degree of reinvention and reinterpretation.

Homes of Heroic Ancestors, Abode of the Gods

A point worth stressing is that none of the Cretan sanctuaries in Bronze Age sites has yielded material evidence for the persistence of cult activities at the same spot from the Bronze into the Early Iron Age. Even if there was a continuity of memory of earlier cult functions, it remains significant that this was not given visible expression until the tenth and especially the later ninth century BC, when newly rising considerations of a socio-political nature provided more acute incentives. In this respect, the phenomenon of Cretan ruin cults ties in with the widespread revival of interest in the Bronze Age or "heroic" past – especially among aristocratic groups – which characterizes much of the Greek world in the Early Iron Age.

Elsewhere the phenomenon is perhaps exemplified by the rise in popularity of the Homeric epics, by the parallel creation of a "heroic" figurative art, and by the inception of cult at Bronze Age tombs, variously interpreted as directed at ancestors, "Heroes" or other legendary beings of past times (Antonaccio 1995). Early Iron Age Cretans, however, expressed their increasing interest in the past in a different way. There is no proof of Cretans engaging in tomb cult at this time, and their receptivity to the Homeric epics was questioned in antiquity. In Plato's *Laws* (III.681C), for instance, the Cretan Klinias is made to say that Homer, "being a foreign poet," was not much read in the island. Moreover, Cretan figurative art – as seen on pottery and metalwork – is thoroughly idiosyncratic. Funerary and combat scenes, popular elsewhere in the Greek world, are rare. Instead, there is a predilection for hunting, often by heavily armed warriors who – in contrast to their mainland colleagues – seem to operate in supernatural settings, as indicated by the addition of sphinxes, goddess figures, and exotic plant life (for examples see Blome 1982).

Cretan interest in the Bronze Age past is most clearly manifested in the establishment of cult places at the sites of long-abandoned Bronze Age complexes. The question remains as to how these Bronze Age complexes were remembered. The example of Palaikastro shows that the memory of an earlier association of the locale with a cult for an important Bronze Age deity may have contributed to the installation of a sanctuary in later times. But were there also other, more specific memories and stories attached to these places? To attempt to answer this question and to reconstruct the specific nature of these memories and stories is a difficult and tentative affair because of the virtual absence of textual evidence. To complicate matters further, the original functions of the Minoan palaces appear to have been manifold and complex. In addition to being places of centralized economic, administrative, and political activities, they also served as royal residences and as important ceremonial or religious centers in ways that may never be fully understood. Just as modern scholars emphasize these functions differently, ancient visitors will have had selective views, each with their own set of cognitive and emotional associations. Two aspects, however, will have been particularly prone to attracting a cult: the site's former function as a sanctuary or religious center, and its former function as seat of powerful rulers, who could have been adopted as ancestral heroes.

The later epigraphic and other written evidence found in the sanctuaries at Bronze Age sites provides no direct evidence for ancestor cults, nor are the associated votives cult-specific enough to point to the veneration of such forefathers. Bronze tripod-cauldrons, which in similar form and technique were already made in the Late Bronze Age, may have borne connotations of a "heroic past" (Maass 1981:18). Yet others emphasize oracular functions for these objects, as exemplified by the tripod in the Apollo cult at Delphi, and by their use in the preparation of the sacrificial meal (Burkert 1985:116). This would suggest that religious motivations of a more general kind lay behind their dedication.

A lack of integrally preserved texts of Cretan making unfortunately prevents us from knowing the details of the heroic, ancestor and religious stories and myths that must have circulated in Early Iron Age Crete. Later Greek writers and scholars sometimes incorporated Cretan stories and traditions in their writings, but with a varying degree of "reworking" and reinterpretation (e.g. S. Morris 1992). We are therefore left with largely unconnected fragments, seen through the eyes of outsiders who were far removed in place and time from the original audiences. Nevertheless, the brief references in the work of later Greek authors do give an impression of the extent of earlier Cretan literature. Well-known is the example of the late seventh- or sixth-century poems by Epimenides, which according to Diogenes Laertius (I.112) included a *Theogony* and a thousands of lines long work *On Minos and Rhadamanthys*. In that light, it is not difficult to imagine how the Early Iron Age foundation of a sanctuary at Bronze Age ruins could have involved the coupling of an ancestor cult with a longer established divine cult, perhaps to raise the importance of the former. This way the rising warrior aristocracy would have been ensured of a direct link, not only with the supernatural world, but also with the powerful rulers of the past. A parallel is found on the Greek mainland, where the shared worship of former kings and deities is more clearly attested. For Athens, where the Athena temple on the Acropolis was built over the remains of the Bronze Age palace, the relationship between the two is elucidated by two passages in the Homeric poems. Both relate to the legendary king of Athens, Erechtheus, who is said to have been visited by Athena in his palace and later to have been worshipped with the goddess in her temple at the Acropolis (*Il.* 2.547; *Od.* 7.80; Nilsson 1950:488). In Crete such a close association between legendary leadership and divinity is reflected in the myths that make Zeus both the father of Minos and the one who provided him with the laws to rule his people.

Despite the lack of direct evidence, the possibility should probably be kept open that the ruined Bronze Age monuments in later times were commemorated both as the abode of gods who had been venerated of old *and* as the homes of heroic ancestors.

Epilogue

The seven Early Iron Age cult places at Bronze Age monuments all remained in use into the Hellenistic period or later, but it is worthy of note that during their long history of use, the appreciation for the presence of the Bronze Age remains seem to have changed. The first signs of such alterations date to the seventh century BC. At Kommos, small retaining walls had been built and maintained around the area of the Early Iron Age sanctuary, apparently in an effort to keep the site from being covered by the accumulating sand. When these efforts were abandoned in the seventh century BC, the high walls of the ashlar Bronze Age complex collapsed and became invisible. The growing number of auxiliary structures in the sanctuary for storage and various industrial activities covered them further (Shaw 1981:233–5). At Ayia Triada the seventh century BC witnessed the gradual failure of what had once been a thriving cult (D'Agata 1998:24).

This does not mean that an association with the Bronze Age past was no longer considered important, but rather that its expressions, scope, and audience changed. In the seventh century BC, there appears to have been an extension of cult practices to less monumental Bronze Age remains at smaller sites. Moldmade female terracottas of seventh-century date have now been discovered at megalithic Bronze Age buildings (alternatively interpreted as watch-towers or farmsteads) south of Palaikastro and at Vamies near Itanos (Chryssoulaki 1994; Kalpaxis et al. 1995:734–6). Evidence from Classical and Hellenistic periods further indicates the great popularity of "ancient" cult places, which acquired almost antiquarian traits. In the same periods, the city of Knossos took pride in issuing coins adorned with images of the legendary Cretan labyrinth and Minotaur. These are just a few of the later manifestations of the continuing interest in the Bronze Age or Minoan past, but they are important in illustrating that two distinctive elements for the Early Iron Age ruin cults seem to have been lost: their exclusive aristocratic character and the emphasis on the physical association with the visible remains of a by-gone age.

References Cited

Antonaccio, C. M. 1995: *An Archaeology of Ancestors. Tomb Cult and Hero Cult in Early Greece.* Lanham: Rowman & Littlefield.

Banti, L. 1941–43: I culti minoici e greci di Haghia Triada. *Annuario della Scuola Archeologica di Atene e delle Missioni Italiane in Oriente*, n.s. 3–5, pp. 9–74.

Blome, P. 1982: *Die figürliche Bildwelt Kretas in der geometrischen und früharchaïschen periode.* Mainz am Rhein: Von Zabern.

Burkert, W. 1985: *Greek Religion*. Cambridge, Mass.: Harvard University Press.

Chatzidakis, I. 1934: *Les Villas Minoennes de Tylissos, Études Crétoises*, vol. 3. Paris: Geuthner.

Chryssoulaki, S. et al. 1994: *Excavation of a Watchtower of the Sea at Karoumes, Zakros. Minoan Roads Research Programme. Report on Proceedings in 1993*. Athens: private edition.

Coldstream, J. N. 1976: Hero-cults in the age of Homer. *Journal of Hellenic Studies* 96, pp. 8–17.

Coldstream, J. N. 1984: Dorian Knossos and Aristotle's villages. In *Aux origines de l'hellénisme: la Crète et la Grèce: hommage à Henri van Effenterre, presente par le Centre G. Glotz*. Paris: Publications de la Sorbonne, pp. 311–22.

Coldstream, J. N. 1988: Some Minoan reflexions in Cretan Geometric art. In *Studies in Honour of T. B. L. Webster*, vol. 2, ed. J. H. Betts, J. T. Hooker and J. R. Green. Bristol: Bristol Classical Press, pp. 23–32.

Coldstream, J. N. 1991: Knossos: an urban nucleus in the Dark Age? *La Transizione dal Miceneo all'Alto Arcaismo. Dal Palazzo alla Città. Atti del Convegno Internazionale Roma, 14–19 marzo 1988*, ed. D. Musti, A. Sacconi, L. Rocchetti, M. Rocchi, E. Scafa, L. Sportiello and M. E. Giannotta. Roma: Consiglio Nazionale delle Ricerche, pp. 287–99.

Coldstream, J. N. 2000: Evans's Greek finds: the Early Greek town of Knossos, and its encroachment on the borders of the Minoan palace. *Annual of the British School at Athens* 95, pp. 259–99.

Coldstream, J. N. and Catling, H. W. (eds.) 1996: *Knossos North Cemetery: Early Greek Tombs*. British School at Athens Supplementary Volume 28. London: British School at Athens.

Crowther, C. 1988: A note on Minoan Dikta. *Annual of the British School at Athens* 83, pp. 37–44.

D'Agata, A. L. 1998: Changing patterns in a Minoan and Post-Minoan sanctuary: the case of Agia Triada. *Post-Minoan Crete, Proceedings of the First Colloquium on Post-Minoan Crete held by the British School at Athens and the Institute of Archaeology, University College London, 10–11 November 1995, British School at Athens Studies* 2, ed. W. G. Cavanagh and M. Curtis. London: British School at Athens, pp. 19–26.

De Polignac, F. 1992: Influence extérieure ou évolution interne? L'innovation cultuelle en Grèce géométrique et archaïque. *Greece Between East and West: 10th–8th Centuries BC. Papers of the Meeting at the Institute of Fine Arts, New York University, March 15–16 1990*, ed. G. Kopcke and I. Tokumaru. Mainz: Von Zabern, pp. 116–27.

Evans, A. J. 1899–1900: Knossos. I. The Palace. *Annual of the British School at Athens* 6, pp. 3–70.

Evans, A. J. 1928: *The Palace of Minos*, Vol. II. London: MacMillan.

Evans, A. J. 1930: *The Palace of Minos*, Vol. III. London: MacMillan.

Hayden, B. 1981: *The Development of Cretan Architecture from the LM III through the Geometric periods*. Philadelphia: University of Pennsylvania Press.

Hood, M. S. F. and Smyth, D. 1981: *Archaeological Survey of the Knossos Area*. British School at Athens Supplementary Volume 14. London: British School at Athens.

Hutchinson, R. W., Eccles, E. and Benton, S. 1939–40: Unpublished objects from Palaikastro and Praisos II. *Annual of the British School at Athens* 40, pp. 38–59.

Kalpaxis, T., Schnapp, A. and Viviers, D. 1995: Rapport sur les travaux menés en collaboration avec l'École Française d'Athènes en 1994. *Itanos (Crète Orientale), Bulletin de Correspondance Hellénique* 119, pp. 713–36.

La Rosa, V. 1985: Preliminary considerations on the problem of the relationship between Phaistos and Ayia Triada. *Scripta Mediterranea* 6, pp. 45–54.

La Rosa, V. 1992: Phaistos. In *The Aerial Atlas of Ancient Crete*, ed. J. W. Myers, E. E. Myers and G. Cadogan. Los Angeles: University of California Press, pp. 232–43.

La Rosa, V. and D'Agata, A. L. 1984: Haghia Triada. In *Creta Antica, Cento anni di archeologia italiana (1884–1984)*. Roma: Di Luca, pp. 161–201.

Lebessi, A. 1991: Flagellation ou autoflagellation. Données iconographiques pour une tentative d'interpretation. *Bulletin de Correspondance Hellénique* 115, pp. 99–123.

Maass, M. 1981: Die geometrischen Dreifüsse von Olympia. *Antike Kunst* 24, pp. 6–20.

MacGillivray, J. A. and Driessen, J. 1990: Minoan settlement at Palaikastro. In *L'habitat égéen préhistorique, Bulletin de Correspondance Hellénique Supplement* 19, ed. P. Darque and P. Treuil. Athens: École Française d'Athenès, pp. 395–412.

MacGillivray, J. A., Sackett, L. H., Driessen, J., Farnoux, A. and Smyth, D. 1991: Excavations at Palaikastro, 1990. *Annual of the British School at Athens* 86, pp. 121–47.

MacVeagh Thorne, S. E. and Prent, M. 2000: The sanctuary of Diktaean Zeus at Palaikastro: a re-examination of the excavations by the British School in 1902–1906. *Prepragmena H' Diethnous Kritologikou Synedriou*. Herakleion, pp. 169–78.

Morgan, C. 1990: *Athletes and Oracles. The Transformation of Olympia and Delphi in the Eighth Century BC*. Cambridge: Cambridge University Press.

Morris, S. 1992: *Daidalos and the Origins of Greek Art*. Princeton: Princeton University Press.

Murray, O. 1983: The symposion as social organization. *The Greek Renaissance of the Eighth Century BC.: Tradition and Innovation, Proceedings of the Second International Symposium at the Swedish Institute in Athens, 1–5 June 1981*, ed. R. Hägg. Stockholm: Svenska Institutet i Athen, pp. 195–9.

Murray, O. 1990: Sympotic history. In *Sympotica. A Symposium on the Symposion*, ed. O. Murray. Oxford: Clarendon Press, pp. 3–13.

Negbi, O. 1992: Early Phoenician presence in the Mediterranean islands: a reappraisal. *American Journal of Archaeology* 96, pp. 599–615.

Nilsson, M. P. 1950: *The Minoan–Mycenaean Religion and its Survival in Greek Religion*. Lund: Gleerup.

Nixon, L. 1990: Minoan settlements and Greek sanctuaries. *Pepragmena tou ST' Diethnous Kritilogikou Synedriou*. Chania: Diethnes Kretologikon Synedrion, pp. 59–67.

Nowicki, K. 2000: *Defensible Sites in Crete, ca. 1200–800 BC*. Aegaeum 21. Liège/Austin: Université de Liège/ University of Texas at Austin.

Pernier, L. 1907: Lavori eseguiti dalla Missione archeologica in Creta nel 1906. *Atti dell' Accademia Nazionale dei Lincei. Rendiconti Rivista di Filologia e d'Istruzione Classica*, 15, pp. 257–303.

Pernier, L. and Banti, L. 1951: *Il Palazzo Minoico di Festòs*. Roma: Istituto d'Archeologia e Storia dell'Arte.

Poland, E. 1932: Minos. In *Paulys Real-Encyclopädie der classischen Altertumswissenschaft* XXX, ed. G. Wissowa et al. Stuttgart: Metzlersche Verlagsbuchhandlung, 1890–1927.

Sackett, L. H. (ed.) 1992: *Knossos from Greek City to Roman Colony. Excavations at the Unexplored Mansion Vol. II*. British School at Athens Supplementary Volume 21. London: British School at Athens.

Sandars, N. K. 1978: *The Sea Peoples. Warriors of the Ancient Mediterranean 1250–1150 BC*. London: Thames and Hudson.

Schäfer, J. (ed.) 1992: *Amnisos. Nach den archäologischen, historischen und epigrafischen Zeugnissen des Altertums und der Neuzeit*. Berlin: Universität Heidelberg.

Schmitt-Pantel, P. 1992: *La Cité au Banquet. Histoire des Repas Publics dans les Cités Grecques, Collections de l'École Française de Rome* 157. Rome: École Française de Rome.

Shaw, J. W. 1981: Excavations at Kommos (Crete) during 1980. *Hesperia* 50, pp. 211–51.

Shaw, J. W. and Shaw, M. C. (eds.) 2000: *Kommos IV. The Greek Sanctuary*. Princeton and Oxford: Princeton University Press.

Snodgrass, A. M. 1980: *Archaic Greece. The Age of Experiment*. London: Dent.

Spyridakis, S. 1970: *Ptolemaic Itanos and Hellenistic Crete*. Berkeley: University of California Press.

Thorne, S. 2000: Diktaian Zeus in later Greek tradition. In *The Palaikastro Kouros. A Minoan Chryselephantine Statuette and its Aegean Bronze Age Context*, ed. J. A. MacGillivray, J. M. Driessen and L. H. Sackett. British School at Athens Studies 6. London: British School at Athens, pp. 149–62.

Van Wees, H. 1992: *Status Warriors: War, Violence and Society in Homer and History, Dutch Monographs on Ancient History and Archaeology* 9. Amsterdam: Gieben.

Willetts, R. F. 1962: *Cretan Cults and Festivals*. London: Routledge.

6
Concrete Memories: Fragments of the Past in the Classic Maya Present (500–1000 AD)

Rosemary A. Joyce

Memory, understood as commemoration, is a topic that seems a natural focus for a study of Classic Maya societies, epitomized by monuments with "historical" inscriptions using a calendar system that allows precise designation of dates of events in a single, continuous, framework. Classic Maya monuments are understood today as marking critical events in political histories. They were often erected at set intervals of five, ten, or twenty of the calendar periods closest to a solar year, a 360 day unit composed of eighteen named groups of twenty days each. Historical dates were recorded as the number of days elapsed from a fixed starting date in 3114 BC, recorded in a base twenty mathematical system as groups of twenty, 400, 8,000 and sometimes higher multiples of the 360 day approximation of the solar year.

Texts on Maya monuments regularly refer back to earlier events as precedents for later actions. The grammatical structures employed to shift time from one framework to another are quite well understood (Houston 1997, 2000), and, like the time-shifting "once upon a time" in English, can be thought of as placing a person in the present in relation to events recalled from the past. Most Maya commemorative inscriptions have a general structure we can paraphrase as "On this day, the ruler of this site dedicated this monument. Many days ago he was born, took office, waged war, or did some form of ritual; some time after that, he did other historically notable actions; and then some time later, came the date of the event that was so important that this monument was created to commemorate it for all time." While biography

This paper was completed while I was a Fellow at the Center for Advanced Study in the Behavioral Sciences in 2001–2002. I am grateful for the financial support provided by Grant 2000–5633 and the "Hewlett Fellow" Grant 98–2124 from the William and Flora Hewlett Foundation. My understanding of cognitive and social psychology models of memory was developed through an informal discussion forum at CASBS organized by Drs. Robert Bjork and Alan Baddeley. I thank them and the other participants in this forum, in particular Drs. Elizabeth Ligon Bjork and John Bargh, for their contributions to my education in this area. Of course, none of these individuals is responsible for any misunderstandings I may have elaborated in recalling what was presented in memory group meetings.

and history are conveyed in these texts, their primary message is one of remembering a monumental past and linking it to the future. Maya calendars and writing
systems, in short, worked as technologies of memory, practices of inscription through
which shared social memories were constructed (Joyce 1998:157–60; Rowlands
1993:143–6).

These obvious technologies of memory were embodied in monuments placed
in spatial relations to each other, as freestanding sculptures (stelae and "altars")
surrounding monumental spaces (plazas), or as carved stairs, lintels, and walls of the
equally monumental buildings surrounding these spaces. The official accounts of the
past were reinforced by the repetition in these spaces of information in different
modes (numerical records, texts, and visual images) and on multiple surfaces, endowed
with striking sensory impact through the talents of the visual artists who created them.

It would seem almost impossible in Classic Maya sites to attend to anything but
such official memory, the memory that legitimated present political circumstances
through appeals to the past. But signs of memory, I argue, were more pervasive in
Classic Maya settlements than even these obvious public inscriptions. The more limited
attention given by modern scholars to less clearly marked materializations of memory
reflects the effectiveness of these other memory cues in naturalizing themselves,
far beyond what historical inscriptions, with their blatant construction of links to the
past, have managed to achieve. Extremely conservative cultural practices, and the material objects reproduced over centuries to enable them, served as mnemonics that cued
implicit memories among more restricted social groups: noble families constructing
social relations over many generations. In some cases, such material cues of implicit
memory were transformed so that they serve today as evidence of explicit commemoration equivalent in content, if not in scale or audience, to the more obvious
medium of commemorative sculpture. I argue that the transformation of objects
employed in practical action into explicit commemorative records, accomplished by
inscribing body ornaments with texts (plate 6.1), changed implicit memory into
explicit recall, merging personal and historical memory.

Thinking about Memory

To explore these other forms of material memory in Classic Maya society, we need
briefly to consider alternative ways of thinking about what memory implies. The
analysis of commemoration, the deliberate marking of something to be remembered,
is only one way of approaching memory. Memory also covers the embodied processes
of recognition and recall through which we gain access to something we already
"know." Without the ability to recall memory and recognize what is known, human
beings would be hard pressed to carry on everyday life. We need to be able to learn,
to commit things to memory where they will be available for recall. We also need to
be able to selectively forget, so that we do not carry with us overlays of obsolete
practical information that has been superseded.

Exploration of the processes by which memory works has attracted considerable
attention in cognitive and social psychology, and perspectives from these fields inform

Plate 6.1 An example of an heirloom inscribed with a text. The first glyph records the possession of the object by the person named in the second glyph. Fragment of a bone orna-ment (possibly a hair pin) recovered at Copan (Peabody Museum catalogue number 92–49–20/C202. Photograph by Steve Burger, courtesy of the Peabody Museum, Harvard University. Used with permission of the President and Fellows of Harvard College)

this paper. Cognitive psychologists differentiate between implicit and explicit memory, where explicit or conscious memory "refers to uses of memory that are accompanied by the subjective experience of remembering" (Kelley and Lindsay 1996:54). Cognitive psychologists agree on a general model of explicit memory as a flow of information processing (Pashler and Carrier 1996). In this "modal model" of memory, sensory inputs are received in a "pre-attentive" process and decay rapidly. Visual perception decays more rapidly than auditory sense information, which persists up to ten times as long (Pashler and Carrier 1996:6–7). Those sensory inputs to which we attend pass into short-term memory, where they must be actively maintained or they will be forgotten.

We rehearse information in short-term memory to maintain it while we work with it, normally in the form of internal speech encoding, regardless of whether the sensory stimuli we receive are visual or auditory (Nairne 1996:109). The transformation from short-term to long-term memory depends on elaborative processes (Kelley and Lindsay 1996:33–4; Pashler and Carrier 1996:18). These include the construction of interactive images, associations with place, and narrativization, the sorts of elaborations that underwrite the effectiveness of the classical system of memory using loci, explored by Frances Yates (1966; see Belleza 1996:349–50, 356–9).

As memory passes from short-term to long-term, it becomes less literal (Bjork 1994). Multiple encoding and variable encoding are effective means to enhance long-term memory. Thus, transcribing information into a new form helps fix it in memory (Baddeley 1990:120–3). We map new information in terms of what we already know, with semantic relationships providing a network structure to memory (Baddeley 1990:235–8, 252–4). The network of memory is associative, not hierarchical or categorical. Associative structures of memory are inherently personalized, uniquely differentiated by experience, within the bounds of similar associations promoted by common enculturation. Through elaboration, memories become less literal. What enters into long-term memory is a translation or representation, taking into account previous knowledge and replacing the sensory input with a new hybrid.

Long-term memory itself cannot be taken as unified. Consciously articulated memory of facts and events (declarative memory) is counterposed to implicit (non-declarative) memory, the kind of memory that underwrites skills and habits (Baddeley 1990:360). Episodic memory, declarative memory of events, is what enables us to mentally travel back into our own past (Baddeley 1990:300–1). Retrieval from long-term to short-term memory, and forgetting, are also active cognitive processes. Retrieval is highly fallible (Baddeley 1990:193–6). Remembering reinforces what is known, because to retrieve a memory is actually to create it anew. Thus, remembering strengthens what has been recalled.

Contextual cuing can help activate or "prime" memories (Baddeley 1990:352–7). Memory studies demonstrate that recall of long-term memory is facilitated in the original context where memory was formed, accessed either literally or in the imagination. Memory studies also indicate that the "priming" of memory through other cues can operate without the conscious knowledge of the remembering subject. Thus, the orchestration of common memory can be understood as an interplay relating remembering to the context in which a memory was formed, the strength of the original perceptual input, and the degree of consciousness of the subject forming and recalling the memory.

Memorization, a highly self-conscious practice for constructing memories, may claim most of our attention. But the continuity of any project in which we are engaged depends on the continuity of memory that is formed continuously and less self-consciously. At the same time, no useful concept of memory can exist without a complementary concept of forgetting (Baddeley 1990:169–89). From the most quotidian perspective, if we were not constantly forgetting things, we would soon be as incapable of functioning as people left without continuous memory. The simple act of remembering one's current telephone number, without having to recall and discard every other telephone number that one has ever used, is a telling illustration of the necessity of forgetting.

For memory as recall – the everyday capacity to remember and forget – the world of things is of critical importance. What distinguishes the context in which an original memory is created will also serve to enhance recall of the memory (Belleza 1996; Roediger and Guynn 1996). The manipulation of the embeddedness of memory in context is at the heart of the classical "art of memory." It is also, I suggest, part of what gives body to practice theories.

My aim in this paper is to give a first trial of a description of memory work in Classic Maya society, taking into account the model of memory sketched out above. I hope to attend to both commemoration and recall, and to single out evidence for the contextual priming of recall that allows for the common understandings of every-day life that are crucial to social existence. In the process, I want to explore how the materiality of everyday life contributes to the construction of social memory, under-stood here following Paul Connerton (1989) as a form of coordinated recall of events by members of a social group. I understand the social nature of memory to imply a number of complex relations. As Suzanne Vromen (1986:57), summarizing Maurice Halbwachs' views, puts it, "memory cannot be considered exclusively an individual faculty, for individuals remember in their capacity as group members. Their interests, their stages in the life cycle, and the social experiences they have lived, shape their memories. Remembering thus implies being tied to collective frameworks of social reference points which allow memories to be coordinated in time and space. Not only are memories acquired through society, they are recalled, recognized, and located socially."

I do not claim to provide a final account of Classic Maya memory work. But simply asking these questions transforms the way we look at material remains from Classic Maya societies, and perhaps can contribute to drawing wider attention to the real challenge memory presented to people in the past.

Everyday Social Memory in the Maya World

I begin with the process of memorizing, remembering, and forgetting which has been so much less a focus of attention in Maya society than commemoration. What evidence might there be for memory as an everyday practice? Given my arguments above, the repetition of actions represented by the physical remains we document archaeologically *is* evidence for the creation and recall of memories. Demonstrating this is most feasible in precisely those circumstances where the sense of memory as something taken for granted is disturbed, where we can see conscious efforts to coor-dinate and constrain personal memories. The incised body ornaments I discuss below are, I suggest, precisely sites where usually implicit memory was made explicit. To understand them requires an initial exploration of the everyday practices from which they are distinguished by their inscriptions.

As Michael Rowlands (1993:144) suggests, "object traditions" serve as a crucial point of access to ongoing memory work in past societies because objects "are culturally constructed to connote and consolidate the possession of past events associated with their use or ownership. They are there to be talked about and invested with the memories and striking events associated with their use." Janet Hoskins (1998) demonstrates that objects in everyday circulation are available as a means to mobilize memory, particularly autobiographical memory. The oral narratives Hoskins recounts, in which common objects serve to embody remembered lives, are a model for my thinking about the Classic Maya object traditions that formed the background for the marked practices of inscription I discuss at length below.

Daily action in Maya settlements was shaped by the performances that a person witnessed while growing up in particular spatial settings, performances providing precedents for later reiteration and for the evaluation of later actions as properly performed (Joyce 2001). Most of the effects of witnessing precedents for later performance would have operated at the level of implicit memory, or recognition, rather than of explicit memory for specific events. Because of the contextuality of memory, different spatial settings could shape and prime different memories of prior performances.

Many objects used in performances enacted in particular settings were commemorated in permanent form through the inscription of visual images on monuments depicting ornaments in meticulous detail (figure 6.1). This move from embodied practices to inscriptional practices transformed the particular, fleeting experience of the person using objects, including the body ornaments I discuss below, into historical precedents for reiteration (Joyce 1998, 2001). Objects removed from spatial contexts of use, I suggest, would have had the potential to cue memories of performances in which they were employed, like those events commemorated in permanent form in visual images. It is thus worth attending to the characteristics of the space of Classic Maya memory in order to begin to address differences in the spatial contexts of formation and social extension of memories contained in, and inscribed on, personal ornaments that circulated through time from these places.

Classic Maya people inhabited spaces that varied in intimacy, visibility, and circulation frequency (Joyce 2001; Joyce and Hendon 2000). Intimacy is partly related to scale, or the size of a group that can be present together and thus share the formation of memory. The interior of individual houses provided a different degree of intimacy than the great exterior plaza spaces where explicit commemorative sculptures are found (compare Meskell, this volume). A number of studies relate the creation of Classic Maya monuments to a desire to externalize in the space of plazas events that actually took place inside buildings (for an explicit discussion, see Bassie-Sweet 1991). Fixed permanently in stone, these commemorations of intimate events formed part of a less intimate material context in which people could form memories of events they had not actually witnessed.

Visibility is a second feature of Classic Maya spatial settings, not unrelated to intimacy but working independently. The least visible settings in Classic Maya sites

Figure 6.1 Drawing of a Maya monument showing how ear spools were worn. Inserted through the ear lobe of the man on the left and the woman on the right, the shafts of the ear spools supported counterweight beads shown hanging below the earlobe, supported by string drawn through holes in the spool. Long counterweight beads emerge from the throats of the spools. The front faces of the ear spools are expanded into flanges with scalloped edges. (Yaxchilan Lintel 26. Drawing by Ian Graham, Corpus of Maya Hieroglyphic Inscriptions. Used by permission)

would have been the subdivided interior spaces of both residences and temples. The memories formed in such settings, unless otherwise replicated and reinforced, would have been the least widely shared. In the process of reinforcing social difference, spatial segregation works in part, I am suggesting, by separating the streams of memory.

The least visible spatial contexts, tombs, were the resting places where archaeologists recovered some of the ornaments I consider below. Because tombs were reused, remodeled, and sometimes simply accidentally encountered by later Maya people, objects in tombs were never completely lost to circulation (compare Lillios, this volume). The placement of Classic Maya costume ornaments with inscriptions in these practically invisible, yet potentially re-visible, locations reinforces the inherent differential visibility of the inscriptions on body ornaments. These small, many-sided objects required handling to reveal written texts and images, obscured when they were worn. Julia Hendon (2000) has argued that in the creation of social distinctions in Classic Maya society, access to space was manipulated to create differential knowledge. Hendon documents that tombs were among the contexts whose locations would have been differentially evident, and whose contents differentially known, to noble residents of wards of Classic Maya sites like Copan. The invisibility of an ornament buried for a time in a tomb, of a surface turned away or covered when in use, or of an ornament unseen by a person distant from actors in social ceremonies, made cues for memory available to some, and concealed them from others.

If we take as given that the actions represented on most Classic Maya commemorative monuments took place somewhere other than the plazas where these sculptures are found, then the creation and placement of monuments exteriorized a certain part of normally less visible memory formation. Monumental architecture, massive terraces that raised some buildings far above ground surface, also coordinated remembrance of things that were not necessarily actually seen. Monumental architecture created highly visible points of reference for memory on the landscape (compare Van Dyke, this volume). Events that took place in the enclosed interiors of temples at the summit of monumental platforms, or at scales beyond the perceptual reach of a single person (such as solstice sightings marked out by multiple buildings), were recalled by monumental architecture for much wider audiences than the immediate participants. This ambiguity of monumental spatial settings, which are themselves highly visible but encapsulate invisible spaces (including the most intimate and invisible, tombs), allowed the construction of common social memories that were simultaneously stratified by relative access to the experience of the episodic events they helped recall.

I have spoken of this contrast primarily in terms of vision, and indeed, memory research suggests that images are powerful stimuli to long-term memory. But these spatial settings also were traversed by sound, as any visitor to these sites today will be reminded, and the absence of sound in our thought about them is a serious gap. Audible sensory input persists longer that visual input, and it is through speech encoding that we rehearse short-term memory. Current understanding of the use of writing in Classic Maya society (Houston 2000; Houston and Stuart 1992) identifies a distinction between writing (as transcription from one medium to another) and reading (which is positioned as speaking a text). The commemorative texts placed throughout Classic Maya sites may well have been prompts for declamation. Intervisibility is most obvious to us today due to the persistence of physical structures. The coordination of memory tied to monumental spatial settings, however, may also have been promoted by sound.

At the same time, I do not think the persistence of the visible is an accidental feature of Classic Maya sites. The translation of memory into striking images tied together in spatial sequences, central to the classical "art of memory," is an effective strategy in the creation of long term memory. The literal construction of built spaces in Classic Maya sites embedded with visual images, channeled the construction of memories over spans far longer than an individual human lifetime. The continuing existence of buildings from the past, carefully incorporated in later site planning, suggests that for the Classic Maya these highly visible buildings were material markers of memory (compare Van Dyke, this volume). At a distance, they were differentiated from more obvious commemorative sculptures by their freedom from textual elaboration. But as privileged visitors with more intimate access knew, monumental buildings, like freestanding commemorative sculptures, were provided with inscriptions that tied them to specific dates, actors, and events.

The final characteristic of the spaces within which everyday memory was formed among the Classic Maya that I want to single out is the frequency and formality of movement through space. As memories are strengthened by their repeated regeneration, the way Classic Maya spaces channeled movement was a means through which memory could be rehearsed and, through recall, strengthened. Ranging from everyday circulation in the house compound, to regular circulation through sites of ritual practice prescribed by common calendars or triggered by unique events in individual lives, movement through Maya sites required implicit, embodied memory of prior performances and, I argue, would have triggered explicit memory. Commemorative sculpture placed along marked routes of circulation, like monuments at the ends of raised formal roadways linking elite residences to the royal plazas of sites like Copan and Seibal, drew on general practical experience of the sequential mobilization of memories primed by movement through familiar space.

My argument is, in short, that the entire material world surrounding Classic Maya people was a medium for the construction of memory over time, giving coherence to the continuity of social life. In the remainder of this paper, I want to offer as support for this general supposition an extended example. The inscription of texts on personal ornaments that were passed on through inheritance within families during the Maya Classic period, and recovered and used as generalized signs of antiquity by later people, would have transformed the effects of objects as cues for memory. I suggest the basic action that begins a new life as a mnemonic for these costume ornaments, inscribing a text, is a material trace of the reconstruction as declarative memory of practices (skills and habits) that previously formed part of the unarticulated reproduction of non–declarative memory.

The site of the remembering I am concerned with first is the grave; the contextual cues framing memory include the images that surrounded actors in their social life; and the memory recalled is that of a practice through which an individual person changed social status. By inscribing the object of this act of memory with a text describing not the scene of memory, but the scene remembered, the actors involved reconstructed and thus strengthened their shared memory of the episode recalled. Converted to an heirloom, the object of memory was conserved and transmitted within a powerful family, and comes to us as a reminder of the small-scale and intimate practice of political memory necessary if the more readily visible commemorative monuments were to have their full impact.

Notes on an Ear Spool

A pair of obsidian ear spools found in the tomb of an adult male noble at Altun Ha, Belize, dated to approximately 550 AD, was incised with a single continuous inscription (Mathews 1979). Stylistically typical of the period between 250 and 400 AD, the text would have been invisible, obscured by the ear, when the spools were threaded through the lobes of the ears of a living person (figure 6.1). Only when the ear spools were handled before their use, for example, before they were placed on the body being buried, could a person have read the text and reflected on it. The text begins with a possessive phrase we read as "his/her ear spool," followed by the titles of the owner. Originally interpreted as a male name, the owner's name begins with a title marking noble women's names. The text continues on the second ear spool with a second clause, introduced by the possessive phrase "his/her mother," followed by two titles, one specific to junior members of a noble house.

Other burials at the site also contain ornaments that were marked with texts. In a burial dating to ca. 600 AD, a pin carved from deer antler was inscribed with a stylistically early text (Peter Mathews, cited in Pendergast 1982:63–4). The text includes a personal name followed by the sign for "child of a woman," introducing the name of the mother, beginning with the sign for "noble woman." The project epigrapher, Peter Mathews, compared this text with a jade ornament from the same burial inscribed with a text in more contemporary style. A woven mat design, symbolic of seats of power, and a brief text that may be glossed "noble woman, his mother, the young noble man," are incised on opposite sides of the later ornament.

A bead pendant in a third tomb, dated to ca. 650 AD, carried a longer text at right angles to the orientation of the suspended bead, and so, like the text on the ear spool, was not legible when the ornament was being worn. The pendant reproduced at small scale the format of a commemorative stone monument. An enthroned male noble was depicted on one side and a long text was on the opposite. Two dates in the text record specific days in the years 569 and 584 AD, making the pendant slightly older than the tomb in which it was laid (Mathews, cited in Pendergast 1982:84–7). On the earlier recorded date, a ritual action took place at a location in the territory of a named title-holder. On the later date, the ruler of Altun Ha assumed a noble title. The ruler named is described as the child of a named noble woman and the offspring of a male person referred to only by title as a lord who had ruled for 20 cycles of 360 days (see also Mathews and Pendergast 1979).

These costume ornaments could not have been intended to display their historical content, since their texts and images were obscured when they were in use. The inscriptions on these ornaments commemorate at an intimate scale the reproduction of succession in rulership and genealogical relationships among nobles. Each ornament was displaced in time in the places where it was recovered by archaeologists, and the sex of the buried person and the named actor are not consistent. I have suggested that such inscribed ornaments served as mnemonics for historical knowledge of alliances among noble houses, transacted through marriage (Joyce 2000b). Here, I want to examine more closely the memory work that these objects accomplished.

Incorporated in closed tombs which could only be re-entered by destroying the covering architecture, in the locations where they were recovered these objects have no audience, and thus have achieved the ideal status of inalienable possessions, no longer in circulation (Weiner 1992). But this status is in theory *unrealizable*, because the end of circulation would mark the end of social connections transacted through these objects. In fact, the ancient Maya reopened tombs, and redistributed their contents, despite the requirement this imposed for architectural reconstruction. I thus treat inscribed objects from Classic Maya tombs as only temporarily at rest. The conversion they generate from implicit to declarative memory must be situated in their inscription and display before burial, as they were used as body ornaments during life, and as objects in funerary rites.

Let us narrow our focus to the ear spools from Tomb A 1/1 at Altun Ha. Massive architectural monuments form the public spaces of this site, but monuments with written texts are unknown there. Were it not for objects like these ear spools, we would know nothing about the political history of the nobles of Altun Ha. Ear spools themselves were not limited in use to nobles. Both visual evidence and burials document general use of ear spools by adults. The preparation of the ears through piercing and progressive widening of the hole in the earlobes was an important body practice used to transform children into adults in Mesoamerica (Joyce 2000a). Ear spools were, consequently, a material reminder of social maturation. The inscription of a title describing a male actor as an immature member of his social group on the Altun Ha ear spools moves this association from a cue for implicit memory, recognition, to an explicit declaration of recalled events.

This biographical script is complemented by text repositioning the same ornament at two other time scales, as a mnemonic of other memories associated with the presentation of ear spools. The kinship statement relating the woman named on one ear spool to the young man as mother to son ties the ear spools to generational succession within a family. Recall that the ear spools were found in a context later than their apparent date of inscription. As the ear spools were transmitted from one generation to the next, they served as a point of reference for kinship relations. By explicitly marking one transition in their history, the inscribed text makes explicit one possible implicit memory, coordinating the recollection of kinship by successive generations using these ornaments in ceremonies of social maturation.

The inscription of text on these ear spools, in other words, is a technique through which certain possible memories are cued, and others, as a consequence, pushed to the background. By marking the ear spools as the property of the woman named as mother of an immature boy who would have used ear spools as signs of his passage into adulthood, the text implies the importance of the mother's family in the life of the child. The events when ear spools were likely displayed, and their histories recounted, would have included social ceremonies during which representatives of the families of mother and father came together to mark transitions in the lives of their offspring through exchanges of goods, including costume ornaments (Gillespie and Joyce 1997). The life cycle ceremonies marking maturation through the adoption of ear spools were only one of these contexts. Mortuary ceremonies resulting in the burials from which ornaments like these were recovered were another occasion for recalling and contesting kinship relations (compare Lillios, this volume).

Memory, Heirlooms, and History

The work that the Altun Ha ear spools accomplished was a form of "elaboration process" through which long-term memories were tied to a specific contextual cue through speech encoding, manifested literally by inscription. This memory work made conscious implicit memory of the habitual body practices that required the preparation of the ear of immature adults for the use of ear spools (Joyce 1998, 2000a). Like the work done by linguistic tagging of chronological relations in Classic Maya monumental texts, the memory work of the ear spools concretized relationships in time and made individual episodic memory into shared social memory, at a temporal and social scale smaller than that encompassed by historical texts on monuments. By their circulation over the long term of precolumbian history, inscribed costume ornaments also established memory at a temporal scale of long duration that historical texts could only pretend to achieve. These objects, converted through their annotation into heirlooms (Joyce 2000b; compare Lillios 1999), themselves converted memory into history.

Many heirloom costume ornaments, like those from Altun Ha, were deposited in burials of nobles within the sites where they were made. Often their inscriptions seem to record actions by persons other than the deceased individual. For example, shell plaques from a male burial at Piedras Negras record the names of a woman (Proskouriakoff 1993:84–7; Stuart 1985). This burial was located within a building associated with the monuments of a particular ruler of the site. The woman named in the inscription on the shells was also mentioned in monuments detailing events in the life of that ruler. The inscription on the shells records the birth of this noble woman in the territory of the Piedras Negras ruler. Dated shortly before the accession of the next ruler of the site, the final action recorded on the shells is described as taking place under the authority of the noble woman, perhaps implying a period of political transition between the male rulers.

Through their explicit reference to events like those commemorated on monuments, these shell ornaments are a medium of historical connection between the two male rulers, but their audience was not the larger social group that could have participated in rituals in the plazas where monuments were set up. Instead, as parts of what was probably a single item of costume, perhaps a headband (compare figure 6.1), the inscription on these shell plaques was likely read only by members of an intimate group. Used during life as regalia in a specific social ceremony, the ornaments were permanently related to that event through their inscription. Transmitted to a later male member of the noble house, their history might be recited when they were worn again. Finally deposited in the grave with one of the deceased members of the group, they evoked implicit memory of the contexts within which they were worn, were inscribed, and were worn again. They literally formed a connection across generations in the noble families that ruled Piedras Negras.

Texts inscribed on other Classic Maya heirlooms focus on the object, naming it as property of a specific historical person while fore-grounding the use of the object itself. These texts create histories for specific objects that transcend individual memories. Dubbed "name-tag" texts, they take the form of possessive statements (see plate 6.1): "his or her [object type], name and titles of a person" (Houston and Taube 1987; Justeson 1983). The Altun Ha Tomb A 1/1 earspools exemplify this kind of text.

Because the grammatical form of the Classic Maya possessive statement is identical to the grammatical form of a third person singular verb, "name-tag" texts suggest the use of the object by the named person: "her earspools" implies "she wore earspools." Viewed from a contemporary western perspective in which commodities are converted into possessions "by endowing them with a personal identity" (Hoskins 1998:194), these texts seem to be intended to mark these objects as personal property. But the common occurrence of objects with a person of a different gender than the person named as their "owner," in contexts dating later than suggested by calendar dates or style of writing, calls into question the simple equation of these texts with markers of personal possessions. Instead, they serve to convert these ornaments into what Hoskins (1993:118–41) has called "history objects," things whose circulation histories create alliances, objects that could be used as evidence in negotiations among noble families. The shift in significance of the "name tag" text on an object of history makes it a focus for the creation of a social memory. For a later male member of the social network through which the Altun Ha ear spools were passed on, the implication of the text became "she wore these earspools then, as I wear them now." The object, text, and action repeated, and thus recalled and commemorated, the earlier implied action.

A jade carving collected in Comayagua, Honduras, in the nineteenth century is another good example (Grube 1992a; Schele and Miller 1986:81–2). The ornament is a modeled portrait head that would have served as the centerpiece of a man's belt, supporting a set of three pendant plaques. Incised on the reverse of the portrait is a partially eroded text that records the name of a lord of Palenque, Mexico. The actions in the text appear to be those involved in sacralizing the belt head itself, a step in its use as an item of ceremonial regalia. The belt head was removed from the western edge of the Maya world to the opposite extreme, perhaps as a consequence of the marriage of a woman of Palenque into the ruling family of Copan (Schele and Mathews 1991). Whenever it was reused, or even simply circulated on to other points on its journey, it carried along the record of its initial preparation and use, as a "history object." Each subsequent use, consequently, evoked and shaped memory.

Texts served to fix the use of these ornaments at particular points in time; they inscribe specific histories for and on the objects (Joyce 2000b). These are histories of being used by specific persons. The names of human beings (also passed down in Classic Maya noble families) are given permanent material form in these heirlooms.

These histories are necessarily carried along as the objects are transmitted from person to person. When they placed heirloom valuables with inscribed histories in tombs, Classic Maya nobles took them out of circulation and transformed them from transactable media into more stable points of historical reference available to those with privileged memory of the circumstances of their use and transmission. Embedded in physically invisible objects, knowledge of the names and histories of specific ornaments might nonetheless be available in memory, providing a basis for the kind of interplay between physical object and memory that Susanne Küchler (1987, 1988) analyzes in her studies of Melanesian *malangan*.

Remembering, Forgetting, and Knowing

While Classic Maya conserved some objects, this was paired with practices that removed objects from circulation, through burial in tombs and caches and patterned destruction like the burning and crushing first noted in objects recovered from the *cenote* (natural well) at Chichen Itza, Mexico. The numerous jade objects dredged from the *cenote* were burned and broken before being thrown into the water, and were laboriously pieced together from fragments by Tatiana Proskouriakoff (1974). Their recovery raises the question of the degree to which incised heirloom ornaments from secondary locations can be considered to have had continued significance as repositories of social memory. The circulation of inscribed Maya ornaments has been regarded as evidence of recycling of raw material, through looting of earlier sites. But the structured nature of the practices in which these items were used is a strong argument against the assumption that they had lost their significance as historical mnemonics.

A formal sequence of ritual disposal of valued objects according to a set procedure of great antiquity within Classic Maya culture has been defined by comparison with the practices of burning and crushing objects recovered at Chichen Itza (Coggins and Shane 1984; Garber 1993:170). Proskouriakoff (1974, 1993:87) suggested that jades from the *cenote* were looted in antiquity from burials, but she was troubled by the inconsistency between this interpretation and her own identification of an undisturbed tomb at Piedras Negras as the probable burial of a ruler named on an ornament recovered at Chichen Itza. Grube (1992b:494), among others, suggests instead that these items were carried to the *cenote* by descendants of the rulers for whom they were manufactured, who had conserved them as heirlooms of great value. "Rendering invisible the representations that act as temporary vehicles of social transmission," through culturally specific practices of destruction, shifts "proprietary rights" from objects to their trace in memory (Küchler 1999:68). The ability to mobilize knowledge from memory was critical in negotiations of relative power among Classic Maya nobility (Hendon 2000). Destroying the material vehicle of historical memories left the final determination of memory of events up to the members of the Maya nobility contesting the meaning of history.

Objects taken out of use in the short term could find their way back into circulation, sometimes being conserved over very long spans of time and used at great distances from their original contexts. Because many objects were forms that continued to be used in contemporary ceremonies (Joyce 2001:112–15), even when removed from the status of "history object" these heirlooms presumably evoked personal memories of experiences and coordinated those into wider social memory. Jade ornaments from the earliest complex societies of the Olmec Gulf Coast of Mexico were recovered and reused by Classic Maya (Andrews 1986; Proskouriakoff 1974; Schele and Miller 1986:219), their Postclassic Maya successors (Friedel and Sabloff 1984:103–4), and the Postclassic Aztecs of Central Mexico (Matos Moctezuma 1996). The lack of added incised texts on most of these objects suggests a less particular significance. Such very old objects might have been understood as antiquities from a primordial civilization (Umberger 1987), their implications depending less on their histories of use than on their status as icons of temporal displacement from, and connection to, the origins of cultural practices. They thus resemble the kinds of "disjunctive" memory discussed by Meskell (this volume).

Not all of the known Classic Maya heirlooms suggest generational transmission within a noble family like the Altun Ha examples discussed above. While the temporal disjunctions are not as great as the 1000 to 2300 year gap between Olmec society and later antiquarian use of Olmec objects, heirlooms passed on over spans beyond the temporal persistence of documented noble families framed and united longer spans of Classic Maya history. There are numerous examples. A Maya burial from Kendall, Belize, dating between 250 and 400 AD, included a pendant carved in a style dating to before 150 AD (Schele and Miller 1986:81). A tomb at Copan with pottery vessels typical of the period after 650 AD, included an incised peccary skull (perhaps originally part of a headdress), with a hieroglyphic date several centuries earlier (Coggins 1988:104–6). In these cases, the reuse of an object, inscribed at an earlier date in a script still being used, promoted ongoing social memory within Classic Maya culture.

Other texts were added long after the original creation of the ornament on which they occur. In these cases, the text connected a contemporary world with a more ancient one, in a more direct way than the kind of antiquarian practice noted above. One Gulf Coast Olmec pendant, likely produced sometime between 800 and 500 BC, has an incised figure and inscription on the reverse, in a style typical of the Maya writing system of around 50–250 AD (Coe 1966; Schele and Miller 1986:119). The text is historical; it records the "seating" in office of a named ruler. The figure incised next to it is shown in the seated position, wearing regalia of office. The implication is that the ancient object figured in the ceremony of installation of the Maya ruler at least 600 years later, giving the ornament (and the practice it embodied) a history longer than Classic Maya society at the time of this inscription.

Several Classic Maya costume ornaments incised with specific notations of political ceremonies were recovered from much later contexts than the dates they carry. The Leiden Plaque, an incised jade belt pendant, was found near the mouth of the Motagua River in Guatemala, with other objects suggesting a date after 800 AD (Morley and Morley 1938). On one side it depicts an image of a standing figure wearing a belt ornamented with sets of three plaques hanging from ornamental masks.

The text refers to a "seating" that took place at the Maya city, Tikal, sometime before 400 AD (Mathews 1985:44, Schele and Miller 1986:118, 120–1). This belt ornament circulated from its original place of creation, probably near to the inland settlement named in its text, for at least 400 years before being carefully deposited with other valuables by later Maya people of the coast. As it moved from point to point on its journey, the text inscribed on it provided a continually legible orientation in time, space, and experience for new users for whom it served as a historical and personal mnemonic.

Texts and images incised on costume ornaments condensed the later use of ornaments with historical precedents for action, making the reading of the text and the use of the ornament both acts of explicit memory recall. One pendant, recovered from the *cenote* at Chichen Itza, where it was deposited sometime after 800 AD, provides a good example (Proskouriakoff 1974). Two sides of this tubular jade bead were carved, at right angles to the orientation as worn. Like the Altun Ha bead pendant, the *cenote* bead replicates the dual-sided structure of a Classic Maya monumental stela, with an image on one side and text on the other. The image shows a young man standing with a heel raised in the Classic Maya stylization of movement. The text refers to events in the life of a young Palenque noble who lived in the eighth century. One clause literally describes him as "taking a step into" or "entering" the succession of rulers, mirroring the action in which the figure is depicted.

A second heirloom jade ornament incised with its history was also recovered from the *cenote* at Chichen Itza (plate 6.2). A single continuous text is incised on the reverse and bottom surfaces of this three-dimensional pendant portrait head (Grube 1992b:494–5; Proskouriakoff 1944). The text records the completion of thirteen calendrical cycles as lord of Piedras Negras, far south and west of Chichen Itza, by an unnamed ruler. The future tense verb refers to a date seven cycles into the future. It states that this date will be the end of the commemorated person's first twenty-cycle period as ruler of the site. The ruler's personal name or titles, largely eroded, end the text. The principal event commemorated as the basis for measuring elapsed time was the adoption of the title of *ahaw* (lord) by the ruler. The ornament itself, a frontal anthropomorphic face, is an iconic version of the *ahaw* title and mimics the textual sign for this title (Fields 1991; Freidel 1993:154–9). It most likely served as the front ornament of a headdress that signified the right to the *ahaw* title, like those depicted in other Maya images (compare figure 6.1).

Even at their furthest remove from their sources of origin, Mesoamerican heirloom items continued to be used in ways consistent with their history as noble house valuables and repositories of powerful histories. Mesoamerican ornaments created at different times, all of which apparently reached lower Central America after 500 AD, were treated in distinct ways. Incised "clam shell" shaped pendants created before 500 BC were generally conserved unaltered or were deliberately terminated in the same fashion as used by the Classic Maya, crushed and burned (Guerrero 1993:193; Hirth and Grant Hirth 1993:186–7). Incised slate mirror backs with Maya texts dating to ca. 250–400 AD were generally preserved intact as well (Baudez and Coe 1966; Stone and Balser 1965). Early Classic Maya jade belt pendant plaques that reached Costa

Plate 6.2   Jade pendant head recovered from the cenote at Chichen Itza, inscribed on reverse with a text referring to events in the history of Piedras Negras (Peabody Museum catalogue number 37–39–20/4885). Probably worn as the front ornament in a head band like that worn by the man on Yaxchilan Lintel 26, on the left in figure 6.1. (Photograph by Steve Burger, courtesy of the Peabody Museum, Harvard University. Used with permission of the President and Fellows of Harvard College)

Rica, in contrast, were always cut in a uniform fashion, split in half lengthwise, separated into quarters (plate 6.3), or further divided into squares, a deliberate dismembering that recognizes the previous markings by systematically distorting them (Graham 1993:23). Even in these very different cultural settings, the ability of objects to concretize particular sequences of action allowed them to serve as sites for the repetition of remembered actions, simultaneously strengthening individual memory and shaping shared social memory.

Thinking about Classic Maya Memory

I began this paper by arguing that Classic Maya sites, with their carefully orchestrated presentation of monumental images depicting the use of objects whose real-world equivalents in turn record depicted actions through both images and inscribed texts, were amenable to understanding from the perspective of contemporary psychological understandings of memory. I distinguished between memory as commemoration, a public marking of specific topics for shared social memory, and the embodied experience of memory as an iterative process of recall and recognition. I suggested that

Plate 6.3   Upper right-hand section of a jade plaque in the form of a celt, used in sets of three as pendants suspended below jade masks on the belts of Classic Maya noble men (Peabody Museum catalogue number 977–4-20/25516). This is an example of a group of Maya ornaments cut into sections found in Costa Rica. The original plaque carried an incised inscription, partly preserved here, in Early Classic style. (Photograph by Steve Burger, courtesy of the Peabody Museum, Harvard University. Used with permission of the President and Fellows of Harvard College)

in explicitly inscribing specific historical texts on objects, Classic Maya people converted what were normally mute cues coordinating memory in relatively unobtrusive fashion into consciously recognized biographical and historical objects, in the senses defined by Janet Hoskins (1993, 1998).

I proceeded to blur the lines between unconscious cues and consciously framed mnemonics by considering the complexities of the histories of specific objects. Drawing on the material apparatus of extremely conservative cultural practices, inscription of texts on Classic Maya objects linked fleeting bodily practices in sequences of reiteration that facilitated the continuity of Classic Maya culture, and of the Mesoamerican cultural tradition of which it was one part (Joyce 2000c). Inscribed memory objects could serve as mnemonics to cue implicit memories among more restricted social groups. The content of these memories was related to that of commemorative monuments, but emphasized the construction of links over generational time and through biography. The succession of generations and connection of biographies at the level of noble families literally took shape through the social ceremonies in which objects like ear spools were used, allowing a merger of personal and social memory and history.

But the effectiveness of the materialization of memory was not limited to circulation of objects inscribed with specific historical content among those who might agree on memory and its meaning. As objects circulated more widely in space, and were conserved, rediscovered, transformed, and passed on over time, they provided occasions for the formulation of more disjunctive forms of memory, notably an antiquarian emphasis on generalized connections to a distant past. Within the time and space of Classic Maya society, the significance of objects as cues for memory figured not only in practices through which they were conserved, marked, and circulated, but also in processes of "forgetting" through which they were taken out of circulation more or less permanently. Knowledge constructed from memory of objects removed from circulation, through burial or destruction, joins other forms of differential knowledge as a resource employed by those engaged in social differentiation in Classic Maya society. Inscriptions on monuments dated by a single continuous calendar may assert the greatest claim for our attention today, but in Classic Maya life, they were embedded in a world of objects, all of them acting as potential foci for acts of remembering and forgetting.

References Cited

Andrews, E. W. 1986: Olmec jades from Chacsinkin, Yucatan, and Maya ceramics from La Venta, Tabasco. In *Research and Reflections in Archaeology and History: Essays in Honor of Doris Stone*, ed. E. W. Andrews. New Orleans: Tulane University, Middle American Research Institute, pp. 11–49.

Baddeley, A. 1990: *Human Memory: Theory and Practice*. Boston: Allyn and Bacon.

Bassie-Sweet, K. 1991: *From the Mouth of the Dark Cave: Commemorative Sculpture of the Late Classic Maya*. Norman: University of Oklahoma Press.

Baudez, C. F. and Coe, M. D. 1966: Incised slate disks from the Atlantic watershed of Costa Rica: a commentary. *American Antiquity* 31, pp. 441–3.

Belleza, F. S. 1996: Mnemonic methods to enhance storage and retrieval. In *Memory*, ed. E. Ligon Bjork and R. A. Bjork. San Diego: Academic Press, pp. 345–80.

Bjork, R. A. 1994: Memory and metamemory: considerations in the training of human beings. In *Metacognition: Knowing about Knowing*, ed. J. Metcalfe and A. Shimamura. Cambridge, Mass.: MIT Press, pp. 185–205.

Coe, M. D. 1966: *An Early Stone Pectoral from Southeastern Mexico*. Washington, D.C.: Dumbarton Oaks.

Coggins, C. C. 1988: On the historical significance of decorated ceramics at Copan and Quirigua and related Classic Maya sites. In *The Southeast Classic Maya Zone*, ed. E. Boone and G. Willey. Washington, D.C.: Dumbarton Oaks, pp. 95–124.

Coggins, C. C. and Shane, O. C. 1984: *Cenote of Sacrifice: Maya Treasures from the Sacred Well at Chichen Itza*. Austin: University of Texas Press.

Connerton, P. 1989: *How Societies Remember*. Cambridge: Cambridge University Press.

Fields, V. 1991: The iconographic heritage of the Maya Jester God. In *Sixth Palenque Round Table, 1986*, ed. M. G. Robertson and V. Fields. Norman: University of Oklahoma Press, pp. 167–74.

Freidel, D. 1993: The jade Ahau: toward a theory of commodity value in Maya civilization. In *Precolumbian Jade: New Geological and Cultural Interpretations*, ed. F. W. Lange. Salt Lake City: University of Utah Press, pp. 149–65.

Freidel, D. and Sabloff, J. A. 1984: *Cozumel: Late Maya Settlement Patterns*. New York: Academic Press.

Garber, J. 1993: The cultural context of jade artifacts from the Maya site of Cerros, Belize. In *Precolumbian Jade: New Geological and Cultural Interpretations*, ed. F. W. Lange. Salt Lake City: University of Utah Press, pp. 166–72.

Gillespie, S. D. and Joyce, R. A. 1997: Gendered goods: the symbolism of Maya hierarchical exchange relations. In *Women in Prehistory: North America and Mesoamerica*, ed. C. Claassen and R. A. Joyce. Philadelphia: University of Pennsylvania Press, pp. 189–207.

Graham, M. M. 1993: Displacing the center: constructing prehistory in Central America. In *Reinterpreting Prehistory of Central America*, ed. M. M. Graham. Niwot: University of Colorado Press, pp. 1–38.

Grube, N. 1992a: Porträtmaske. In *Die Welt der Maya: archaologische Schatze aus drei Jahrtausenden*, ed. E. Eggebrecht, A. Eggebrecht and N. Grube. Mainz am Rhein: P. von Zabern, pp. 488–9.

Grube, N. 1992b: Anhänger. In *Die Welt der Maya: archaologische Schatze aus drei Jahrtausenden*, ed. E. Eggebrecht, A. Eggebrecht and N. Grube. Mainz am Rhein: P. von Zabern, pp. 494–5.

Guerrero, M. J. V. 1993: The context of jade in Costa Rica. In *Precolumbian Jade: New Geological and Cultural Interpretations*, ed. F. W. Lange. Salt Lake City: University of Utah Press, pp. 191–202.

Hendon, J. A. 2000: Having and holding: storage, memory, knowledge, and social relations. *American Anthropologist* 102, pp. 42–53.

Hirth, K. G. and Grant Hirth, S. 1993: Ancient currency: the style and use of jade and marble carvings in central Honduras. In *Precolumbian Jade: New Geological and Cultural Interpretations*, ed. F. W. Lange. Salt Lake City: University of Utah Press, pp. 173–90.

Hoskins, J. 1993: *The Play of Time: Kodi Perspectives on Calendars, History, and Exchange*. Berkeley: University of California Press.

Hoskins, J. 1998: *Biographical Objects: How Things Tell the Stories of People's Lives*. London: Routledge Press.

Houston, S. 1997: Shifting now: aspect, deixis, and narrative in classic Maya texts. *American Anthropologist* 99, pp. 291–305.

Houston, S. 2000: Into the minds of ancients: advances in Maya glyph studies. *Journal of World Prehistory* 14, pp. 121–201.

Houston, S. and Stuart, D. 1992: On Maya hieroglyphic literacy. *Current Anthropology* 33, pp. 589–93.

Houston, S. and Taube, K. 1987: Name-tagging in Classic Mayan script. *Mexikon* IX(2), pp. 38–41.

Joyce, R. A. 1998: Performing the body in Prehispanic Central America. *RES: Anthropology and Aesthetics* 33, pp. 147–65.

Joyce, R. A. 2000a: Girling the girl and boying the boy: the production of adulthood in ancient Mesoamerica. *World Archaeology*, 31, pp. 473–83.

Joyce, R. A. 2000b: Heirlooms and houses: materiality and social memory. In *Beyond Kinship: Social and Material Reproduction in House Societies*, ed. R. A. Joyce and S. D. Gillespie. Philadelphia: University of Pennsylvania Press, pp. 189–212.

Joyce, R. A. 2000c: High culture, Mesoamerican civilization, and the Classic Maya tradition. In *Order, Legitimacy, and Wealth in Ancient States*, ed. J. Richards and M. Van Buren. Cambridge: Cambridge University Press, pp. 64–76.

Joyce, R. A. 2001: Negotiating sex and gender in Classic Maya society. In *Gender in Pre-Hispanic America*, ed. C. Klein. Washington, D.C.: Dumbarton Oaks, pp. 109–41.

Joyce, R. A. and Hendon, J. A. 2000: Heterarchy, history, and material reality: "communities" in Late Classic Honduras. In *The Archaeology of Communities: A New World Perspective*, ed. M-A. Canuto and J. Yaeger. London: Routledge Press, pp. 143–59.

Justeson, J. 1983: Mayan hieroglyphic "name-tagging" of a pair of rectangular jade plaques from Xcalumkin. In *Recent Contributions to Maya Hieroglyphic Decipherment, Number 1*, ed. S. D. Houston. New Haven: Human Relations Area Files, Inc., pp. 40–3.

Kelley, C. M. and Lindsay, D. S. 1996: Conscious and unconscious forms of memory. In *Memory*, ed. E. Ligon Bjork and R. A. Bjork. San Diego: Academic Press, pp. 31–63.

Küchler, S. 1987: Malangan: art and memory in a Melanesian society. *Man* 22, pp. 238–55.

Küchler, S. 1988: Malangan: objects, sacrifice, and the production of memory. *American Ethnologist* 15, pp. 625–37.

Küchler, S. 1999: The place of memory. In *The Art of Forgetting*, ed. A. Forty and S. Küchler. Oxford: Berg, pp. 53–72.

Lillios, K. T. 1999: Objects of memory: the ethnography and archaeology of heirlooms. *Journal of Archaeological Method and Theory* 6(3), pp. 235–62.

Mathews, P. 1979: The glyphs from the ear ornament from Tomb A 1/1. In *Excavations at Altun Ha, Belize, 1964–1970, Volume 1*, ed. D. Pendergast. Toronto: Royal Ontario Museum, pp. 79–80.

Mathews, P. 1985: Maya Early Classic monuments and inscriptions. In *Considerations of the Early Classic Period in the Maya Lowlands*, ed. G. R. Willey and P. Mathews. Albany: Institute for Mesoamerican Studies, State University of New York, pp. 5–54.

Mathews, P. and Pendergast, D. 1979: The Altun Ha jade plaque: deciphering the inscription. In *Studies in Ancient Mesoamerica, IV*, ed. J. A. Graham. Berkeley: University of California Archaeological Research Facility, pp. 197–214.

Matos Moctezuma, E. 1996: Deity mask. In *Olmec Art of Ancient Mexico*, ed. E. P. Benson and B. de la Fuente. Washington D.C.: National Gallery of Art, p. 252.

Morley, F. and Morley, S. G. 1938: The age and provenance of the Leyden Plate. In *Contributions to American Anthropology and History No. 24*. Washington, D.C.: Carnegie Institution of Washington, pp. 1–17.

Nairne, J. S. 1996: Short-term/working memory. In *Memory*, ed. E. Ligon Bjork and R. A. Bjork. San Diego: Academic Press, pp. 101–26.

Pashler, H. and Carrier, M. 1996: Structures, processes, and the flow of information. In *Memory*, ed. E. Ligon Bjork and R. A. Bjork. San Diego: Academic Press, pp. 3–29.

Pendergast, D. 1982: *Excavations at Altun Ha, Belize, 1964–1970, Volume 2.* Toronto: Royal Ontario Museum.

Proskouriakoff, T. 1944: An inscription on a jade probably carved at Piedras Negras. *Notes on Middle American Archaeology and Ethnology 2.* Cambridge, Mass.: Carnegie Institution of Washington, Division of Historical Research, pp. 142–7.

Proskouriakoff, T. 1974: *Jades from the Cenote of Sacrifice, Chichen Itza, Yucatan.* Cambridge, Mass.: Harvard University, Peabody Museum of Archaeology and Ethnology.

Proskouriakoff, T. 1993: *Maya History.* Austin: University of Texas Press.

Roediger, H. L., III and Guynn, M. J. 1996: Retrieval processes. In *Memory*, ed. E. Ligon Bjork and R. A. Bjork. San Diego: Academic Press, pp. 197–236.

Rowlands, M. 1993: The role of memory in the transmission of culture. *World Archaeology* 25, pp. 141–51.

Schele, L. and Mathews, P. 1991: Royal visits and other intersite relationships among the Classic Maya. In *Classic Maya Political History: Hieroglyphic and Archaeological Evidence*, ed. T. P. Culbert. Cambridge: Cambridge University Press, pp. 226–52.

Schele, L. and Miller, M. E. 1986: *The Blood of Kings: Dynasty and Ritual in Maya Art.* Fort Worth: Kimbell Art Museum.

Stone, D. Z. and Balser, C. 1965: Incised slate disks from the Atlantic watershed of Costa Rica. *American Antiquity* 30, pp. 310–29.

Stuart, D. 1985: The inscriptions on four shell plaques from Piedras Negras. In *Fourth Palenque Round Table, 1980, Vol. VI*, ed. M. G. Robertson and E. P. Benson. San Francisco: Pre-Columbian Art Research Institute, pp. 175–83.

Umberger, E. 1987: Antiques, revivals, and references to the past in Aztec art. *Res: Anthropology and Aesthetics* 13, pp. 63–106.

Vromen, S. 1986: Maurice Halbwachs and the concept of nostalgia. *Knowledge and Society: Studies in the Sociology of Culture Past and Present* 6, pp. 55–66.

Weiner, A. 1992: *Inalienable Possessions: The Paradox of Keeping-While-Giving.* Berkeley: University of California Press.

Yates, F. A. 1966: *The Art of Memory.* London: Routledge and Kegan Paul.

Part II
Memory Studies in Prehistory

7
Creating Memory in Prehistory: The Engraved Slate Plaques of Southwest Iberia

Katina T. Lillios

Introduction

Prehistory is not simply time before history, not merely that vast temporal void before the first Mesopotamians took stylus to clay. With respect to memory, prehistory is more accurately conceived not by what follows it, but in reference to itself. Individuals and groups communicated and remembered their pasts through the recitation of oral traditions and genealogies, the sacralization and transformation of landscapes (Bradley 2000), the construction of monuments, the performance of dance, song, and ritual, and, of course, the production and use of material culture. Thus, prehistoric peoples should not, in any sense, be thought of as memory-challenged.

It is we, as archaeologists, who have the problem with memory. Although many anthropologists now question the notion of a Great Divide separating prehistory from history (Street and Besnier 1994), relatively few prehistorians, with the notable exception of Marshack (1991), have taken seriously the possibility that decorative motifs on ancient artifacts were material mnemonics, or memory aids, that can actually be deciphered or 'read' in the present day. Archaeologists are generally reluctant to ascribe meaning to symbols, particularly those that are non-representational, and thus we unwittingly continue to reify the distinction between prehistoric and historic societies. In this paper, I examine the case of the slate plaques of Iberia found in the collective burials of southern Portugal and Spain and dated to the Late Neolithic and Copper Age (3000–2500 BC), and I develop the hypothesis that their engraved designs

I wish to thank Ruth Van Dyke and Susan Alcock for organizing such a stimulating session at the 2001 AIA meetings and for their insightful questions, comments, and suggestions. I am also grateful for the many conversations I have had with friends and colleagues about the plaques, although not all might agree with my interpretations. I want especially to thank Bettina Arnold, Paul Axelrod, Elizabeth Barber, Donald Crowe, Cidália Duarte, Antonio Gilman, Victor Gonçalves, Stephen Houston, Mary Helms, Petya Hristova, Evelyn Kain, Isabel Gomes Lisboa, Sarah McGowan, Jean Moore, Teresa Orozco-Köhler, Jeffrey Quilter, Andrew Rich, James Sackett, Morten Schlütter, Stephanie Serlin, John Steinberg, and João Zilhão.

recorded lineage affiliation and genealogical histories. Indeed, the slate plaques of Iberia may be the earliest evidence for heraldry in the world.

The Iberian plaques have long engaged and stimulated the imagination of European archaeologists (Almagro Gorbea 1973; Bueno Ramirez 1992; Correia 1917; Frankowski 1920; Rodrigues 1986a and b; Siret 1913; Vasconcellos 1897, 1906; Veiga 1887). The occasional appearance of anthropomorphic features on the plaques inspired nineteenth and early twentieth century prehistorians to assume that they were representations of the Mother Goddess, whose cult had supposedly diffused from the eastern Mediterranean and whose worshippers brought other components of "civilized" life, such as copper metallurgy and fortified settlements, to Iberia. Although this model was overturned in the 1960s when radiocarbon dates and their calibration demonstrated that metallurgy and other features of "civilized" life in Iberia were con- temporary with, or actually predated, their "sources" (Renfrew 1976), some prehisto- rians still see the anthropomorphic plaques as depictions of the Mother Goddess (Almagro Gorbea 1973; Gonçalves 1992, 1999; Rodrigues 1986a and b).

Recently, Lisboa (1985) disputed the Mother Goddess attribution of the slate plaques for the same reasons as did Frankowski (1920) and Fleming (1969): only a few of the plaques unquestionably depict anthropomorphic figures, and none are obviously females or deities. She proposed that the plaques be seen as "ordered and meaningful, in the sense that they (were) used to transmit messages" and suggested that "they had a heraldic function" not necessarily associated with individuals (Lisboa 1985:193). Lisboa did not, however, offer any test of this model.

In this paper, I develop Lisboa's suggestion that these plaques − or at least a large number of them − were material mnemonics, and I further propose, contrary to what Lisboa argued, that they were indeed associated with individuals. In doing so, I address the formal qualities of the plaques and their cultural contexts, with the assumption that these attributes provide signposts to the function and meaning of the plaques. Finally, I recontextualize the plaques within the prehistoric politico-economic land- scape in which they are found and present a new model for the role of memory in the emergence of social inequalities during late prehistoric Iberia.

This study is based on 680 illustrated plaques published in a variety of sources, the principal one being the multi-volume series *Die Megalithgräber der Iberischen Halbinsel* (Leisner 1965, 1998; Leisner and Leisner 1943, 1951, 1956, 1959). All the plaques from these publications were coded for context (geographic location of tomb, date of tomb) and formal attributes (size, form, compositional structure, design elements). There are, not surprisingly, many plaques that have not been illustrated, that are unpublished, or that exist in publications that I have not yet consulted. Based on estimates provided by Gonçalves (2001, personal communication) and my tally of published and unpublished plaques, I estimate there to be between 1,000 and 2,000 plaques excavated to date.

Contextualizing the Iberian Slate Plaques

In their depositional contexts, form, compositional structure, and decorative elements, the slate plaques of Iberia appear to possess a distinctive unity; yet in fact no two plaques are identical. In this section, I describe the commonalities among the plaques as well as their variability by context, form, and design, and then develop the hypothesis, first posed by Lisboa, that they were heraldic in nature.

The slate plaques have been found only in southwestern Iberia (map 7.1) and are principally recovered in the collective burials typical of the time; these include megaliths, caves, rockshelters, rock-cut tombs, and corbel-vaulted tombs. In these burials, the plaques are generally found in association with undecorated pottery, flint blades, and unused polished stone tools. A few plaques, principally fragments, have been found at settlements (Spindler 1981:224–5). Given the preponderance of plaques in burials and their rarity in settlements, it seems reasonable to postulate that they were produced close to the time of death of an individual. If they had been owned and used during life, one would expect many more broken or lost pieces in settlement contexts, especially given the fragility of slate. This important "biographical" question, however, merits further research.

Although found throughout southwestern Iberia, the plaques are not evenly distributed throughout this territory. Approximately 50 percent were recovered in the Portuguese district of Évora alone. The range in plaque numbers by tomb is also striking. The site of Anta Grande do Olival da Pega (Évora) was found with 134 plaques (Leisner and Leisner 1951:240), while the contemporary burial of Anta 1 do Cebolinho (Évora) had only 31 (Leisner and Leisner 1951:276–9). Furthermore, not all individuals within a tomb were buried with plaques. At the site of Cabeço da Arruda 1 (Lisboa), the minimum number of individuals buried was 19, yet there were only 11 slate plaques recovered (Silva 1999:356–7; Spindler 1981:224).

Although the precise dating of the plaques is problematic, they are generally placed within the late fourth-early third millennium BC (Gonçalves 1999:117). Their chronology has been difficult to ascertain primarily because late prehistoric burial sites in Iberia were repeatedly reused, sometimes until the Early Bronze Age, so artifacts and skeletal remains are often found disturbed. Furthermore, the acidic soils of the regions where many of these burials are located do not regularly preserve skeletal remains, and thus, direct dating of associated individuals is difficult.

A range of raw materials was used to make the plaques. Although most plaques were made of slate, some were also made of schist and sandstone. No provenance studies have yet been undertaken to identify the precise sources of these plaques; however, their raw materials are found in southwestern Iberia, close to their depositional contexts (Instituto Técnológico GeoMinero de España 1994).

In their form, the Iberian plaques display a certain consistency. They are generally trapezoidal, roughly 10–20 cm in height and approximately 10 cm in maximum width. Yet there are also some plaques that are rectangular and others with a composite shape, with a triangular or rectangular form extending from the narrower width. Approximately 30 percent of the plaques share a common compositional structure. This group of plaques, which I have termed "classic," has a bipartite compositional structure, consisting of a narrower one-third (top) of the plaque and a wider bottom two-thirds of the plaque (base) (figure 7.1). I refer to the narrower section as the "top" because it is often perforated (with one or two holes), and the plaques appear to have been hung from here (possibly on a person's neck or a post). On some plaques,

Map 7.1   Number of slate plaques in study, by district (Portugal) or province (Spain). Map also shows sources of amphibolite, in black

the perforations are perfectly sharp and give the appearance that the plaque was never worn or suspended; yet on others, a range of wear is exhibited, suggesting they were worn or hung (Vasconcellos 1897:159). The top also has an empty triangular field in the center with bands ("straps"), either horizontal (touching the sides of the triangle) or vertical (touching the top of the base). Sometimes separating the top and base are single or multiple horizontal bands that can be undecorated or decorated with cross-hatching, triangles, or some other geometric design. There are also plaques without

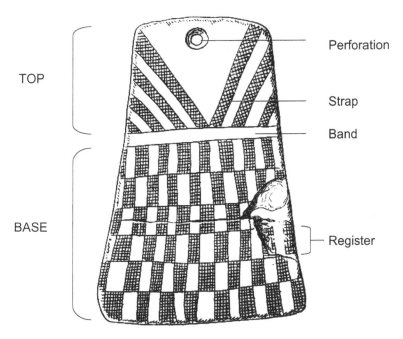

Figure 7.1   Anatomy of a classic Iberian plaque. Plaque from Folha da Amendoeira, Beja (ht. 18 cm) (Leisner and Leisner 1959: Tafel 42, 2, 24)

this separating band, and with only a horizontal line separating the top from the base. The base is where the decorative elements are concentrated, and one (or more) of six repeating geometric motifs are found here: checkerboard, vertical bands, triangles, chevrons, herringbone, and zigzags. The checkerboard and triangle motifs are organized generally along horizontal registers, while the chevrons and herring-bones are organized along vertical registers. The zigzag and vertical band motifs use the entire base as their compositional field.

As noted above, approximately half of the plaques have been found in the district of Évora, and it is also in Évora where we see the full range of forms, compositional structures, and decorative motifs. Thus, it seems logical to begin the interpretive process in this district and in the surrounding region of the Alentejo (which also includes the districts of Portalegre and Beja). Archaeologically, the Alentejo is known principally for hundreds of megaliths in the form of passage graves, menhirs, and stone circles; understandably, the character of the Alentejo as a ritual landscape has traditionally been emphasized. More recently, however, Portuguese archaeologists have identified late prehistoric settlements in the Alentejo and have demonstrated that the region was not an empty landscape, visited only during solstices, full moons, or funerals. Rather, it was inhabited by groups, probably pastoralists and farmers, who built most of their settlements in relatively perishable materials (Gonçalves 1997).

The Alentejo was also important for being the principal regional source of amphi-bolite, used to make the polished stone tools that were traded and used throughout southern Portugal (map 7.1). Amphibolite was a durable and highly workable meta-morphic stone. Even when local hard stone, such as basalt, was available and some-times used, communities – even those far from the sources – still preferred amphibolite. At Late Neolithic and Copper Age sites between 70–150 km away, such as Zambujal, Leceia, and Vila Nova de São Pedro, over 50 percent of the ground-stone tools were made of amphibolite; at Leceia, almost 80 percent were made of amphibolite (Lillios 1997). Thus, the value and importance of this stone was widely recognized throughout southern Portugal in later prehistory.

The association between amphibolite tools and slate plaques becomes closer when one compares their color (dark grey, green, or blue), luster (shiny) and their form (trapezoidal). Furthermore, in the few representations of hafted adzes in late prehis-toric Portugal, many of the same features as the slate plaques appear, such as the bipar-tite compositional structure, the horizontal bands between the top and base (probably depictions of hafting), and even the triangle motif (figure 7.2a) (Larsson 1998; Lillios 1997; Vasconcellos 1922:292). For these reasons, I suggest that the slate plaques semi-otically referred to the amphibolite tools that were so important to the economic and social life of ancient peoples in the Alentejo.

It is also clear that some plaques were meant to depict beings, whether humans, animals, or deities (figure 7.2b). The arms, eyes, and noses on these plaques are quite unambiguous. If Iberian plaques represent part of some relatively coherent visual com-munication system, axes may well have acted as metaphors for humans (Tilley 1999), much as Battaglia (1983, 1990:133–5) argued in her study of the Sabarl Islanders of Melanesia. In the context of the agricultural and complex societies of late prehistoric Portugal, in which the symbolic and social potency of axes as transformative objects would have been great, the metaphorical fusion of axes and humans seems eminently reasonable. Plaques may have taken on more anthropomorphic qualities under con-ditions of social stress, such as war and/or social stratification, when new leaders emerged who assumed greater control over the means of economic production and social reproduction.

How can we explain the decoration of the plaques? The answer lies, I suggest, with the anthropomorphic plaques. Although rarely noted in published references, many of the "beings" represented are clearly wearing clothing (figure 7.2b). Furthermore, the decorative motifs on these clothes are also those found on the non-anthropomorphic plaques. There are also some plaques that, with their decorated borders, are evocative of woven rugs or blankets. Thus, it seems logical to consider textiles such as cloth-ing, blankets, or carpets as the inspiration or basis for the decorative motifs on the slate plaques. There is a great deal of evidence, such as loom weights and spindle whorls, for a thriving textile industry in the Late Neolithic and Copper Age of Iberia (Castro Curel 1984; Cardito Rollán 1996). Furthermore, all the motifs found on the plaques are weaves easily reproducible by card or tablet weaving or on a simple loom (Held 1978; Barber, personal communication 2002). Finally, there are the few pre-served textiles themselves. Two fragments of linen (including a fragment painted with horizontal bands) have been found covering metal axes in two Portuguese Copper Age burials (Formosinho et al. 1953/1954; Viana et al. 1948).

I would like to suggest, however, that the primary function of the design on the slate plaques (as is also so often the case with clothing) was to communicate the

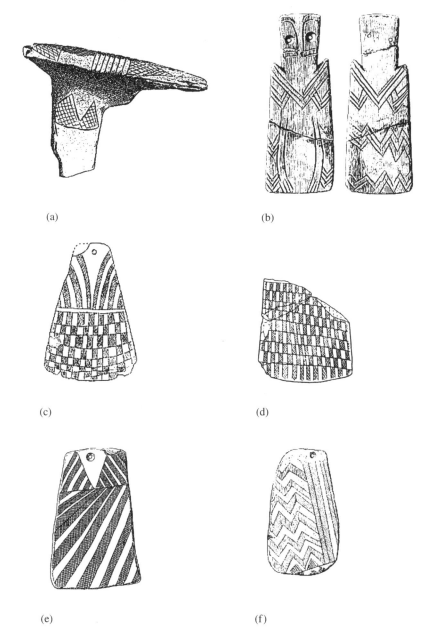

Figure 7.2a–f Artifacts discussed in text. (a) Limestone hafted adze from São Martinho de Sintra (Lisboa) (Vasconcellos 1922: Est. XVII). (b) Plaque from Idanha-a-Nova (Castelo Branco), ht. 19.5 cm (Leisner 1998: Tafel 75). (c) Plaque from Anta 1 da Herdado do Passo (Évora), ht. 16.2 cm (Leisner and Leisner 1951: Est. XXI, 21). (d) Plaque (fragment) from Anta Grande do Olival da Pega (Évora), ht. 12 cm (Leisner and Leisner 1951: Est. XXVIII, 57). (e) Plaque from Folha da Amendoeira (Beja), ht. 16.5 cm (Leisner and Leisner 1959: Tafel 42, 23). (f) Plaque fragment recycled into pendant from Ribeira de Odivelas (Évora), ht. 12 cm (Leisner and Leisner 1959: Tafel 34, 9, 2)

deceased individual's membership within a social group. The regular compositional structure of the plaques and the relatively small number of decorative elements, in combination with the uniqueness of each plaque, all point to such a codified communication system. Other indicators of the personal nature of at least some of the plaques are suggested by their discovery, when context is recorded, along the side or on the chest of individual bodies (Gonçalves 1999).

Material mnemonics recording genealogical status are well-known in the ethnographic literature. For example, in the knobs along the wooden *whakapapa,* or genealogy, staffs of the New Zealand Maori, generations of ancestors were recorded. The knobs, used as memory aids, were touched by a chief in the recitation of genealogies that were so critical to the identity and political authority of chiefly Maori. Similar to the *whakapapa* staffs are other wooden staffs from Borneo, Myanmar, Sumatra, and Rarotonga which, in their vertical arrangement of anthropomorphic figures, notches, or knobs, were used to record ancestry, community organization, or numbers of enemies killed by the deceased (Schuster and Carpenter 1996:64–5).

The Iberian Slate Plaques as Material Mnemonics?

Viewing heraldic design as an example of an active form of emblemic style created to communicate a set of information about a person's affiliation and identity (Wiessner 1983; Wobst 1977), I make the assumption that the most visible decorative attributes signify the most inclusive social categories. On the plaques, these attributes are found on the base. By contrast, attributes found on the top third of the plaque are either less visible or more ambiguous. Although in the future I plan to analyze the attributes concentrated on the top of the plaque (the straps and bands), I wish to focus here on those more visible and unambiguous attributes on the base.

As a working hypothesis, I propose that, for the classic plaques, the design motifs on the base were emblematic of lineage affiliation, and the number of horizontal registers indicated the generational distance between the deceased person and an important ancestor. If this was indeed the case, the following five test implications should be confirmed:

1   There should not be a relationship between the number of registers and the size of the plaque.
2   There should be more plaques with high numbers of registers and fewer plaques with low numbers of registers.
3   Plaques with low numbers of registers should be found over a small area, and those with larger numbers of registers should be more widely dispersed.
4   Assuming tombs and tomb groups housed closely related people over many generations, there should be plaques in continuous sequences of register numbers, by motif, within these tombs or tomb groups.
5   Those plaques with higher numbers of registers should postdate those with lower numbers of registers, by motif.

I now review these five test implications in light of the data set available. The four motifs that will be considered in this discussion are the triangle, checkerboard, zigzag, and chevron. There are very few classic plaques with the herringbone (n = 1) and vertical band (n = 4) motifs, so I will not include them here.

1 *Design independent of material constraints.* It is necessary to rule out the determining role of raw material constraints if the engraved design on the plaques is to be taken seriously on its own. When the relationship between the height of complete plaques and the number of their registers, by motif, is examined, an interesting pattern becomes clear. Specifically, there is no correlation between the height of the plaque and the number of registers on that plaque. The correlation coefficient for plaques with zigzag motifs = 0.01, chevrons = 0.27, triangles = 0.28, and checkerboards = −0.10. Large plaques sometimes have few registers, and smallish plaques were used to engrave high numbers of registers. Furthermore, the mean height of the plaques (15 cm) is virtually identical by motif. These data suggest that the quarrying and initial shaping of the plaque was done to satisfy a basic size requirement, and then the requisite design was applied, perhaps by another person.

Furthermore, when the *chaîne opératoire* of the engraved designs can be gleaned, we again see a priority attached to design over raw material constraints. In a few cases, for example, there appears to have been an attempt to "squeeze" registers at the bottom of the base to produce the desired number of registers (figure 7.2c). These "squeezed in" registers are often irregular in size and in the straightness of their lines. And, on other plaques, there seems to have been ample room to create an additional register, but this was not done (figure 7.2d). These observations and analyses suggest that the number of registers on the plaques was more important than specific material constraints or any regularity in design.

2 *More plaques with more registers vs. fewer plaques with lower numbers of registers.* Over time, more and more people could count themselves as descendants of a founding ancestor. Thus, there should be more plaques with high numbers of registers, and fewer plaques with low numbers of registers. When the number of plaques in relation to the number of registers is examined, support for this test implication is found (figure 7.3). In all four motifs, there is an increase in the number of plaques as the register numbers increase, however, this is then followed by a sharp decrease. This may simply reflect that it gets progressively more difficult to draw more registers on a plaque. However, a larger piece of slate could have been selected, and indeed rather high numbers of registers were at times drawn – up to 14 in some cases. What this could also indicate is a process in which the reckoning of generations assumed less importance over time or that people found other media on which to record their genealogies.

3 *Geographic dispersion.* Over time, we would expect that the descendants of an ancestor dispersed over a region, and that the burial of their plaques should reflect this (map 7.2a–d). Indeed, as the number of registers increases by motif, there is a geographic dispersal of the plaques. In the case of the triangle plaques, this is a particularly notable trend (map 7.2d). While there are numerous 2-registered plaques in the eastern half of Portugal, there are no 2-registered plaques in the western half of

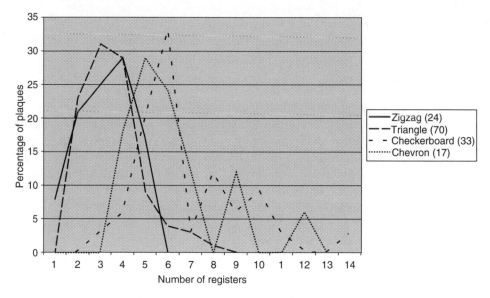

Figure 7.3   Percentage of plaques by registers and motif

Portugal, suggesting an east–west gradient in the movement of peoples. Such directionality is consistent with the east–west flow of the major riverways – the Sado and Tejo.

4 *Lineage continuity within tombs.* If we assume that tombs and tomb groups housed closely related family members over many generations, we would expect to see continuities in the register numbers. When plaques in each tomb are sequenced by their number of registers, by motif, intriguing support for this test implication can be found (figure 7.4a–d). There are, indeed, many tombs with continuous sequences or near-continuous sequences, in which there is a skip of one register. The continuities are most common for plaques with the triangle motif, although there are continuities for all the plaque motifs. For the triangles, sequences can be found at Anta Grande do Olival da Pega (Évora), Escoural (Évora), Anta 1 do Cebolinho (Évora), Brissos (Évora), and at a number of other sites in Badajoz and Lisboa (figure 7.4d). Also significant is the fact that Anta Grande do Olival da Pega (the site with one of the largest numbers of plaques, and indeed one of the largest megalithic tombs in Portugal) and Herdade do Passo have sequences for three of the four motifs. This may indicate that the tombs were particularly special burial grounds for chiefly lineages.

With regard to sequences in general, all the classic plaques seem to fall into one of two categories: either they occur in continuous (or near-continuous) sequences or they occur as isolates. Very few plaques occur in discontinuous series. And, given that there are many incomplete plaques and fragments that were not counted in this tally, the percentage of plaques in discontinuous sequences could actually be close to zero. In this bimodal distribution, we may be looking at the material expression of post-marital residence rules, in which the members of one sex were expected to stay in

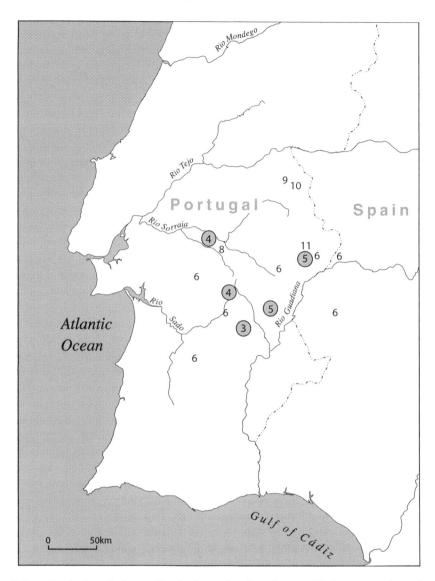

Map 7.2a   Checkerboard plaque distributions, showing plaque with lowest number of registers at site. The lowest number of plaques in the sequence is highlighted

their natal territory, with members of the opposite sex leaving this territory upon marriage. Only analyses of associated skeletal remains, including DNA work, could confirm this.

5   *Relative dating.* Plaques with higher numbers of registers should postdate those with lower numbers of registers. Unfortunately, the heavily disturbed and weathered condition of the skeletal remains in the tombs and the relatively poor resolution of

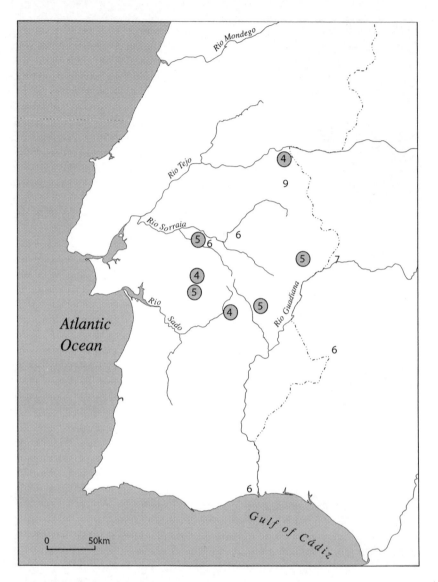

Map 7.2b　Chevron plaque distributions, showing plaque with lowest number of registers at site. The lowest number of plaques in the sequence is highlighted

radiocarbon dates, at least with respect to pinpointing generational differences, make this difficult to test.

At the burial site of Pedra Branca (Setúbal), however, there is a sequence of burials (with plaques) in two different stratigraphic levels: Late Neolithic/Copper Age and Late Copper Age/Beaker. Unfortunately, the later Late Copper Age/Beaker plaques are not of the classic form and so are not useful for our immediate problem. Nonetheless, the Pedra Branca sequence is significant for establishing a general relative dating

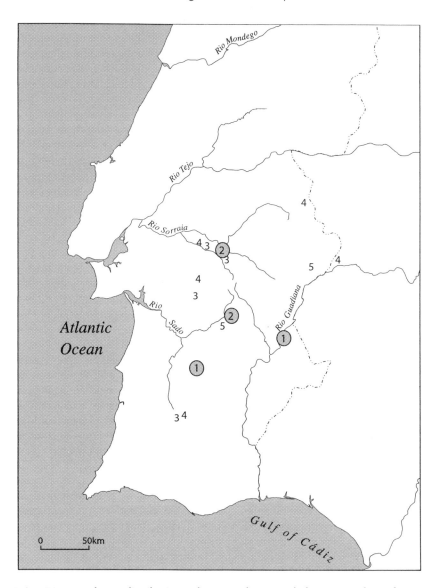

Map 7.2c   Zig zag plaque distributions, showing plaque with lowest number of registers at site. The lowest number of plaques in the sequence is highlighted

sequence of the plaques (Ferreira et al. 1975). Through the use of the Pedra Branca sequence and a seriation of the plaques as a whole, one might be able to determine whether this final test implication finds support in the data. Future research will be devoted to creating such a seriational sequence.

To summarize, the plaques' distribution and iconography strongly suggest their use as genealogical records. There does not appear to be a relationship between the size

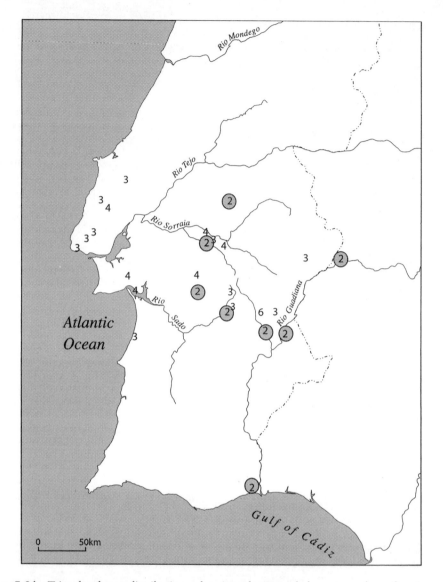

Map 7.2d   Triangle plaque distributions, showing plaque with lowest number of registers at site. The lowest number of plaques in the sequence is highlighted

of the plaque and the number of registers, indicating that the raw material did not present constraints to what was depicted on the plaques. Furthermore, representing the correct number of registers seems to have been more important than representing registers of regular appearance. Additional support for the model is found in the greater numbers of plaques by register number, as one would expect more people could trace their descent from an ancestor over time. There is also a distributional spread from a core area of plaques with low numbers of registers to a larger area with plaques with higher numbers of registers, suggestive of demic diffusion. Finally, perhaps the strongest evidence for the plaques' use as genealogical records are the continuous sequences of plaques by each motif in tombs and tomb groups.

Other possible explanations for the register sequences can be offered, but none of these explanations can account for the data. For example, one might posit that the plaques recorded land holdings or economic transactions, as with early Mesopotamian texts. However, if this were the case, it is difficult to imagine why such plaques do not appear on settlements, where they would have been most useful, and why sequences in tombs and a distributional spread occur. Another hypothesis is that the plaques were records of the age at death of the deceased individual or the number of children they had. Again, however, the data do not seem consistent with such hypotheses; why would tombs have continuous sequences of registers and why the distributional spread? One, therefore, must conclude that the best explanation for the plaques' distribution and iconography is that they recorded lineage histories.

Re-contextualizing the Iberian Slate Plaques

If the Iberian plaques indeed functioned as genealogical mnemonics, how does our view of Iberian prehistory, and prehistory in general, change? First, if the Iberian plaques were heraldic, they would be the oldest known examples of objects in Europe – if not the world – used to record genealogical information, predating medieval European heraldry by four millennia (Brooke-Little 1978:2). The point is not to claim that the Iberian plaques were models for medieval heraldry. Rather, this suggests that what we have in the Iberian plaques is the fortuitous preservation of heraldic arti-facts, which are known ethnographically to have often been made on perishables, such as textiles and wood, or inscribed on the body, such as with tattoos (Schuster and Carpenter 1996; Simmons 1986; Weiner and Schneider 1989). The identification of the Iberian plaques as mnemonics also points to the possibility that other objects in the prehistoric record were similarly used, but have not yet been interpreted as such.

Heraldic reckoning systems have been created to satisfy particular social and polit-ical needs, for example, to identify individuals in times of conflict or competition or to reinforce social or economic privilege (Davis 1985:152). The socio-economic land-scape of southwestern Iberia in the fourth and third millennia BC – particularly the Alentejo with its valued stone resources – could well have provided the conditions which made it necessary for some groups and individuals to distinguish themselves in order to legitimate access to territory or to amphibolite outcrops. By the middle of the third millennium BC, however, those needs apparently disappeared, although the decorative motifs of the plaques persisted (were remembered and recalled?) in the representational vocabulary of Iberians, quite probably with new meanings. Indeed, all the motifs on the Iberian plaques are found on later, Bell-Beaker pottery in Iberia (Harrison 1974:185).

The plaques' form and depositional context also suggest that new interpretations of ancient prehistoric ritual in Iberia may be offered. The plaques, which appear to

(a) CHECKERBOARD SEQUENCES

NUMBER OF REGISTERS

SITE	3	4	5	6	7	8	9	10	11	12	13	14
Cebolinho 1 (Évora)	1											
Vale de Rodrigo 1 (Évora)		1										
Brissos (1 and 6) (Évora)		1	1	1								
Olival da Pega (1 and 2) (Évora)			5	1	1		1	2				
Alto do Poço Novo (Portalegre)			1									
Herdade do Passo (Évora)				3		2						
Carvão (Evora)				1								
Comenda da Igreja (Évora)				1								1
Torre de Arcas 5 (Portalegre)				1								
Malpica (Badajoz)				1								
Barcarrota (Badajoz)				1		1						
Folha da Amendoeira (Beja)				1								
Caeira 7 (Évora)						1						
Castelo de Vide (Portalegre)							1					
Cabeço (Portalegre)								1				
Sobreira 2 (Portalegre)									1			
TOTAL	1	2	7	11	1	4	2	3	1	0	0	1	33

(b) CHEVRON SEQUENCES

NUMBER OF REGISTERS

SITE	4	5	6	7	8	9	10	11	12
Anta Grande da Comenda da Igreja (Évora)	1	1		1					1
Herdade do Passo (Évora)	1								
Maxial (Portalegre)	1								
Herdade da Comenda (Évora)		1							
Escoural (Évora)		1							
Brissos 6 (Évora)		1							
Camuge (Portalegre)		1							
Lapeira (Évora)			1						
Ordem 1 (Portalegre)			1						
Jerez de los Caballeros (Badajoz)			1						
Marcella (Faro)			1						
Granja de Cespedes (Badajoz)				1		1			
Lameira (Portalegre)						1			
TOTAL	3	5	4	2	0	2	0	0	1	17

Figure 7.4a–d Register continuity by motif and tomb and tomb group: (a) checkerboard, (b) chevron, (c) zigzag, (d) triangle

represent both axes and human beings, reflect the ambiguous status of the dead, particularly the newly dead. Like the dead, the plaques are neither entirely person nor thing, animate nor inanimate, subject nor object. Prehistoric Iberians may have even believed that the dead person not only became an ancestor but perhaps even stone – amphibolite? – itself. Similar beliefs are known among aboriginal groups in western Arnhem Land, Australia (Taçon 1991). Thus, the plaques may have aided the dead to

(c) ZIGZAG SEQUENCES

NUMBER OF REGISTERS

SITE	1	2	3	4	5
Folha da Amendoeira (Beja)	1				
Olival da Pega (Evora)	1	2		1	2
Caeira 7 (Evora)		2			
Herdade do Passo (Evora)		1	1		
Monte Velho (Beja)			1		
Escoural (Evora)			2	1	
Lapeira 1 (Evora)			1		
Capela S. Dionísio (Evora)			1		
Montenegro (Beja)				1	
Comenda da Igreja (Evora)				1	
Brissos (Evora)				1	
Anta da Marquesa (Portalegre)				1	
Anta da Malpica (Badajoz)				1	
Cebolinho 1 (Evora)					1
Poço Novo (Portalegre)					1
TOTAL	2	5	6	7	4	24

(d) TRIANGLE SEQUENCES

NUMBER OF REGISTERS

SITE	2	3	4	5	6	7	8
Marcella (Faro)	1						
Tholos de Farisoa (Évora)	1						
Escoural (Évora)	2	2	2	1			
Brissos (Évora)	1	1	1				
Olival da Pega (Évora)	7	3	2	1			
Cebolinho 1 (Évora)	1	1	1				1
Cavaleiros 6 (Portalegre)	1						
Granja de Cespedes (Badajoz)	2	2	2				
Herdade do Passo (Évora)		2		1			
Matalote 1 (Évora)		1					
Vale de Rodrigo 1 (Évora)		1					
Barrocal 1 (Évora)		1					
Camuge (Portalegre)		1					
Pedra Branca (Setúbal)		2		3	1		
Dolmen das Conchadas (Lisboa)		1	1				
Cabeço da Arruda (Lisboa)		1	1			1	
Praia das Maçãs (Lisboa)		1	1				
Furadouro da Roche Forte (Lisboa)		1	1				
Alapraia 2 (Lisboa)		1					
Caeira 6 (Évora)			1		1		
Oliveira (Évora)			1				
Anta da Velada (Évora)			1				
Palmela (Setúbal)			3				
Praia de S. Torpes (Setúbal)			1				
Cova da Moura (Lisboa)			1				
Herdade da Comenda 2 (Évora)					1		
Horta Velha do Reguengo (Portalegre)						1	
TOTAL	16	22	20	6	3	2	1	70

proceed safely in completing the cycle of regeneration, a characteristic goal of burial rituals (Bloch and Parry 1982).

On a more practical level, the slate plaques could have helped the living identify deceased individuals in the collective tombs in which they were placed. This would have been especially useful in those areas where acidic soils destroyed the skeleton, such as in the Alentejo. Perhaps the identification of individuals made a difference in determining the location of subsequent burials or in demonstrating continuity of use. As signifiers, the plaques may have also been viewed to help the dead identify each other and to reconstitute their social world in the afterlife.

Perhaps most importantly, by distinguishing particular individuals at death, by recording their histories, and by memorializing their being, the plaques also created and enhanced social differences. Some dead could be remembered through their plaques, while others were forgotten. These inequalities are also evidenced in a variety of other ways in the material record of late prehistoric Iberia, such as in the variability of grave good distributions and the concentration of long-distance trade items at some settlements (Chapman 1997; Gilman 1987).

Conclusion

Memory is an important ingredient in the constitution of power, whether this power is based on economic control of important resources, social or political alliances, or military might (Connerton 1989). But memories are also highly ephemeral and, thus, vulnerable to loss. Humans regularly seek to objectify memories that are critical to political identity (Lillios 1999; Joyce, this volume). Of course, in the process of objectifying memory, and indeed in the construction of something that can be called a "memory," selective processes are at work. Memories are not primarily about revisiting the past, but are about defining the present and managing the future of individuals and groups within meaningful, yet shifting, contexts. Thus, the control of memory and objects of memory is an important component of power. The need to control individual and collective memory might partially explain why the plaques were deposited in tombs with the dead – out of sight and inaccessible to acquisitive hands. Their primary role may have been in relation to the burial rituals of subsequent individuals. Ironically, the plaques' vulnerability was also greatest at this time, when tombs were reopened. It is interesting to speculate about the heightened tensions associated with the performance of these funerary rites, as collective tombs were reopened, the previous dead revisited and remembered, and their emblems of identity and power made visible once again.

If memory is a basis for power, evidence of challenges or resistance to it should also be expected. While this is difficult to detect with assurance in the case of the plaques, we might be able to view the eccentric plaques – those plaques that withstand and, indeed, defy classification (figure 7.2e) – as possible evidence for the rejection of normative mnemonic behaviors. In a perhaps less provocative way, the reuse of old plaque fragments (scavenged from tombs?) as pendants may also be evidence for the challenging of elite memory, or at least the transformation of ancestral objects of memory into more personal and private domains (figure 7.2f). Finally, the fragmentation of so many of the plaques may be partially explained by the intentional destruction of plaques, in acts designed to wipe out the memory of individuals or groups (Hoffman 1999).

Central to memory studies, of course, is the question of agency (Gell 1998). How can we be certain that people were actively working to remember or to record something or were simply passively or unconsciously copying a model master or teacher? These are not easy questions to answer, and indeed, one could argue that these two behaviors represent two kinds of remembering – one more conscious (or declarative) and one more embedded in the unconscious (or non-declarative) (Joyce, this volume). However, I would argue that with creative thinking, careful observation of *chaînes opératoires*, and a bit of preservational good fortune, as we have in the Iberian plaques, some glimpse into the intentionalities and conscious remembering of individuals can be detected.

The future of Iberian slate plaque studies – and archaeological studies of material mnemonics in general – lies in our taking seriously the need for human groups to remember their past and ancestry. Of course, the precise nature of these memories and of these acts of remembrance are situated in and constrained by particular social, political, and historical conditions (Hoskins 1998; Küchler 1988; Kwint et al. 1999; Marshack 1991; Weiner 1992). In the Hawaiian chiefdoms, for example, the ability to recall lineage histories was a key component in the legitimation of chiefly status and power, and memory specialists were enlisted to keep track of chiefly genealogies. Commoners did not have access to these specialists (Earle 1997:36).

If the Iberian plaques are ever fully "decoded," archaeologists could justifiably entertain the possibility of reconstructing lineage histories, marriage patterns, and kinship structures of ancient Iberian societies. Indeed, we may be able to learn something about the fine-grained history, however constructed and however remembered, of a prehistoric people. To paraphrase Eric Wolf, some of Europe's own "people without history" may some day have histories of their own.

References Cited

Almagro Gorbea, M. J. 1973: Los idolos del Bronce I Hispano. *Bibliotheca Praehistorica Hispana*, vol. XII. Madrid: Consejo Superior de Investigaciones Científicas.

Battaglia, D. 1983: Projecting personhood in Melanesia: the dialectics of artefact symbolism on Sabarl Island. *Man* 18, pp. 289–304.

Battaglia, D. 1990: *On the Bones of the Serpent: Person, Memory, and Mortality in Sabarl Island Society*. Chicago: University of Chicago Press.

Bloch, M. and Parry, J. (ed.) 1982: *Death and the Regeneration of Life*. Cambridge: Cambridge University Press.

Bradley, R. 2000: *An Archaeology of Natural Places*. London: Routledge.

Brooke-Little, J. P. 1978 (1950): *Charles Boutell's Heraldry*. London: Frederick Warne.

Bueno Ramirez, P. 1992: Les plaques décorées alentéjaines: approche de leur étude et analyse. *L'Anthropologie* 96(2–3), pp. 573–604.

Cardito Rollán, L. M. 1996: Las manufacturas textiles en la prehistoria: las placas de telas en el calcolítico peninsular. *Zephryus* 49, pp. 125–45.

Castro Curel, Z. 1984: Notas sobre la problemática del tejido en la Peninsula Ibérica. *Kalathos* 3–4, pp. 95–110.

Chapman, R. 1997: *Emerging Complexity: The Later Prehistory of South-east Spain, Iberia, and the West Mediterranean*. Cambridge: Cambridge University Press.

Connerton, P. 1989: *How Societies Remember*. London: Cambridge University Press.

Correia, V. 1917: Arte pré-histórico: los idolos-placas. *Terra Portuguesa* 12, pp. 29–35.

Davis, D. D. 1985: Hereditary emblems: material culture in the context of social change. *Journal of Anthropological Archaeology* 4, pp. 149–76.

Earle, T. 1997: *How Chiefs Come to Power: The Political Economy in Prehistory*. Palo Alto, Calif.: Stanford University Press.

Ferreira, O. da V., Zbyszewski, G., Leitão, M., North, C. T. and Sousa, H. R. da 1975: The megalithic tomb of Pedra Branca, Portugal: preliminary report. *Proceedings of the Prehistoric Society* 41, pp. 167–78.

Fleming, A. 1969: The myth of the mother-goddess. *World Archaeology* 1, pp. 247–77.

Formosinho, J., Ferreira, O. da V. and Viana, A. 1953/1954: Estudos arqueológicos nas Caldas de Monchique. *Trabalhos de Antropologia e Etnologia* 14.

Frankowski, E. 1920: Estelas Discoideas da la Península Ibérica, Mem. 25. *Comisión de Investigaciones Paleontológicas y Prehistóricas*. Madrid: Museu Nacional de Ciencias Naturales.

Gell, A. 1998: *Art and Agency: An Anthropological Theory*. Oxford: Oxford University Press.

Gilman, A. 1987: Unequal development in copper age Iberia. In *Specialization, Exchange and Complex Societies*, ed. E. M. Brumfiel and T. K. Earle. Cambridge: Cambridge University Press, pp. 22–9.

Gonçalves, V. S. 1992: *Revendo as Antas de Reguengos de Monsaraz*. Cadernos da Uniarq 2. Lisbon: Instituto Nacional de Investigação Científica.

Gonçalves, V. S. (ed.) 1997: Muitas Antas, Pouca Gente? Actas do I Colóquio Internacional Sobre Megalitismo. *Trabalhos de Arqueologia* 16. Lisbon: Instituto Português de Arqueologia.

Gonçalves, V. S. 1999: *Reguengos de Monsaraz: Territórios Megalíticos*. Lisbon: Câmara Municipal de Reguengos de Monsaraz.

Harrison, R. J. 1974: Origins of the Bell Beaker cultures. *Antiquity* 48, pp. 99–109.

Held, S. E. 1978: *Weaving: A Handbook of the Fiber Arts*. New York: Holt, Rinehart and Winston.

Hoffman, C. R. 1999: Intentional damage as technological agency: breaking metals in late prehistoric Mallorca, Spain. In *The Social Dynamics of Technology, Practice, Politics, and World Views*, ed. M.-A. Dobres and C. R. Hoffman. Washington, D.C.: Smithsonian University Press, pp. 103–23.

Hoskins, J. 1998: *Biographical Objects: How Things Tell the Stories of People's Lives*. New York: Routledge.

Instituto Técnologico GeoMinero de España 1994: Mapa Geológico de la Península Ibérica, Baleares y Canarias. 1:1,000,000. Madrid.

Küchler, S. 1988: Malangan: objects, sacrifice and the production of memory. *American Ethnologist* 15, pp. 625–37.

Kwint, M., Breward, C. and Aynsley, J. (eds.) 1999: *Material Memories: Design and Evocation*. Oxford: Berg.

Larsson, L. 1998: Rock, stone and mentality. Stones that unite, stones that subjugate – a megalithic tomb in Vale de Rodrigo, southern Portugal. In *The World-view of Prehistoric Man. Papers presented at a symposium in Lund, 5–7 May 1997*, ed. L. Larsson and B. Stjernquist. Kungl: Vitterhets Historie och Antikvitets Akademien, pp. 137–55.

Leisner, G. and Leisner, V. 1943: *Die Megalithgräber der Iberischen Halbinsel: Der Süden, Römisch-Germanische Forschungen*, Vol. 17. Berlin: Walter de Gruyter.

Leisner, G. and Leisner, V. 1951: *Antas do Concelho de Reguengos de Monsaraz*. Lisbon: Instituto para a Alta Cultura.

Leisner, G. and Leisner, V. 1956: *Die Megalithgräber der Iberischen Halbinsel: Der Westen. Madrider Forschungen*, Vol. I, 1. Berlin: Walter de Gruyter.

Leisner, G. and Leisner, V. 1959: *Die Megalithgräber der Iberischen Halbinsel: Der Westen. Madrider Forschungen*, Vol. I, 2. Berlin: Walter de Gruyter.

Leisner, V. 1965: *Die Megalithgräber der Iberischen Halbinsel: Der Westen. Madrider Forschungen*, Vol. I, 3. Berlin: Walter de Gruyter.

Leisner, V. 1998: *Die Megalithgräber der Iberischen Halbinsel: Der Westen. Madrider Forschungen*, Vol. I, 4. Berlin: Walter de Gruyter.

Lillios, K. T. 1997: Amphibolite tools of the Portuguese Copper Age (3000–2000 BC): a geoarchaeological study of prehistoric economics and symbolism. *Geoarchaeology* 12(2), pp. 37–163.

Lillios, K. T. 1999: Objects of memory: the ethnography and archaeology of heirlooms. *Journal of Archaeological Method and Theory* 6(3), pp. 235–62.

Lisboa, I. M. G. 1985: Meaning and messages: mapping style in the Iberian Chalcolithic. *Archaeological Review from Cambridge* 4(3), pp. 181–96.

Marshack, A. 1991: *The Roots of Civilization*. New York: Moyer Bell Ltd.

Renfrew, C. 1976: *Before Civilization*. Cambridge: Cambridge University Press.

Rodrigues, M. C. M. 1986a: *Código Para a Análise das Placas de Xisto Gravadas do Alto Alentejo – Nova Estratégia para o Tratamento de Dados em Arqueologia*, Vol. I. Castelo de Vide: Câmara Municipal de Castelo de Vide.

Rodrigues, M. C. M. 1986b: *Estudo Ideológico-Simbólico das Placas de Xisto Gravadas – Alto Alentejo*, Vol II. Castelo de Vide: Câmara Municipal de Castelo de Vide.

Schuster, C. and Carpenter, E. 1996: *Patterns that Connect: Social Symbolism in Ancient and Tribal Art*. New York: Harry N. Abrams.

Silva, A. M. 1999: A necrópole neolítica do Cabeço da Arruda (Torres Vedras, Portugal): os dados paleobiológicos. In *II Congrés del Neolític a la Península Ibèrica, Saguntum*, Extra-2, ed. J. Bernabeu Aubán and T. Orozco-Köhler. Valencia: Universitat de Valencia, pp. 355–60.

Simmons, D. R. 1986: *Ta Moko: The Art of Maori Tattoo*. Auckland: Reed Publishing.

Siret, L. 1913: *Questions de chronologie et d'ethnographie Ibériques*. Paris: Paul Geuthner.

Spindler, K. 1981: Cova da Moura. *Madrider Beiträge* 7. Mainz am Rhein: Philipp von Zabern.

Street, B. and Besnier, N. 1994: Aspects of literacy. In *Companion Encyclopedia of Anthropology*, ed. T. Ingold. London: Routledge, pp. 527–63.

Taçon, P. 1991: The power of stone: symbolic aspects of stone use and tool development in western Arnhem Land, Australia. *Antiquity* 65, pp. 192–207.

Tilley, C. 1999: *Metaphor and Material Culture*. Oxford: Blackwell.

Vasconcellos, J. L. de 1897: *Religiões da Lusitania*, Vol. 1. Lisboa: Imprensa Nacional.

Vasconcellos, J. L. de 1906: Bibliographia – Portugalia. *O Arqueólogo Português*, II, pp. 321–79.

Vasconcellos, J. L. de 1922: Encabamento de instrumentos de pedra prehistóricos. *O Arqueólogo Português* 25, pp. 288–98.

Veiga, S. P. M. E. da 1887: *Antiguidades Monumentaes do Algarve*, Vol. 2. Lisboa: Imprensa Nacional.

Viana, A., Formosinho, J. and Ferreira, O. da V. 1948: Duas raridades arqueológicas. *Revista do Sindicato Nacional dos Engenheiros Auxiliares, Agentes Técnicos de Engenharia e Condutores* 24.

Weiner, A. B. 1992: *Inalienable Possessions: The Paradox of Keeping-While-Giving*. Berkeley: University of California Press.

Weiner, A. B. and Schneider, J. (ed.) 1989: *Cloth and Human Experience*. Washington D.C.: Smithsonian Institution Press.

Wiessner, P. 1983: Style and social information in Kalahari San projectile points. *American Antiquity* 48(2), pp. 253–76.

Wobst, H. M. 1977: Stylistic behavior and information exchange. In *For the Director: Research Essays in Honor of James B. Griffin, Anthropology Papers* 61, ed. C. Cleland. Ann Arbor: Museum of Anthropology, University of Michigan, pp. 317–42.

8
Mounds, Memory, and Contested Mississippian History

Timothy R. Pauketat and Susan M. Alt

The Indian tradition[s] give an acc[oun]t of those works they say . . . [were] the works of their forefathers . . . formerly as numerous as the Trees in the woods . . . on the Mississippi . . . (George Rogers Clark 1928 [1778])

Overgrown earthen mounds in the wooded valleys and hilltops of eastern North America urge us to remember the past. In the shadows of these tumuli we see the myths, beliefs, and rituals of native people. We recognize mound-building "traditions" in the upper Midwest, the Midsouth, and the Gulf Coast (Bense 1994; Squier and Davis 1998; Thomas 1985[1894]). We sense deep roots to these ancient traditions, perpetuated in the precolumbian era by the building of mounds themselves. And we ask ourselves, what did these mounds mean? For what purposes were they used?

Typically, they are said to have signified fundamental Native American beliefs concerning sacred and secular, past and present, and earth and sky (see Buikstra et al. 1998; Hall 1997; Knight 1989). They are thought to have embodied the fundamental cultural "structures," or traditions, of entire ethnic groups, if not all native North Americans (in the sense of Levi-Strauss 1967[1958]). Archaeologists often suspect that these traditions arose owing to the social, economic, or political pressures of specific time periods. Mounds are said to have marked territory, reinforced ideologies, and elevated native aristocrats above commoners (see Dillehay 1990; Knight 1989; Lindauer and Blitz 1997; Smith 1978).

However, there are severe theoretical drawbacks to these structuralist and functionalist explanations. Those drawbacks stem from the weak conceptual devices that

The National Science Foundation (SBR 99-96169), the National Geographic Society (6319-98), the Cahokia Mounds Museum Society, and the University of Illinois at Urbana-Champaign supported the upland Mississippian research cited in this paper. We would like to thank Ruth Van Dyke and Susan Alcock for inviting us to contribute to this volume even though we were not participants in the original symposia. Their critical comments on an earlier draft of this paper were greatly appreciated. All problems of thought or fact are our own.

underlie the business of interpreting meanings and inferring functions. On the one hand, merely identifying a "cultural structure" or tradition does not address the question of *how* such standardized and shared knowledge would have been transmitted uniformly across space and through time. Appeals to this kind of reasoning simply assume that structures, traditions, or cultures are widely shared and change at a glacial pace. On the other hand, ascribing functions to mounds relies on even weaker conceptual devices. Functionalist explanations assume that society was an organic whole such that knowing the constituent elements allows us to analyze the system without worrying much about the history of people. Archaeologists who analyze functions in this manner believe that mounds were constructed with an intent revealed in the mound's form. From this point of view, it may seem that the need to delineate the potential complexities of mound-construction history is obviated. But was it the *mound* that was the goal of the builders, or the *act of construction* itself? Following Knight (1986, 1989), Pauketat (1993, 2000b) has argued that annual mound building would have regularly integrated those who took part in the construction. If so, then what about those social situations where the interests or beliefs of laborers who built a mound were at odds with those of a ritual overseer? Would not the laborers' interests or beliefs get "built-into" the tumulus somehow, perhaps even affecting its size, shape, use-life, or construction history?

In this chapter, we argue that appeals to cultural structures or mound functions obscure the processes whereby Native Americans constructed both mounds and traditions. We suggest that the patterns of mound building in the Mississippi valley and beyond necessitate a more nuanced view of how people "lived culture" at local sites through the active and contested recollection of the past (Van Dyke and Alcock, this volume). Those same processes of living culture or, better, "culture making" or "tradition building" are yet ongoing today (consider Appadurai 1996; Wolf 1982:387). Here, we juxtapose the evidence of "microscale" cultural practices (see Shennan 1993) from the Greater Cahokia region and the "macroscale" patterns of spatial and temporal disjunctures across the Mississippi valley. We pay particular attention to the Coles Creek, Plum Bayou, and American Bottom (a.k.a. Greater Cahokia) cultural regions along the Arkansas and Mississippi Rivers (map 8.1; see Phillips et al. 1951; Rolingson 1982, 1998). The point, of course, is to understand how cultural regions, as macroscale phenomena, were continuously constructed by people through their microscale practices (see Pauketat in press).

Our purpose is to promote an appreciation of memory in the cultural interstices between supposed macroscale traditions and the everyday practices involved in localized negotiations of identity, power, and meaning. Our focus is on a series of flat-topped pyramidal mounds built over a several century span (ca. 700–1500 AD) in the Midwest and Midsouth, rather than on the sepulcher or animal effigy mounds of other parts of the Eastern Woodlands. We begin by outlining a commonly accepted Mississippi-valley culture history. Following this, we explore the implications of this culture history in terms of the construction of social memory. We then turn to consider the evidence for mound construction at Cahokia, ca. 1050 AD, and how that may have involved contestation over meanings and memories by a diverse group of actors. Finally, we reassess the potential importance of disjunctures in

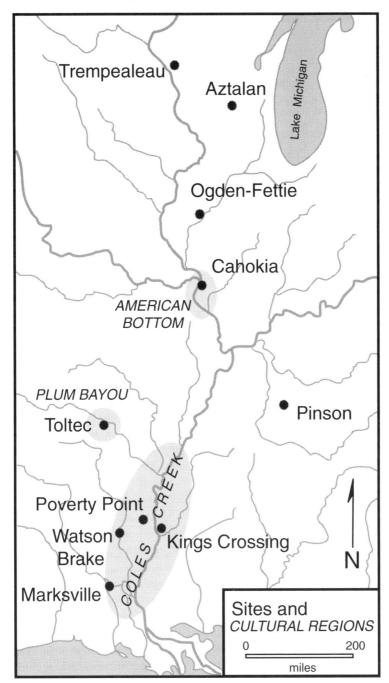

Map 8.1   Map of selected sites and cultural complexes in the precolumbian Mississippi Valley

patterns of Mississippi valley mound-construction with respect to an archaeology of memory.

Mississippi Valley Culture History

The earliest known earthen mounds in the New World are found in Louisiana at the Watson Brake site (Saunders et al. 1997). Dated to the fourth millennium BC, this oval arrangement of flat-topped mounds already suggests a degree of social complexity that appears and disappears through time in a spatially discontinuous fashion across the east until Indian depopulation and removal (Sassaman and Heckenberger 2001). Other complex mound sites follow; the well-known Poverty Point site and nearby late Archaic period sites in Louisiana date to the three centuries after 1600 BC (Gibson 2000). Subsequent Woodland-period mounds dot the eastern United States. These include, by the first century or two BC, conical burial mounds, earthen embankments, and four-sided, flat-topped earthen pyramids. Middle Woodland period platform mounds are less well known than the other mound types, given the early antiquarian attentions paid to enigmatic geometric enclosures and the tombs beneath conical mounds. However, large platform mounds were built between ca. 200 BC–300 AD (e.g., Mainfort 1988; Rafferty 1990). Some, as at the Pinson site in Tennessee, were quite large, reaching heights of up to 18 m. These appear to have been platforms for ritual performances and were not surmounted by "temples" or other buildings.

In the lower Mississippi River valley, mounded "Middle Woodland" Marksville-culture centers appear to give rise to later Woodland "Baytown" (Troyville) and then "Coles Creek" centers (or similar cultural cognates, e.g., Ford 1951; Kidder 1992, 1998; Phillips et al. 1951; Williams and Brain 1983). The latter are modest arrangements of one to ten rectangular platforms around rectangular plazas (figure 8.1). We will return to the issue of plazas later. For now, suffice it to say that, like their Middle Woodland precursors, the Coles Creek mounds do not seem to have been substructural platforms for buildings (until 900 AD or later, see Kidder 1998). Few if any of the Coles Creek centers are thought to have supported large populations, although the largest such complexes cover areas around 30 ha. The people living at or near any given center appear to have had minimal interests in trade with outsiders, given the "parochial" character of the material assemblages (Kidder 1992, 1998). Then again, by 1100 AD if not earlier, various Coles Creek residents do seem to have met and exchanged with Cahokians far to the north.

The mound-plaza arrangements of the Coles Creek sites conjured up images of Mesoamerica for mid-twentieth-century analysts (see Smith 1984). The lower Mississippi valley centers, it was thought, might have served as a kind of cultural conduit of Mesoamerican knowledge up the Mississippi to places like Cahokia. Others looked to the "Caddoan" culture area of Texas and Oklahoma as a conduit to the north (see Phillips and Brown 1978:170–4). Although the Mesoamerican conduit argument has fallen from favor, there are gross similarities of the Coles Creek centers to a series of later (post 1050 AD) Mississippian sites to the north, especially Cahokia. Likewise, the apparent similarities between certain Mississippian complexes in the

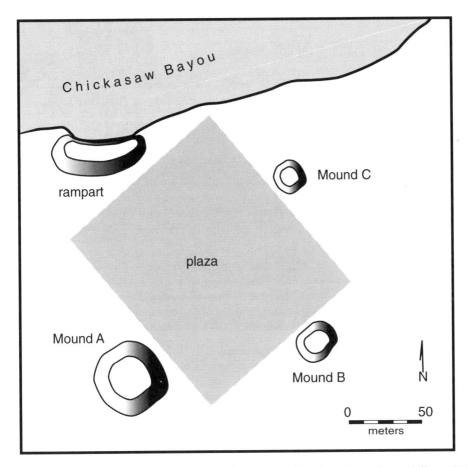

Figure 8.1 The Kings Crossing Site near Vicksburg, Mississippi (redrawn from Phillips 1970: Figure 181)

trans-Mississippi south and Huastecan sites in northeastern Mexico have also been noted (Hall 1991; Phillips and Brown 1978).

The relevance of such macroscale parallels lies in what they tell us about the spatial and temporal discontinuities of mound building. These can be illustrated using the known cultural–historical details from the central Arkansas River and central Mississippi River valleys. In the former, the largest Coles-Creek-like regional complex, the Plum Bayou culture, featured a large central ceremonial center named "Toltec" (Nassaney 1991, 1992, 1994, 2001; Rolingson 1982, 1998). There are 18 rectangular or oval platform mounds at Toltec reaching heights of 15 m, all arranged around two probable rectangular plazas, located near a bayou and ringed by an earthen embankment enclosing some 42 ha (plate 8.1). The mounds themselves appear to have been built over the period 750–1000 AD during a series of relatively large-scale construction events (e.g., Rolingson 1998). Their summits do not seem to have been used for buildings. Unusual refuse suggestive of public feasting involving sacred or valuable

Plate 8.1   Mound A at the Toltec Site, Arkansas

material symbols (including crystals and novaculite) is found scattered in the construction fills and possible feasting refuse associated with these mounds. Nassaney
(1992, 1994, 2001) interprets the political economy of Toltec and its hinterland as one
filled with contradiction, as emerging regional inequality was balanced by repeated
acts that memorialized community and, presumably, equality.

That balance was not maintained. The Toltec site, along with much of the central
Arkansas River valley, appears to have been abandoned sometime before 1100 AD.
The few small settlements known in the twelfth century Arkansas valley, and in
adjacent portions of the Mississippi valley, have produced broken earthenware vessels
and microlithic or expedient-core technologies that betray Cahokian origins or inspiration (Buchner 1998; House 1996; Johnson 1987; David Kelley, personal communication, 2001; Koldehoff and Carr 2001; Mainfort 1996). The Cahokian connection is
noteworthy, as a dramatic social and demographic centralizing process was well under-
way in that northern location at the same time as the abandonment of the Arkansas
valley.

The history of mound construction in the central Mississippi River valley is quite
different than the Arkansas or lower Mississippi regions. Emerson and McElrath
(2001:204) have characterized the 140-km stretch of Mississippi River floodplain, also
called the "American Bottom," as a border zone prior to 1000 AD. To the north along
the Illinois River, Middle Woodland people built burial mounds near large horticul-
tural villages like those of the well-known Hopewell peoples of Ohio or the

Marksville people of the lower Mississippi drainage. At the Ogden–Fettie site, one Middle Woodland mound may have been a rectangular platform like those at Pinson and points south; there may have been a couple of others at nearby sites (D. Esarey, personal communication, 2002). But in the American Bottom, only a handful of modest Middle Woodland mounds are known, and those are in the northern expanse of floodplain bordering the Illinois River (see Fortier 1998; McElrath and Fortier 2000). As far as we know, none of them were platform mounds.

Moreover, few to no mounds are known in the region during the subsequent Late Woodland period (300–1050 AD). Certainly, there are no Toltec-sized centers. Most Late Woodland sites up to ca. 900 AD were relatively modest-sized hamlets, or villages of at most a few dozen people. Between 900 and 1050 AD some villages (formerly called "Emergent Mississippian") in the American Bottom proper did become enlarged (see Fortier and McElrath 2000). There *may* have been two or three of these large villages (of which Cahokia was one) with only a few modest earthen platforms. However, the evidence for mound construction at this time (at the Lunsford-Pulcher and perhaps Morrison sites) is equivocal at best (Kelly 1990; Lopinot et al. 1998; Milner 1998; Pauketat 1994, 1998). The case for Cahokia is even less secure, based as it is on a single radiocarbon date from a core sample of the lower levels of Cahokia's Monks Mound (Reed et al. 1968). It is certain that the Late Woodland people living in the hilly uplands on either side of the linear floodplain of the American Bottom did not construct platform mounds.

One could argue that the existing Middle Woodland mounds, or remembered places in the region, such as cemeteries, remained meaningful features of the landscape (see Chesson 2001; Joyce 2001:13). For instance, one Mississippian mound at the Horseshoe Lake site was built at least partially over a Middle Woodland burial ground (Pauketat et al. 1998; notes on file, University of Illinois). Another possible Woodland conical mound atop the bluffcrest overlooking the American Bottom, locally called "Sugarloaf Mound" and measuring about 7 m in height, was probably visible from Cahokia (certainly it was from atop Monks Mound). It was located along a historic Indian trail that led from an outlying Mississippian town site to Cahokia (Koldehoff et al. 1993).

Such instances doubtless indicate the lasting power of landscapes as inscribed social memories. Perhaps the landscape was a constant reminder of the "works of their forefathers" during the several centuries when few to no people engaged in the physical construction of earthen mounds in the American Bottom and adjacent uplands. Nonetheless, the recognition of a mound-building past by a people would not in itself constitute the continuity of a mound-building tradition (compare Meskell, this volume). A long-term social memory of mound building may have existed through the Late Woodland construction hiatus, but the social memories constructed by the viewing of ancient tumuli would have been much different from those constructed as part of the physical inscription of the landscape. If nothing else, the soil engineering knowledge evidenced in the profiles of mound excavations – never mind cultural meanings – might have been more than a little difficult to retain during the interim. "We can infer that a group, perhaps a class, of individuals with a specialized knowledge of soils (soils or mound engineers) were responsible for directing construction of the mound" (Bareis 1975:13). What would happen to this "specialized knowledge" if mounds were not built for a period of decades, if not centuries?

Given the obvious hiatus and its potential implications, the amplitude of pyramidal mound construction beginning around 1050 AD in the Greater Cahokia region can be startling to the contemporary archaeologist (for a chronological overview, see Pauketat 1998; Pauketat and Emerson 1997). At that time, construction began on scores of platform mounds, including the largest ever built in North America. Monks Mound at Cahokia reached a height of 30 m and was surrounded in a 30 sq km area by the ongoing construction of about 200 other earthen tumuli, most of which were substructure platforms topped with one or more oversized houses, temples, or council buildings (Pauketat 1997). Platform mound construction was initiated more or less simultaneously at a minimum of five and perhaps as many as a dozen other town sites in the region. Thus, to a great extent, the scale of mound construction at Cahokia, if not also the very fact of mound construction there, was unprecedented in the middle of the eleventh century.

Because of this, Cahokia's historical effects on the other native peoples living in the Midsouth, upper Midwest, and eastern Plains may have been profound. While mercantile explanations are not supported by archaeological evidence (Emerson and Hughes 2000; Milner 1998; Pauketat 1998), there are artifactual, iconographic, and architectural reasons to suspect that Cahokians may have traveled to obtain exotic raw materials or that distant people may have visited and then "emulated" Cahokia (Hall 1991, 1997). For instance, ceramic wares and nonlocal arrowheads from the Plum Bayou and Coles Creek cultural regions are found at tenth and eleventh century sites in the Greater Cahokia region. In another instance, an early Mississippian mounded site at Trempealeau, Wisconsin, seems strategically located near an unusual lithic resource, Hixton Silicified Sediment (Green and Rodell 1994). The distinctive Hixton material was used by Cahokians to make projectile points, among other things, including some made to look like southern Lower Mississippi Valley styles (Ahler 2000). These and other exotic arrowhead styles (with many made from available local cherts) are featured in the famous eleventh-century caches from Mound 72 (Fowler et al. 2000).

Sites as far north as southern Minnesota and South Dakota have produced Cahokian or Cahokia-like objects, styles, and architectural forms. A number of these sites evince clear "founding" phases where the objects, styles, and forms appear "intrusive" to the localities in question, almost as if they fell out of the sky (see Emerson 1991; Stoltman 1991). Because of this settlement and artifact-assemblage evidence, researchers have suggested that factions of Cahokians may have moved northward, perhaps to escape conditions deemed unpleasant in the American Bottom or perhaps to set up "colonies" or short-term extractive outposts of sorts (Emerson 1991; Stoltman 1991, 2000). In a few locations, platform mounds were constructed as part of these northern "site unit intrusions." Multi-terraced platform mounds – thought possible copies of Cahokia's largest pyramid – were built late in the eleventh or early twelfth century at the Aztalan and Trempealeau sites in Wisconsin (plates 8a and b; Green and Rodell 1994:352; see also Overstreet 2000).

Plate 8.2a and b   Platform mounds compared: (a) Aztalan, and (b) Cahokia (Aztalan photo courtesy William C. Millhouse, Galena, Illinois)

In any event, nearly as abruptly as it began, mound construction ceased in the American Bottom at ca. 1250–1300 AD. The Greater Cahokia region was largely abandoned by 1350 AD, although mound construction continued to the south of the American Bottom in the central and lower Mississippi valleys. There, other newly founded Mississippian centers, with their own four-sided and flat-topped substructure mounds, arose to become seats of government for numerous southeastern chiefdoms.

There, earthen mounds are arranged around open, rectangular plazas, in patterns that suggest nearly immutable "sacred landscapes" to some (Lewis and Stout 1993). These spaces have been associated with "cult institutions" (i.e., cultural structures) and are thought to be imbued with cosmological and cosmographic symbolism said to have been common to Mississippian peoples everywhere (Knight 1986). Mississippian symbolism and the use of mounds as platforms were apparent to the first Europeans traveling through the Southeast. Such symbolism, and the creation of meaning annually at ritual grounds, continues today (e.g., Howard 1968; Moore 1994). Today, the rate and amplitude of mound and plaza construction is clearly unlike the Mississippian past. Then again, if we look deeper into the ancient Mississippian mounds, we can see a lack of uniformity in mode, scale, and rate of mound construction there too (cf. Anderson 1994; Knight 1989; Pauketat 1993).

The Implications of Mounds and Plazas

Woodland and Mississippian traditions could be said to "survive" in vestigial form to this day in the practices of various southeastern people, altered to a degree through contact with Europeans and their diseases (e.g., Hudson 1976). Perhaps as a result of this perceived continuity, archaeologists tend to envision change as exogenous to the identities or cultures of Eastern Woodlands peoples. Hence, long-term changes in the Woodlands are still attributed in many archaeological accounts to population growth, political–economic cycles, social–organizational dynamics, environmental fluctuations, and migrations (e.g., Anderson 1994; Blitz 1999; Nassaney 1992; M. Williams 1994; S. Williams 1990). Except perhaps for migrations, these explanations leave aside the question of *how* mound-construction knowledge was transmitted across generational divides, regions, and linguistic boundaries (but see Drechsel 1994).

Why worry about explaining how mound knowledge was conveyed? For some, the fact that mound-construction knowledge was transmitted is by itself sufficient. This position assumes that cultural "structures" or traditions were conveyed in a relatively uniform manner, as if these were pieces of information that could be communicated without significant disruption. The standard mound forms found across the Woodlands, as noted above, seemingly affirm the uniform-transmission assumption. A pyramidal mound is a pyramidal mound, or so the logic goes that holds meanings and functions constant across space and through time. But just this kind of logic has clearly misled archaeologists in the past.

In southeastern North America, four-sided rectangular mounds were thought to correlate with a maize-based agricultural system managed by hereditary chiefs. Until recently, archaeologists had a difficult time accepting that many platform mounds dated to the Middle Woodland period, since maize and hereditary chiefship were not thought to characterize this period (but see, for example, Knight 1990; Mainfort 1988; Rafferty 1990). Likewise, Coles Creek peoples were thought to be the earliest hierarchical chiefdoms based in maize agriculture, despite a lack of evidence to support such a position (Steponaitis 1986; but see Fritz and Kidder 1993; Kidder 1992; Kidder and Fritz 1993; Nassaney 2001)!

Without a doubt, the archaeology of the last 30 years points to fundamental problems inherent with ahistorical (structuralist or functionalist) explanations. In part owing to the growing discordance within these older paradigms, various "historical-processual" perspectives (i.e., practice-theoretical, agent-centered, feminist, phenomenological, and even neo-Darwinian schools of thought) are promulgating a sense of "traditions" as dynamic phenomena (Pauketat 2001a, following Wolf 1982:387–91; see also Van Dyke and Alcock, this volume). Traditions for such theorists are not normative, static, and epiphenomenal. They are "practiced," put into action, and made and remade continuously by people through time. They can even be "invented" (Hobsbawm and Ranger 1983). In effect, *traditions are the media of change*, co-opted and promoted in ways that selectively draw from the past (Trouillot 1995). Whole community, ethnic, and national identities are "imagined" through such selective recollections of traditions (Anderson 1983).

Given this selective, dynamic quality, it follows that traditional knowledge is not a fixed quantity accessible to all or to be recollected in the same way from the past by all. "Memory is historically conditioned, changing . . . according to the emergencies of the moment; . . . it is progressively altered from generation to generation . . . [and] is inherently revisionist and never more chameleon than when it appears to stay the same" (Samuel 1994:10). It does not stay the same; it cannot be transmitted as a structure or as information without incurring change. Trouillot (1995:14–16) is critical of viewing traditions as fixed collective memories that can be retrieved uniformly by living people. Consider an individual's memory: it "is not always a process of summoning representations of what happened" in one's lifetime (Trouillot 1995:14). For instance, knowledge of one's own childhood may derive from what one was told later, such that these later informants actually contribute to the creation of an individual's history based on their own imperfect (and etic) recollection. Few people can remember details of various earlier life experiences, leaving certain recollections weighted in ways more proportionate to the context of recollection than to the importance of the experience at the time (see also Connerton 1989; Meskell, this volume).

> Given that the individual's history tends to be constructed in these ways, surely the problems of determining what belongs to the past multiply tenfold when that past is said to be collective. . . . We may want to assume for purposes of description that the life history of an individual starts with birth. But when does the life of a collectivity start? At what point do we set the beginning of the past to be retrieved? How do we decide – and how does the collectivity decide – which events to include and which to exclude? (Trouillot 1995:16)

Memories may be fixed to a degree if incorporated in mnemonic devices – liturgical recitations, ritual processions, music, song, prayer, etc. – and through the inscription of them in material culture, the human body, and space (Van Dyke and Alcock, this volume; see also Abercrombie 1998; Connerton 1989; Hagedorn 2001:77; Joyce 2000, this volume; Joyce and Hendon 2000; Kus 1997; Meskell, this volume; Rouget 1985:121; Rowlands 1993). Written history clearly constitutes such a case of inscription (see Papalexandrou, this volume). However, mounds are also a kind of inscription of social memory in space. Each instance of mound construction is an inscriptive act of "memorialization" (Meskell, this volume). Such inscriptive practices in space are said, of course, to create places (Van Dyke and Alcock, this volume). People "being in the world" unavoidably transform spaces into places, linking personal histories to cultural identities (Thomas 1996:83, citing Heidegger 1962). Certain "places are deliberate creations of past actors" (Joyce and Hendon 2000), especially apparent when places are named and so imbued with cultural meanings (Tilley 1994:18). "All locales and landscapes are therefore embedded in the social and individual times of memory . . . personal biographies, social identities and a biography of place" (Tilley 1994:27). The meanings of these places change as their biographies were actively created (e.g., Gosden and Marshall 1999; Holtorf 1998; Joyce 2000, this volume; Sinopoli, this volume; H. Williams 1998).

This is not to say that meanings associated with places necessarily change gradually. No, there appear to be any number of cases where mounds in the Eastern Woodlands did not develop gradually within particular regions but were built at specific historical moments. That these were "deliberate creations of past actors" has already been implied by the uneven pan-Mississippi-valley pattern of mound construction, noted earlier. It is further evident in comparisons of regional Mississippian histories that point to abrupt flashpoints when polities were "consolidated" (King 2000; Knight 1997; Pauketat 2000a). It may also be palpable in the "intrusive" appearance of various northern Mississippian refugees, colonies, or outposts. Certainly the construction of copies of Cahokia's Monks Mound far to the north in Wisconsin, if indeed that is what the Trempealeau and Aztalan mounds represent, would have constituted landmark historical changes for those localities.

That mounds mark the deliberate creations of past actors is also illustrated by a series of earth-moving events related to the founding of a number of mounded centers. This is easiest to argue on the basis of the plazas at these centers. Dalan (1997) and associates (Holley et al. 1993) were the first to realize the significance of the discovery that Mississippian plazas were not just empty spaces but had been physically constructed. Based on her geophysical surveys and the archaeological excavations of the "Grand Plaza" at Cahokia by others, including the authors, it is now well established that this 19 ha rectangular space was built over a short span of time (around 1050 AD) by cutting and filling an enormous naturally undulating surface (see also Alt and Pauketat, report in preparation; Holley et al. 1993; Pauketat and Rees 1996; Pauketat 2001b; Pauketat et al. 2002). The plaza is flat, with a slight dip from north to south and a sandy construction fill that may have improved drainage.

Since Dalan's initial work, evidence of additional land reclamation has been found at Cahokia and at the related East St. Louis site (Kelly 1997; Koldehoff et al. 2000; Pauketat, report in preparation). Low areas were occasionally filled to create flat surfaces. Similar land leveling practices were employed elsewhere, the plaza at the Etowah site in Georgia being a prominent example (Dalan 1997:101, citing Larson 1989:136). Recently, Kidder (2002) has made similar observations at the Coles Creek site of Raffman, in Louisiana, and has implied that central plazas dating as far back as the Late Archaic sites of Poverty Point and Watson Brake may also have been so constructed. Such plazas, he further suggests, cannot be dissociated from the earthen pyramids that surround them. The fact of plaza construction, that is, necessitates that site plans were inscribed on landscapes at specific points in time. This, in turn, necessitates considerable labor coordination at the very inception of construction and a pervasive alteration of landscape (and, presumably, social memories).

The scale of the mound-center constructions and the evidence of northern intrusions suggests that the "adoption," founding, or penetration of new ideas in various localities is not a trait-unit-diffusionary process, but a package deal. At Cahokia and in the northern Midwest, everything from art to architecture took on putative Mississippian characteristics after 1050 AD or so. How did this happen? Hall (1991, 1997) has suggested that the historically known practice of ritual adoption, potentially homologous to the Calumet or "peace pipe" ceremonies, explains how fictive kin ties were created and, thus, how the northern Midwest and eastern Plains regions were "Mississippianized" (see also Green 2001). Rock art in Missouri and Wisconsin dating to the middle eleventh century AD does appear to depict the "intrusion" of mythical superhuman figures associated in later centuries with ritual adoption (Diaz-Granados and Duncan 2000; Diaz-Granados et al. 2001; Salzer and Rajnovich 2000). In such an adoption ceremony, art forms, technological styles, and monuments presumably would have embedded an integrated suite of myths, meanings, and practices in landscapes. The result would have been a syncretic field of local knowledge and cultural practices superimposed by adopted myths, symbols, and practices that archaeologists call Mississippian after the fact.

However, the creation of place is not merely a one-time fixing of meanings or mythological associations in time and space (Joyce, this volume; Meskell, this volume; Sinopoli, this volume). Meanings and associations change constantly (but not necessarily gradually). The "life histories of things and the biographies of people intersect" in space to create "multivocal" places (Joyce and Hendon 2000, following Rodman 1992). It is this multivocality of place that permits the continuing transformation of meaning and function. Thus, in the end, appearances are deceptive. Cultural structures and macroregional traditions are illusory except as memories recollected and brought forward through ongoing practices (see also Pauketat 2001a, 2001c). Such structures and traditions were not so fundamental as to obviate the need to understand how localized practices might have transmogrified them with each instance of mound building.

We cannot even assume that all flat-topped pyramidal mounds – even within just one region or during just one phase – meant the same thing or functioned in the same ways. While platform mound construction in Wisconsin "may seem superficially analogous" to that at Cahokia or Toltec or Kings Crossing, "the discursive reasons" for each construction "were very different" (Meskell, this volume). Here, the idea of social memory (as constructed under multivocal and syncretic conditions) is necessary to explain how the labor-intensive creations of the Eastern Woodlands mound-plaza complexes simultaneously could be the realization of the "deliberate" plans of a few actors *and* the inclusive constructions of all people.

To make this point, we should first ask: exactly what was transmitted from place to place or across generational lines, when and how was that done, and by whom? The answers are to be found within the layers of Cahokia's mounds and among the residential remains of contemporary farming villages recently excavated in the Greater

Cahokia region. The layers of Cahokia's mounds reveal an unprecedented regularity to construction – unlike documented mound constructions elsewhere – that we interpret as evidence of inclusion. At the same time, the farming villages indicate that those who were presumably included in construction projects did not necessarily speak or act with one voice.

Practice, Pluralism, and the Creation of Cahokia

At about 1050 AD, events accelerated the centralizing tendencies of agricultural life in the American Bottom (for a regional-historical overview, see Pauketat 1998). Over the span of the tenth through early eleventh centuries, a series of agricultural villages grew to sizeable proportions. Cahokia itself may have had a thousand-plus residents in the early eleventh century; a handful of other villages may have reached population levels of several hundred residents (Pauketat and Lopinot 1997). The reasons for this growth are poorly understood, although the evidence at Cahokia of possible trade with foreigners, if not the presence of foreign potters themselves, suggests processes that in the very least attracted the attention of outsiders.

Then, in dramatic fashion at about 1050 AD, a planned capital center was constructed over the former village, entailing a series of massive labor projects and a kind of urban renewal never before seen in North America. The new 19 ha Grand Plaza and perimeter platform mounds were built over a short period of time. The earth for construction was taken from borrow pits surrounding the central earthworks, at least one of which was refilled with rich organic residues and sumptuary goods apparently left over from public feasts with political–religious overtones (Pauketat et al. 2002). The population of the central capital swelled rapidly to 10,000–16,000 people in an area of under 2 sq. km; many of them lived in a new style of house and were engaged to some extent in crafting an array of "invented" local symbols (*sensu* Hobsbawm and Ranger 1983). Additional living space and more people occupied the East St. Louis and St. Louis "centers" which appear to be part of a continuous residential sprawl connected to Cahokia.

Elsewhere, we have argued that the construction of earthen platform mounds at Cahokia embodied a distinctive negotiation of many different groups of people of all statuses and identities (Alt 2001a; Pauketat 2000b). The negotiation, contingent on the history of all of the peoples involved, was a synergistic process wherein people who lived (or used to live) in outlying agricultural settlements accommodated the representations and interests of Cahokians, and vice versa. While power and identity-politics were definite underlying currents of Cahokia's inception, the practices of farmers are thought to have greatly contributed to the shape of what Cahokia would become. Cahokia, by one or more orders of magnitude the largest of native North American political–cultural formations, was large precisely owing to the kind of participatory "promotion" that a Cahokian community embodied. The place was itself the negotiated compromises between people and their memories of the past (Pauketat 1997, 2000a, 2000b; Pauketat and Emerson 1999).

Mound building evidence

The stratigraphic evidence of earthen pyramid construction at and around Cahokia shows clearly that mound building was a regularly prosecuted, communal effort (Pauketat 1993, 2000b; Pauketat and Rees 1996; Pauketat et al. 1998; Porter 1974; Reed et al. 1968; Smith 1969). With each major building event, laborers appear to have demolished the temples and houses atop the platforms, laid down one or two mantles of earth, and rebuilt the surmounting architecture. Excavations into the Emerald, Kunnemann, Horseshoe Lake, Red (#49), and East St. Louis mounds appear to affirm the use of alternating light and dark or sandy and clayey fills, some of which appear "engineered" (see Bareis 1975; M. Kolb, personal communication, 2001; Pauketat 1993; Pauketat and Rees 1996; Pauketat et al. 1998).

The most salient feature of mound construction in the Greater Cahokia region is the "blitz" in which it was pursued (V. J. Knight, personal communication, 1998). More than other Mississippian mounds to the south and east, Cahokia's mounds betray innumerable vertical and horizontal "stage enlargements," "blanket mantles," and various other modifications to mound faces, surmounting buildings, and marker posts (see overview in Pauketat 1993; cf. Anderson 1994; Knight 1989; Lindauer and Blitz 1997). The pre-Mississippian platform mounds of the Coles Creek and Plum Bayou regions were not built in the "blitz" mode of early Cahokia's mounds. Larger mound stages there were added during construction events that were probably *not* annual affairs (see Rolingson 1982, 1998). However, in the best-documented Cahokian examples, something seems to have happened to the mound every year.

While the central pyramids of "downtown" Cahokia may possess massive clayey cores built ca. 1050 AD, other mounds clearly began as mere lenses of fill beneath important buildings. In the case of the Kunnemann, Horseshoe Lake, and at least one East St. Louis mound, the earliest "stages" of a particular platform were sometimes only a few centimeters high (Pauketat 1993; Pauketat, report in preparation; Pauketat et al. 1998). These blanket mantles probably would have not been visible from a distance, at least relative to the large buildings constructed atop them. Some time and several blanket mantles or stage enlargements later, the shape of a platform may have finally become evident. However, it seems reasonable to assert that in these cases, an imposing mound was not the goal of mound construction. Possibly, the goal of construction in these cases was the act of construction itself (and all that this entailed). Presumably, the greater the frequency of communal construction, the greater the integrative effects on a disparate population.

By contrast, the creation of an imposing monument seems to have been a likely goal of the laborers who built the Grand Plaza and the early stages of its perimeter pyramids, especially Monks Mound. This was a grand memorializing act (in the sense of Collins and Chalfant 1993). Its form and scale appear to have established, through the relations of monuments and the people and values associated with them, the grounds for a new kind of community. Subsequently, and even in the case of the 30 m high prominence, a regular and likely routinized annual construction cycle seems evident in the many thin blanket mantles observed in platform mound excavations (see Pauketat 2000b:Figure 9.3). In the end, with scores of pyramids under construction simultaneously, year after year within the period 1050–1150 AD, Cahokia's laborers appear to have been involved regularly in a labor-extensive, if not also labor-intensive, building process. Given that pyramids are found at outlying towns as well, it would seem that most people within the region were actively involved in the continuous and symbolically charged rhythms of this new living landscape.

One could say, if predisposed toward structuralist explanations, that Cahokia's Mississippian culture was reaffirmed every year in this way: mound building was merely an expression of relatively static traditions. If predisposed toward functionalist explanations, one could claim that such a construction cycle was an ideological strategy that, by elevating Mississippian elites, ensured the continued functioning of a hierarchically based political economy. Static traditions in this case would have been a means to an end.

But both structuralist and functionalist explanations, while perhaps not entirely wrong, fail to explain either *how* all people would have come to share in such static traditions in the first place, or *why* they might have been duped into affirming it in the second. A third explanation involves raising the possibility that Cahokia was an unintended consequence of social negotiations at an unprecedented scale between Cahokians and a diverse farming population. These negotiations were contentious and dynamic, and the scale of Cahokian construction is a memorial to the unification of one Mississippian community from such a contentious and continually changing field. Identifying the participants in this process is a necessary first step in situating memory in the construction of mounds and the production of Mississippian history.

Upland Mississippian pluralism

Since 1995, the authors have been engaged in (1) a survey of a portion of these uplands (now called the "Richland Complex") to locate early Mississippian sites coeval with Cahokia's coalescence, and (2) the excavation of large portions of these upland sites to delineate how villagers lived ca. 1050–1150 AD (Alt 1999, 2000, 2001a, 2001b; Pauketat 1998, 2000a, 2003). Other survey and excavation recently conducted in this same vicinity has resulted in the identification and excavation of additional Cahokia-related villages in the hilly uplands surrounding the American Bottom (e.g., Hargrave and Hedman 2001; Holley et al. 2000, 2001; Jackson 2000).

A total of 255 domiciles and hundreds of related pit, hearth, and post features have been excavated at 15 Richland-Complex settlements dating to the eleventh century AD (see Alt 2001a, 2001b; Pauketat 2003). Based on this substantive database, these upland Richland peoples are known to have originated from elsewhere within – and possibly beyond – the American Bottom floodplain. At a point around 1050 AD, hundreds and possibly thousands of pre-Mississippian farmers resettled in a zone of open forest and prairie some 10 to 20 km east and southeast of Cahokia proper. Once there, villagers appear to have retained a good deal of autonomy in their everyday routines (Alt 2001a). Yet, these village farmers lived only a day's walk from the new plaza and pyramids of Cahokia, a distance deemed insufficiently great to impart any real political autonomy (Pauketat 2003, following Hally 1993). The relationship between Cahokians and these hill farmers is, in fact, revealed by quantitative measures of artifact density in domestic refuse. There, the resharpening debitage from chipped stone hoe blades is found in exceedingly high densities relative to Cahokia or other floodplain sites; conversely, the finely crafted wares and exotic raw materials possibly obtained through Cahokia are found in the lowest densities known from the region (Pauketat 1998:Figure 6).

Alt (2001a, 2001b) has analyzed the material culture of the Richland villagers, casting further light on the relationship of the immigrant upland farmers and Cahokians. For example, by contrasting settlement plans, architecture, and sizes of ceramic cooking pots, she has deduced two features of social life in the Greater Cahokia region. First, the upland villagers lived a more communal existence than did their floodplain neighbors. They conducted daily life in and around clusters of "traditional" post-wall buildings around small courtyards. In the floodplain, and particularly at Cahokia proper, pre-Mississippian post-wall house styles were all but eliminated at 1050 AD; the small courtyards of the pre-Mississippian village were replaced with neighborhoods; novel tool forms and technologies became prevalent; communal cemeteries may have been localized at Cahokia proper; certain public or community symbols or practices – pipe smoking, marker posts, and the gaming pieces for a popular competitive sport ("chunkey") – were centralized at Cahokia and its subsidiary towns (see DeBoer 1993; Pauketat 1994, 1997, 1998, 2000a). Yet, the outlying upland villages retained their own chunkey stones, ca. 10 cm wide stone disks used to play a high-stakes team sport. These same villages were associated with cemeteries where the dead were arranged in patterns reminiscent of the nearby domestic courtyards (Emerson et al. 2002; Hargrave and Hedman 2001; Holley et al. 2000).

Second, social diversity within and between contemporaneous upland settlements was potentially profound. The material aspects of Cahokia adopted by these villagers, along with the timing of adoption, seem to have varied from village to village. In addition, particular individuals within some settlements, and possibly some villages more than others, produced craft goods ranging from cloth to shell beads and stone axheads (Alt 1999, 2001a). Production of such goods, comparable to the early Mississippian pattern at and nearer to Cahokia proper, suggests an integrated Cahokia-centric economy that pulled goods and labor from a hinterland (Pauketat 1997; see also Emerson and Hughes 2000).

Given the (1) possible regional economic integration, (2) evidence for the physical movement of Richland villagers into the uplands at the same time horizon as Cahokia's abrupt coalescence ca. 1050 AD, and (3) signs of practical differences between those upland people and their Cahokian counterparts, we believe that the early Mississippian population of Greater Cahokia was not so homogeneous as often assumed (compare Pauketat 2003 with Kelly 1990 or Milner 1998). Rather, cultural pluralism, albeit possibly village-level in scale, may have been an important factor underlying the character of the social negotiations that defined early Cahokia (see also Emerson and Hargrave 2000). The diverse practices of distinct villages within the

Cahokian sphere are believed to have profoundly influenced the manner in which labor was mobilized to build Cahokia's impressive earthen pyramids.

Discussion

It seems increasingly unlikely that Cahokia's resettled farmers, apparently called upon to craft goods and till the soil as part of a regional Cahokian order, accommodated all Cahokia-centric changes with equal affability. It seems unlikely that Cahokia's labor and product expropriations were entirely commensurate with the practices of farmers at ca. 1050 AD. Instead, the diverse contexts of experience among farmers prior to 1050 AD would have ensured an embedded resistance to Cahokians. And yet Cahokia was built, forcing us to ask: what elements of tradition and community did Cahokians seek to emphasize? What traditions and meanings did the outlying farmers participating in Cahokia's construction promote? More to the point, how was a compromise struck between the two and then embedded in Cahokia's mound-and-plaza plan at 1050 AD? How did the "life" of this particular "collectivity" begin? Who decided at 1050 AD "which events to include and which to exclude" from memory so as to legitimate the unprecedented construction of a massive public place (Trouillot 1995:16)?

At this point it should be noted that the homelands of some of the earliest Cahokians could have been to the south (cf. Smith 1984). Perhaps such a migration might help explain the dramatic disjuncture represented by the timing and scale of Cahokia's earliest known mound-and-plaza construction. In such a scenario, some segment of a Plum Bayou or Coles Creek population – with a working knowledge of how and why to build four-sided platform mounds – would have arrived at the large village of Cahokia before 1050 AD and superimposed their interests on a local population (compare Morse 1977; Morse and Morse 2000; Perino 1971). The pan-Mississippi-valley settlement pattern – particularly the abandonment of the Plum Bayou region – may lend credence to an explanation for population shifts, if not directly to Cahokia then certainly across the regions of the Midwest and Midsouth.

Whether migration was involved or not, the founding of the Mississippian site of Cahokia at 1050 AD was a major cultural disjuncture. Particular individuals might have acted as founding figures (DeBoer and Kehoe 1999:264; Pauketat 1994). Their individual memories of mounds and plazas may have been the basis for that memorialized in the newly built center. However, founding figures – even charismatic leaders – could not have built plazas and pyramids without collaborators, making the founding of Cahokia an inclusive, social phenomenon that cannot be reduced to a Great Man explanation (in the sense of Scott 1990:221; see Pauketat 2000b). The social construction of memory holds the key to understanding this founding event.

To wit, most of the pre-Mississippian peoples of the American Bottom at 1050 AD would have possessed only vague, unmarked senses of what mounds signified. The cross-generational or pan-regional transmission of more than this – that is, the special knowledge about the functions and meanings of mounds – would have been inhibited by the temporal and spatial gaps in mound construction across the Mississippi valley. Under these circumstances, the de-centered cultural practices of peoples and the disparate loci of memory construction could have been co-opted and arrayed under the banner of a new kind of Cahokian community (Pauketat and Emerson 1999; Pauketat 2001a). Whatever cultural resistance there may have been to such a Cahokian co-optation of space, labor, and meaning – perhaps only realized at the moment of attempted "domination" (sensu Scott 1990:27) – could have been subsumed within the multivocality and inclusive character of the place.

This does definitely entail that the platform mounds seen elsewhere, even if consciously emulated by a founding figure, could not have been built in the same way at Cahokia as they were at other places. Cultural structures could not have been transplanted intact from the south to Cahokia any more than the idea of Cahokia could have been emulated without significant change at Trempealeau, Aztalan, or elsewhere. The history of the people doing the building would have shaped differently each locality, if not each mound, regardless of the original plan. The mounds of Cahokia necessarily would have become vehicles for cultural compromises rather than intact cultural structures imported from elsewhere. The construction of social memories, in the context of the eleventh-century American Bottom, was materialized *as* a distinctly Cahokian variant of the platform mound. Each instance of mound construction there, or anywhere in the Mississippi valley, would have been different from the next because the memories of them were always locally constructed.

Ultimately, it seems that the tensions in the process of creating Cahokia also pulled it apart. Factionalism has been identified within the region and it may be evidenced in the form of possible intrusive "refugee" settlements to the north midway through the twelfth century (see Emerson 1991; Pauketat 1992; Pauketat and Emerson 1997). Palisade constructions at this same time emphasize that Cahokia and its associated town sites had become highly contested grounds (Pauketat 1998:71). In Cahokia's case, political disintegration was accompanied by an overall abandonment of the region, a process probably more or less complete by 1350 AD. As with its initial consolidation at 1050 AD, Cahokia's abandonment was part of an apparent midcontinent-wide movement of peoples, opening up large "vacant" zones between former polities, if not between emergent ethnicities (e.g., S. Williams 1990).

That Cahokia rose and fell during the early Mississippian period before many other Mississippian complexes developed to the south might suggest that its historical role was as a founding capital (for regional comparisons of histories, see King 2001; Knight 1997; Pauketat 1998). Perhaps the rest of the Mississippian world consisted of attempts to recreate the distant memory of Cahokia (Anderson 1997). Such an idea would be consistent with the degree to which outsiders had looked to Cahokia as a place of pilgrimage during the eleventh through twelfth centuries. "Remembered places have often served as symbolic anchors of community for dispersed people" and that same effect may well be extended to the pan-regional influence of places as singular as Cahokia (Gupta and Ferguson 1997:289)

Clearly the thousands of people who had resided in the Greater Cahokia region left and went elsewhere. How was the memory of Cahokia's earthen pyramids reconstructed in the locations where the Cahokians ended up? This question remains a puzzle, although it does seem apparent in the juxtaposition of macroregional cultural complexes ("traditions") that Cahokia splintered and various groups ended up in the eastern Plains, to the west, and perhaps amidst other "Mississippians," to the south (see Pauketat and Emerson 1997). The fact that immigrants from the north moved into the American Bottom following 1350 AD, along with evidence of twelfth- and thirteenth-century Cahokian interactions primarily with the south, would seem to preclude significant counter-movements northward on the part of Cahokians. Several scholars have favorably compared the material culture, historic accounts, and iconic representations of Dhegiha Souian speakers, like the Osage of the eastern Plains or the Quapaw of Arkansas, to the supposed features of the earlier Mississippians of Greater Cahokia (Diaz-Granados and Duncan 2000; Gartner 1996; Hall 1991; Hoffman 1994; Kehoe 2001).

In any event, it is instructive that no southern Mississippian groups ever matched the mound construction frenzy of their Cahokian forebearers. Even more instructive, however, is the fact that earthen platform mounds were *not* being built among the Dhegihans at the times of contact. Perhaps more than any other line of evidence, the possible termination of mound construction by Dhegiha-Souian speakers affirms that mounds are matters of memory creation. Those mounds are inextricably linked to the places through the construction of memory, and cannot be excised from those places.

Conclusion

In the Mississippi valley, the construction of earthen pyramids was at one time thought to be a hallmark of hierarchy and of a deep-seated and widely shared "Mississippian" belief system. Although the archaeological evidence accumulated over the last 30 years has eroded this line of reasoning, archaeologists have not adequately explained the process whereby four-sided and flat-topped earthen pyramids were built by different peoples at different times, from Coles Creek, to Cahokian, to later Mississippi valley landscapes. The common-sense appeal to cultural structures in earlier analyses, while not entirely wrong, remains unsatisfactory.

That four-sided platform mound construction stretched across the Mississippi valley and lasted in some form or another for millennia probably attests to the power of the inscription of social memory in landscapes. Mounds were powerful media that shaped the lived experiences of people. And yet the hundreds of kilometers and temporal hiatuses that separate mound-building peoples in parts of the Mississippi valley, along with the localized variability in the mode of mound construction, are suggestive of *dynamic* traditions.

There are few regions anywhere in the Eastern Woodlands where mound building persisted from the fourth millennium BC to contact (northeastern Louisiana is the only candidate). That fact emphasizes the importance of pilgrimages, regional demographic shifts, and migrations in the history of places. And it emphasizes the potential significance of the construction of social memory in the punctuated history of mound construction in the Mississippi valley. There, regions were abandoned, unusual places were founded, and memories were actively constructed – and perhaps in the case of Cahokia's abandonment – intentionally forgotten (DeBoer and Kehoe 1999:267). The construction and abandonment of mounds was a matter of building memories and, not incidentally, alternately underwriting or undoing central authority.

Our analysis locates the platform-mound-building "tradition" of the Mississippi valley in the local processes of cultural construction involving the practices of every-day people. We find that merely attributing platform mounds to some antecedents and assuming a uniform transferal of structures or behaviors is insufficient. Yes, Coles Creek centers were probably invoked as memories in the construction of Cahokia, and Cahokia may have been a memory for those Mississippians who sought to emulate that powerful archetype. But people constructed their pasts in contested fields and at multiple loci. Mounds were features of living landscapes, observed by all, recollected differently by many, liable to be co-opted and intruded as statements of inclusion or hegemony.

Given the archaeological traces of trans-Mississippi contacts and migrations, there is no reason to invoke widely shared or deeply imbued structures to explain the mounds. In our reanalysis, practices in the context of founding events, pilgrimages, migrations, and resettlements explain the putative structural continuities of the Mississippi valley. Such events necessitate memory construction in wholly new con-texts, allowing for old forms to take on novel meanings even while retaining the old appearances. Thus, we translate structures into memories, and allow the past to have been actively constructed by all of the peoples of that past.

References Cited

Abercrombie, T. A. 1998: *Pathways of Memory and Power: Ethnography and History Among an Andean People.* Madison, Wisc.: University of Wisconsin Press.

Ahler, S. R. 2000: Projectile point caches. In *The Mound 72 Area: Dedicated and Sacred Space in Early Cahokia,* ed. M. L. Fowler, J. Rose, B. Vander Leest and S. R. Ahler. Springfield: Illinois State Museum, Reports of Investigations, No. 54, pp. 101–15.

Alt, S. M. 1999: Spindle whorls and fiber production at early Cahokian settlements. *South-eastern Archaeology* 18, pp. 124–33.

Alt, S. M. 2000: Identity, tradition, and accommodation during the rise of Mississippianism in the American Bottom. Paper presented at the 57th Annual Southeastern Archaeological Conference, November 8–11, Macon, Georgia.

Alt, S. M. 2001a: Cahokian change and the authority of tradition. In *The Archaeology of Tradi-tions: Agency and History Before and After Columbus,* ed. T. R. Pauketat. Gainesville: University Press of Florida, pp. 141–56.

Alt, S. M. 2001b: Keeping order in the uplands: a look at a Cahokian administrative center. Paper presented at the 58th Annual Meeting of the Southeastern Ceremonial Conference, November 14–17, Chattanooga, Tennessee.

Anderson, B. 1983: *Imagined Communities: Reflections on the Origins and Spread of Nationalism.* London: Verso.

Anderson, D. G. 1994: *The Savannah River Chiefdoms: Political Change in the Late Prehistoric Southeast.* Tuscaloosa: University of Alabama Press.

Anderson, D. G. 1997: The role of Cahokia in the evolution of Southeastern Mississippian society. In *Cahokia: Domination and Ideology in the Mississippian World*, ed. T. R. Pauketat and T. E. Emerson. Lincoln: University of Nebraska Press, pp. 248–68.

Appadurai, A. 1996: *Modernity at Large: Cultural Dimensions of Globalization*. Minneapolis: University of Minnesota Press.

Bareis, C. J. 1975: Report of 1972 University of Illinois-Urbana excavations at the Cahokia site. In *Cahokia Archaeology: Field Reports*, ed. M. L. Fowler. Springfield: Illinois State Museum Papers in Anthropology Number 3, pp. 12–15.

Bense, J. A. 1994: *Archaeology of the Southeastern United States: Paleoindian to World War I*. San Diego: Academic Press.

Blitz, J. H. 1999: Mississippian chiefdoms and the fission-fusion process. *American Antiquity* 64, pp. 577–92.

Buchner, C. A. 1998: A forked eye Ramey Incised jar from Mississippi County, Arkansas. *Field Notes: Newsletter of the Arkansas Archeological Society* 283, pp. 8–9.

Buikstra, J. E., Charles, D. K. and Rakita, G. F. 1998: *Staging Ritual: Hopewell Ceremonialism at the Mound House Site, Greene County, Illinois*. Kampsville Studies in Archeology and History 1. Kampsville, Illinois: Center for American Archeology.

Chesson, M. S. 2001: Social memory, identity, and death: an introduction. In *Social Memory, Identity, and Death: Anthropological Perspectives on Mortuary Rituals*, ed. M. S. Chesson. Washington, D.C.: Archeological Papers of the American Anthropological Association Number 10, pp. 1–10.

Clark, G. R. 1928 [1778]: *The Life of George Rogers Clark*, by J. A. James. Chicago: University of Chicago Press.

Collins, J. M. and Chalfant, M. L. 1993: A second-terrace perspective on Monks Mound. *American Antiquity* 58, pp. 319–32.

Connerton, P. 1989: *How Societies Remember*. Cambridge: Cambridge University Press.

Dalan, Rinita 1997: The construction of Mississippian Cahokia. In *Cahokia: Domination and Ideology in the Mississippian World*, ed. T. R. Pauketat and T. E. Emerson. Lincoln: University of Nebraska Press, pp. 89–102.

DeBoer, W. R. 1993: Like a rolling stone: the chunkey game and political organization in eastern North America. *Southeastern Archaeology* 12, pp. 83–92.

DeBoer, W. R. and Kehoe, A. B. 1999: Cahokia and the archaeology of ambiguity. *Cambridge Archaeological Journal* 9, pp. 261–67.

Diaz-Granados, C. and Duncan, J. R. 2000: *The Petroglyphs and Pictographs of Missouri*. Tuscaloosa: University of Alabama Press.

Diaz-Granados, C. M., Rowe, W., Hyman, M., Duncan, J. R. and Southon, J. R. 2001: AMS radiocarbon dates from three rock paintings and their associated iconography. *American Antiquity* 66, pp. 481–92.

Dillehay, T. D. 1990: Mapuche ceremonial landscape, social recruitment and resource rights. *World Archaeology* 22, pp. 223–41.

Drechsel, E. J. 1994: Mobilian jargon in the "prehistory" of southeastern North America. In *Perspectives on the Southeast: Linguistics, Archaeology, and Ethnohistory*, ed. P. B. Kwachka. Athens: University of Georgia Press, pp. 25–43.

Emerson, T. E. 1991: Some perspectives on Cahokia and the northern Mississippian expansion. In *Cahokia and the Hinterlands: Middle Mississippian Cultures of the Midwest*, ed. T. E. Emerson and R. B. Lewis. Urbana: University of Illinois Press, pp. 221–36.

Emerson, T. E. and Hargrave, E. 2000: Strangers in paradise? Recognizing ethnic mortuary diversity on the fringes of Cahokia. *Southeastern Archaeology* 19, pp. 1–23.

Emerson, T. E., Hargrave, E. and Hedman, K. in press: Death and ritual in early rural Cahokia. In *Theory, Method, and Technique in Modern Archaeology*, ed. R. J. Jeske and D. K. Charles. Westport: Bergin and Garvey.

Emerson, T. E. and Hughes, R. E. 2000: Figurines, flint clay sourcing, the Ozark Highlands, and Cahokian acquisition. *American Antiquity* 65, pp. 79–101.

Emerson, T. E. and McElrath, D. L. 2001: Interpreting discontinuity and historical process in midcontinental Late Archaic and Early Woodland societies. In *The Archaeology of Traditions: Agency and History Before and After Columbus*, ed. T. R. Pauketat. Gainesville: University Press of Florida, pp. 195–217.

Ford, J. A. 1951: *Greenhouse: A Troyville-Coles Creek Period Site in Avoyelles Parish, Louisiana*. Anthropology Papers, Volume 44(1). New York: American Museum of Natural History.

Fortier, A. C. 1998: Pre-Mississippian economies in the American Bottom of southwestern Illinois, 3000 BC–AD 1050. *Research in Economic Anthropology* 19, pp. 341–92.

Fortier, A. C. and McElrath, D. 2001: Revisiting the Emergent Mississippian concept in the American Bottom: the case for the Terminal Late Woodland (ca. AD 800–1050). Paper presented at the 47th annual meeting of the Midwest Archaeological Conference, October 12–14, La Crosse, Wisconsin.

Fowler, M. L., Rose, J., Vander Leest, B. and Ahler, S. R. 2000: *The Mound 72 Area: Dedicated and Sacred Space in Early Cahokia*. Springfield: Illinois State Museum, Reports of Investigations, No. 54.

Fritz, G. J. and Kidder, T. R. 1993: Recent investigations into prehistoric agriculture in the Lower Mississippi Valley. *Southeastern Archaeology* 12, pp. 1–14.

Gartner, W. G. 1996: Archaeoastronomy as sacred geography. *Wisconsin Archeologist* 77, pp. 128–50.

Gibson, J. L. 2000: *The Ancient Mounds of Poverty Point: Place of Rings*. Gainesville: University Press of Florida.

Gosden, C. and Marshall, Y. 1999: The cultural biography of objects. *World Archaeology* 31, pp. 169–78.

Green, W. 2001: Chiwere sociopolitical complexity?: reconciling mythology and archaeology. Paper presented at the 47th annual meeting of the Midwest Archaeological Conference, October 12–14, La Crosse, Wisconsin.

Green, W. and Rodell, R. L. 1994: The Mississippian presence and Cahokia interaction at Trempealeau, Wisconsin. *American Antiquity* 59, pp. 334–59.

Gupta, A. and Ferguson, J. 1997: Beyond "culture": space, identity, and the politics of difference. In *Culture, Power, and Place: Explorations in Critical Anthropology*, ed. A. Gupta and J. Ferguson. Durham: Duke University Press, pp. 33–57.

Hagedorn, K. J. 2001: *Divine Utterances: The Performance of Afro-Cuban Santería*. Washington, D.C.: Smithsonian Institution Press.

Hall, R. L. 1991: Cahokia identity and interaction models of Cahokia Mississippian. In *Cahokia and the Hinterlands: Middle Mississippian Cultures of the Midwest*, ed. T. E. Emerson and R. B. Lewis. Urbana: University of Illinois Press, pp. 3–34.

Hall, R. L. 1997: *An Archaeology of the Soul*. Urbana: University of Illinois Press.

Hally, D. J. 1993: The territorial size of Mississippian chiefdoms. In *Archaeology of Eastern North America: Papers in Honor of Stephen Williams*, ed. J. B. Stoltman. Jackson, Mississippi: Archaeological Report No. 25, Mississippi Department of Archives and History, pp. 143–68.

Hargrave, E. A. and Hedman, K. 2001: *The Halliday Site (11-S-27): Investigations into Early Mississippian Mortuary Behavior*. Illinois Transportation Archaeological Research Program, Research Reports No. 50. Urbana-Champaign: University of Illinois Press.

Heidegger, M. 1962: *Being and Time*, trans. J. Macquarrie and E. Robinson. Oxford: Blackwell.

Hobsbawm, E. and Ranger, T. (eds.) 1983: *The Invention of Tradition*. Cambridge: Cambridge University Press.

Hoffman, M. P. 1994: Ethnic identities and cultural change in the Protohistoric period of eastern Arkansas. In *Perspectives on the Southeast: Linguistics, Archaeology, and Ethnohistory*, ed. P. B. Kwachta. Athens: The University of Georgia Press, pp. 61–70.

Holley, G. R., Dalan, R. A. and Smith, P. 1993: Investigations in the Cahokia site Grand Plaza. *American Antiquity* 58, pp. 306–19.

Holley, G. R., Parker, K. E., Watters, H. W. Jr., Harper, J. N., Skele, M., Ringberg, J. E., Brown, A. J. and Booth, D. L. 2000: *The Prehistoric Archaeology of the Knoebel Locality, Scott Joint-Use Archaeological Project*. Report submitted to the Illinois Department of Transportation, Southern Illinois University, Edwardsville.

Holley, G. R., Parker, K. E., Watters, H. W. Jr., Harper, J. N., Skele, M. and Ringberg, J. E. 2001: *The Prehistoric Archaeology of the Lembke Locality, Scott Joint-Use Archaeological Project*. Report submitted to the Illinois Department of Transportation, Southern Illinois University, Edwardsville.

Holtorf, C. J. 1998: The life-histories of megaliths in Mecklenburg-Vorpommern (Germany). *World Archaeology* 30, pp. 23–38.

House, J. H. 1996: East-central Arkansas. In *Prehistory of the Central Mississippi Valley*, ed. C. H. McNutt. Tuscaloosa: University of Alabama Press, pp. 137–54.

Howard, J. H. 1968: *The Southeastern Ceremonial Complex and Its Interpretation*. Columbia, Missouri: Missouri Archeological Society Memoir No. 6.

Hudson, C. 1976: *The Southeastern Indians*. Knoxville: University of Tennessee Press.

Jackson, D. 2000: The Mississippian community at the Grossmann site. Paper presented at the 57th Annual Southeastern Archaeological Conference, November 8–11, Macon, Georgia.

Johnson, J. K. 1987: Cahokia core technology in Mississippi: the view from the South. In *The Organization of Core Technology*, ed. J. K. Johnson and C. A. Morrow. Boulder, Colorado: Westview Press, pp. 187–206.

Joyce, R. A. 2000: Heirlooms and houses: materiality and social memory. In *Beyond Kinship: Social and Material Reproduction in House Societies*, ed. R. A. Joyce and S. D. Gillespie. Philadelphia: University of Pennsylvania Press, pp. 189–212.

Joyce, R. A. 2001: Burying the dead at Tlatilco: social memory and social identities. In *Social Memory, Identity, and Death: Anthropological Perspectives on Mortuary Rituals*, ed. M. S. Chesson. Washington, D.C.: Archeological Papers of the American Anthropological Association Number 10, pp. 12–26.

Joyce, R. A. and Hendon, J. A. 2000: Heterarchy, history, and material reality: "communities" in Late Classic Honduras. In *The Archaeology of Communities: A New World Perspective*, ed. M. A. Canuto and J. Yaeger. London: Routledge, pp. 143–60.

Kehoe, A. B. 2001: Osage texts and Cahokia data. Manuscript in possession of the authors.

Kelly, J. E. 1990: The emergence of Mississippian culture in the American Bottom region. In *The Mississippian Emergence*, ed. B. D. Smith. Washington, D.C.: Smithsonian Institution Press, pp. 113–52.

Kelly, J. E. 1991: The evidence for prehistoric exchange and its implications for the development of Cahokia. In *New Perspectives on Cahokia: Views from the Periphery*, ed. J. B. Stoltman. Monographs in World Archaeology 2. Madison, Wisc.: Prehistory Press, pp. 65–92.

Kelly, J. E. 1997: Stirling-phase sociopolitical activity at East St. Louis and Cahokia. In *Cahokia: Domination and Ideology in the Mississippian World*, ed. T. R. Pauketat and T. E. Emerson. Lincoln: University of Nebraska Press, pp. 141–66.

Kidder, T. R. 1992: Coles Creek period social organization and evolution in northeast Louisiana. In *Lords of the Southeast: Social Inequality and the Native Elites of Southeastern North America*, ed. A. W. Barker and T. R. Pauketat. Washington, D.C.: American Anthropological Association, Archaeological Papers 3, pp. 145–62.

Kidder, T. R. 1998: Mississippi period mound groups and communities in the Lower Mississippi Valley. In *Mississippian Towns and Sacred Spaces: Searching for an Architectural Grammar*, ed. R. B. Lewis and C. Stout. Tuscaloosa: University of Alabama Press, pp. 123–50.

Kidder, T. R. 2002: Investigating the plaza at the Raffman site (16MS20), northeast Louisiana. Manuscript in possession of the authors.

Kidder, T. R. and Fritz, G. J. 1993: Subsistence and social change in the Lower Mississippi Valley: excavations at the Reno Brake and Osceola sites, Louisiana. *Journal of Field Archaeology* 20, pp. 281–97.

King, A. 2001: Long-term histories of Mississippian centers: the developmental sequence of Etowah and its comparison to Moundville and Cahokia. *Southeastern Archaeology* 20, pp. 1–17.

Knight, V. J. 1986: The institutional organization of Mississippian religion. *American Antiquity* 51, pp. 675–87.

Knight, V. J. 1989: Symbolism of Mississippian mounds. In *Powhatan's Mantle: Indians in the Colonial Southeast*. Lincoln: University of Nebraska Press, pp. 279–91.

Knight, V. J. 1990: *Excavation of the Truncated Mound at the Walling Site: Middle Woodland Culture and Copena in the Tennessee Valley*. Alabama State Museum of Natural History, Division of Archaeology, Report of Investigations No. 56. Tuscaloosa, Alabama: University of Alabama.

Knight, V. J. 1997: Some developmental parallels between Cahokia and Moundville. In *Cahokia: Domination and Ideology in the Mississippian World*, ed. T. R. Pauketat and T. E. Emerson. Lincoln: University of Nebraska Press, pp. 229–47.

Koldehoff, B. and Carr, P. J. 2001: Chipped stone technology: patterns of procurement, production, and consumption. In *Excavations at Wickliffe Mounds*, by K. Wesler, Chapter 10 (CD-ROM). Tuscaloosa: University of Alabama Press.

Koldehoff, B., Pauketat, T. R. and Kelly, J. E. 1993: The Emerald site and the Mississippian occupation of the central Silver Creek valley. In *Highways to the Past: Essays on Illinois Archaeology in Honor of Charles J. Bareis*, ed. T. Emerson, A. Fortier and D. McElrath. *Illinois Archaeology* 5, pp. 331–43.

Koldehoff, B., Witty, C. O. and Kolb, M. 2000: Recent investigations in the vicinity of Mounds 27 and 28 at Cahokia: the Yale Avenue borrow pit. *Illinois Archaeology* 12, pp. 199–217.

Kus, S. 1997: Archaeologist as anthropologist: much ado about something after all? *Journal of Archaeological Method and Theory* 4, pp. 199–213.

Larson, L. H., Jr. 1989: The Etowah site. In *The Southeastern Ceremonial Complex: Artifacts and Analysis*, ed. P. Galloway. Lincoln: University of Nebraska Press, pp. 133–41.

Levi-Strauss, C. 1967[1958]: *Structural Anthropology*. New York: Doubleday.

Lewis, R. B. and Stout, C. (eds.) 1993: *Mississippian Towns and Sacred Spaces: Searching for an Architectural Grammar*. Tuscaloosa: University of Alabama Press.

Lindauer, O. and Blitz, J. H. 1997: Higher ground: the archaeology of North American platform mounds. *Journal of Archaeological Research* 5, pp. 169–207.

Lopinot, N. H., Conner, M. D., Ray, J. H. and Yelton, J. K. 1998: *Prehistoric and Historic Properties on Mitigation Lands, Horseshoe Lake Peninsula, Madison County, Illinois*. St. Louis District Historic Properties Management Report No. 55. St. Louis: U.S. Army Corps of Engineers.

Mainfort, R. C., Jr. 1988: Middle Woodland ceremonialism at Pinson Mounds, Tennessee. *American Antiquity* 53, pp. 158–73.

Mainfort, R. C., Jr. 1996: The Reelfoot Lake basin, Kentucky and Tennessee. In *Prehistory of the Central Mississippi Valley*, ed. C. H. McNutt. Tuscaloosa: University of Alabama Press, pp. 77–96.

McElrath, D. L. and Fortier, A. C. 2000: The early Late Woodland occupation of the American Bottom. In *Late Woodland Societies: Tradition and Transformation across the Midcontinent*, ed. T. E. Emerson, D. L. McElrath and A. C. Fortier. Lincoln: University of Nebraska Press, pp. 97–121.

Milner, G. R. 1998: *The Cahokia Chiefdom: The Archaeology of a Mississippian Society.* Washington, D.C.: Smithsonian Institution Press.

Moore, J. H. 1994: Ethnoarchaeology of the Lamar peoples. In *Perspectives on the Southeast: Linguistics, Archaeology, and Ethnohistory*, ed. P. B. Kwachka. Athens: University of Georgia Press, pp. 126–41.

Morse, D. F. 1977: The penetration of northeast Arkansas by Mississippian culture. In *For the Director: Research Essays in Honor of James B. Griffin*, ed. C. E. Cleland. Museum of Anthropology Anthropological Papers 61. Ann Arbor: University of Michigan, pp. 186–211.

Morse, D. F. and Morse, P. A. 2000: Social interaction between the American Bottom of Cahokia and the Crowley's Ridge Lowlands Division of the Lower Mississippi River AD 800–1200. In *Mounds, Modoc, and Mesoamerica: Papers in Honor of Melvin L. Fowler*, ed. S. R. Ahler. Scientific Papers 28. Springfield: Illinois State Museum, pp. 347–60

Nassaney, M. S. 1991: Spatial-temporal dimensions of social integration during the Coles Creek period in central Arkansas. In *Stability, Transformation, and Variation: The Late Woodland Southeast*, ed. M. S. Nassaney and C. R. Cobb. New York: Plenum, pp. 177–220.

Nassaney, M. S. 1992: Communal societies and the emergence of elites in the prehistoric American Southeast. In *Lords of the Southeast: Social Inequality and the Native Elites of Southeastern North America*, ed. A. W. Barker and T. R. Pauketat. Washington, D.C.: Archeological Papers of the American Anthropological Association No. 3, pp. 111–43

Nassaney, M. S. 1994: The historical and archaeological context of Plum Bayou culture in central Arkansas. *Southeastern Archaeology* 13, pp. 36–55.

Nassaney, M. S. 2001: The historical-processual development of Late Woodland societies. In *The Archaeology of Traditions: Agency and History Before and After Columbus*, ed. T. R. Pauketat. Gainesville: University Press of Florida, pp. 157–73.

Overstreet, D. F. 2000: Cultural dynamics of the late prehistoric period in southern Wisconsin. In *Mounds, Modoc, and Mesoamerica: Papers in Honor of Melvin L. Fowler*, ed. S. R. Ahler. Scientific Papers 28. Springfield: Illinois State Museum, pp. 405–38.

Pauketat, T. R. 1992: The reign and ruin of the lords of Cahokia: a dialectic of dominance. In *Lords of the Southeast: Social Inequality and the Native Elites of Southeastern North America*, ed. A. W. Barker and T. R. Pauketat. Washington, D.C.: Archeological Papers of the American Anthropological Association 3, pp. 31–51.

Pauketat, T. R. 1993: *Temples for Cahokia Lords: Preston Holder's 1955–1956 Excavations of Kunnemann Mound.* Museum of Anthropology Memoir No. 26. Ann Arbor: University of Michigan.

Pauketat, T. R. 1994: *The Ascent of Chiefs: Cahokia and Mississippian Politics in Native North America.* Tuscaloosa: University of Alabama Press.

Pauketat, T. R. 1997: Cahokian political economy. In *Cahokia: Domination and Ideology in the Mississippian World*, ed. T. R. Pauketat and T. E. Emerson. Lincoln: University of Nebraska Press, pp. 30–51.

Pauketat, T. R. 1998: Refiguring the archaeology of Greater Cahokia. *Journal of Archaeological Research* 6, 45–89.

Pauketat, T. R. 2000a: Politicization and community in the pre-Columbian Mississippi valley. In *The Archaeology of Communities: A New World Perspective*, ed. M. A. Canuto and J. Yaeger. London: Routledge, pp. 16–43.

Pauketat, T. R. 2000b: The tragedy of the commoners. In *Agency in Archaeology*, ed. M.-A. Dobres and J. Robb. London: Routledge, pp. 113–29.

Pauketat, T. R. 2001a: A new tradition in archaeology. In *The Archaeology of Traditions: Agency and History Before and After Columbus*, ed. T. R. Pauketat. Gainesville: University Press of Florida, pp. 1–16.

Pauketat, T. R. 2001b: A waterline through Cahokia's Grand Plaza. *Cahokian* (Spring), pp. 10–12.

Pauketat, T. R. 2001c: Practice and history in archaeology: an emerging paradigm. *Anthropological Theory* 1, pp. 73–98.

Pauketat, T. R. 2003: Resettled farmers and the making of a Mississippian polity. *American Antiquity* 68.

Pauketat, T. R. in press: Materiality and the immaterial in historical-processual archaeology. In *Current Issues in Archaeological Method and Theory*, eds. T. L. VanPool and C. S. VanPool. Salt Lake City: University of Utah Press.

Pauketat, T. R. and Emerson, T. E. 1997: Introduction: domination and ideology in the Mississippian world. In *Cahokia: Domination and Ideology in the Mississippian World*, ed. T. R. Pauketat and T. E. Emerson. Lincoln: University of Nebraska Press, pp. 30–51.

Pauketat, T. R. and Emerson, T. E. 1999: The representation of hegemony as community at Cahokia. In *Material Symbols: Culture and Economy in Prehistory*, ed. J. Robb. Occasional Paper No. 26. Carbondale: Southern Illinois University, pp. 302–17.

Pauketat, T. R., Kelly, L. S., Fritz, G. J., Lopinot, N. H., Elias, S. and Hargrave, E. 2002: The residues of feasting and public ritual at early Cahokia. *American Antiquity* 67, pp. 257–279.

Pauketat, T. R. and Lopinot, N. H. 1997: Cahokian population dynamics. In *Cahokia: Domination and Ideology in the Mississippian World*, ed. T. R. Pauketat and T. E. Emerson. Lincoln: University of Nebraska Press, pp. 103–23.

Pauketat, T. R. and M. A. Rees 1996: Early Cahokia Project 1994: excavations at Mound 49, Cahokia (11-S-34-2). Springfield: Report submitted to the Illinois Historic Preservation Agency.

Pauketat, T. R., Rees, M. A. and Pauketat, S. L. 1998: *An Archaeological Survey of the Horseshoe Lake State Recreation Area, Madison County, Illinois*. Quaternary Studies Program, Technical Report Number 95-899-34. Springfield: Illinois State Museum.

Perino, G. 1971: The Mississippian component at the Schild site (No. 4), Greene County, Illinois. In *Mississippian Site Archaeology in Illinois I*. Urbana: Illinois Archaeological Survey, Bulletin 8.

Phillips, P. 1970: *Archaeological Survey in the Lower Yazoo Basin, Mississippi, 1949–1955*. Papers of the Peabody Museum of Archaeology and Ethnology 60. Cambridge, Mass.: Harvard University.

Phillips, P. and Brown, J. A. 1978: *Pre-Columbian Shell Engravings from the Craig Mound at Spiro, Oklahoma, Part I*. Cambridge, Mass.: Peabody Museum Press.

Phillips, P., Ford, J. A. and Griffin, J. B. 1951: *Archaeological Survey in the Lower Mississippi Alluvial Valley, 1940–1947*. Papers of the Peabody Museum of Archaeology and Ethnology 25. Cambridge, Mass.: Harvard University.

Porter, J. W. 1974: *Cahokia Archaeology as Viewed from the Mitchell Site: A Satellite Community at AD 1150–1200*. Ph.D. dissertation, Department of Anthropology, University of Wisconsin, Madison.

Rafferty, J. 1990: Test excavations at Ingomar Mounds, Mississippi. *Southeastern Archaeology* 9, pp. 103–15.

Reed, N. A., Bennett, J. W. and Porter, J. W. 1968: Solid core drilling of Monks Mound: technique and findings. *American Antiquity* 33, pp. 137–48

Rodman, M. 1992: Empowering place: multilocality and multivocality. *American Anthropologist* 94, pp. 640–56.

Rolingson, M. A. (ed.) 1982: *Emerging Patterns of Plum Bayou Culture: Preliminary Investigations of the Toltec Mounds Research Project*. Fayetteville: Arkansas Archeological Survey Research Series No. 18.

Rolingson, M. A. (ed.) 1998: *Toltec Mounds and Plum Bayou Culture: Mound D Excavations*. Fayetteville: Arkansas Archeological Survey, Research Series No. 54.

Rouget, G. 1985: *Music and Trance: A Theory of the Relations Between Museum and Possession*. Chicago: University of Chicago Press.

Rowlands, M. 1993: The role of memory in the transmission of culture. *World Archaeology* 25, pp. 141–51.

Salzer, R. J. and Rajnovich, G. 2000: *The Gottschall Rockshelter: An Archaeological Mystery*. St. Paul, Minn.: Prairie Smoke Press.

Samuel, R. 1994: *Theatres of Memory*. London: Verso.

Sassaman, K. E. and Heckenberger, M. J. 2001: Roots of the Theocratic Formative of the Archaic Southeast. Paper presented at the Southern Illinois University Visiting Scholar Conference "Hunters and Gatherers in Theory and Archaeological Research," March 23–24, 2001, organized by G. Crothers. Carbondale, Illinois.

Saunders, J. W., Mandel, R. D., Saucier, R. T., Allen, E. T., Hallmark, C. T., Johnson, J. K., Jackson, E. H., Allen, C. M., Stringer, G. L., Frink, D. S., Feathers, J. K., Williams, S., Gremillion, K. J., Vidrine, M. F. and Jones, R. 1997: A mound complex in Louisiana at 5400–5000 years before the present. *Science* 277, pp. 1796–9.

Scott, J. C. 1990: *Domination and the Arts of Resistance: Hidden Transcripts*. New Haven: Yale University Press.

Shennan, S. J. 1993: After social evolution: a new archaeological agenda? In *Archaeological Theory: Who Sets the Agenda?*, eds. N. Yoffee and A. Sherratt. Cambridge: Cambridge University Press, pp. 53–9.

Smith, B. D. 1978: Variation in Mississippian settlement patterns. In *Mississippian Settlement Patterns*, ed. B. D. Smith. New York: Academic Press, pp. 479–503.

Smith, B. D. 1984: Mississippian expansion: tracing the historical development of an explanatory model. *Southeastern Archaeology* 3, 13–32.

Smith, H. M. 1969: The Murdock Mound: Cahokia site. In *Explorations into Cahokia Archaeology*, ed. M. L. Fowler. Urbana: Illinois Archaeological Survey Bulletin 7, pp. 49–88.

Squier, E. G. and Davis, E. H. 1998: *Ancient Monuments of the Mississippi Valley* (originally published 1848). Washington, D.C.: Smithsonian Institution Press.

Steponaitis, V. P. 1986: Prehistoric archaeology in the southeastern United States, 1970–1985. *Annual Review of Anthropology* 15, 363–404.

Stoltman, J. B. 1991: Cahokia as seen from the peripheries. In *New Perspectives on Cahokia: Views from the Periphery*, ed. J. B. Stoltman. Monographs in World Archaeology No. 2. Madison, Wisc.: Prehistory Press, pp. 349–54.

Stoltman, J. B. 2000: A reconsideration of the cultural processes linking Cahokia to its northern hinterlands during the period AD 1000–1200. In *Mounds, Modoc, and Mesoamerica: Papers in Honor of Melvin L. Fowler*, ed. S. Ahler. Springfield, Ill.: Illinois State Museum Scientific Papers 28, pp. 439–54.

Thomas, C. 1985[1894]: *Report on the Mound Explorations of the Bureau of Ethnology*. Washington, D.C.: Smithsonian Institution Press.

Thomas, J. 1996: *Time, Culture, and Identity*. Oxford: Routledge.

Tilley, C. 1994: *A Phenomenology of Landscape: Places, Paths, and Monuments*. Oxford: Berg.

Trouillot, M.-R. 1995: *Silencing the Past: Power and the Production of History*. Boston: Beacon Press.

Williams, H. 1998: Monuments and the past in early Anglo-Saxon England. *World Archaeology* 30, pp. 90–108.

Williams, M. 1994: The origins of the Macon Plateau site. In *Ocmulgee Archaeology 1936–1986*, ed. D. J. Hally. Athens: University of Georgia Press, pp. 130–37.

Williams, S. 1990: The Vacant Quarter and other late events in the Lower Valley. In *Towns and Temples Along the Mississippi*, ed. D. H. Dye. Tuscaloosa: University of Alabama Press, pp. 170–80.

Williams, S. and Brain, J. P. 1983: *Excavations at the Lake George Site, Yazoo County, Mississippi, 1958–1960*. Papers of the Peabody Museum of Archaeology and Ethnology, No. 74. Cambridge, Mass.: Harvard University.

Wolf, E. 1982: *Europe and the People Without History*. Berkeley: University of California Press.

9
Memory and the Construction of Chacoan Society

Ruth M. Van Dyke

Social memory is deeply implicated in the narrative traditions of contemporary native inhabitants of the North American Southwest. The Hopi, for example, tell of ancestral clan migrations across the landscape. These memories are materially evidenced through archaeological sites, rock art, and shrines. Traditional links to past landscapes are woven into contemporary Puebloan constructions of authority and identity. Puebloan architecture contains direct references to memory and the past. For example, unusual stones may be set into walls to remind the builder of specific events in his or her life (R. Ellis 1997:2). The *sipapu* is a small hole in a kiva floor that, according to Puebloan mythology, represents the place of emergence from earlier worlds into this one, connecting the present world to past mythic events (Smith 1972). But what of the use of social memory a millennium ago, in the Ancestral Puebloan past? We can safely infer that memories are used and constructed by all societies, but the archaeological reconstruction of memory in prehistoric contexts might seem so difficult as to be impossible.

Ethnographic analogy provides one starting point, and the intertwined nature of memory and place provides another. Place – the intersection of time, space, and self – is, for existentialist philosophers the most fundamental form of embedded experience (Casey 1996; Heidegger 1962; Merleau-Ponty 1981[1962]). As humans create

Research at the Red Willow and Los Rayos sites was undertaken during June 1998 with the permission of the Navajo Nation Historic Preservation Department, Permit No. A9807. An earlier version of this paper was presented at the 64th Annual Meeting of the Society for American Archaeology in Chicago, March 1999. Portions of this paper were completed while I was a National Endowment for the Humanities Resident Scholar at the School of American Research – my thanks to NEH and to the staff of the School for their support. Thanks to Chuck Riggs for his improvements and additions to some of my original figures. I am indebted to many people, particularly Sue Alcock, James Brooks, Cathy Cameron, Gary Gossen, Bob Powers, Mary Eunice Romero, Marni Sandweiss, Wolky Toll, Phil Tuwaletstiwa, and Tom Windes for suggestions and comments on the structure of the paper and the ideas presented here. Any errors or lapses of memory, however, remain my own.

and move through spatial milieus, the mediation between spatial experience and perception reflexively creates, legitimates, and reinforces social relationships and ideas (Lefebvre 1991; Soja 1996). Human existence is apprehended through dwelling, through practice, through daily experience that transforms spaces into places, charging them with meaning (Bourdieu 1977). A sense of place rests upon, and reconstructs, a history of social engagement with the landscape (Basso 1996). We cannot know or recognize a place, we cannot lend it meaning, without prior experience of a literal or figurative nature (De Certeau 1984). Based on these phenomenological premises, it is possible to attempt to construct past senses of place and, by extension, past social memories, at least insofar as these are spatially represented (Gosden 1994; Thomas 1996; Tilley 1994).

Many of the papers in this volume illustrate how memory may be used to naturalize authority and to consolidate social identity. In this chapter, I argue that this was no less true in the prehistoric Chacoan era in the American Southwest. At Chaco, architecture and landscape were employed to reference the past as part of the construction of new social configurations. Symbolic appropriations of ancestral beliefs and events lent legitimacy to Chacoan leaders and helped create a sense of community.

The Chacoan World

The arid mesas, plateaus, and canyons of northwest New Mexico were home to prehistoric Ancestral Puebloan (Anasazi) peoples who grew corn, beans, and squash, and who produced plain and corrugated grayware and black-on-white pottery. During the first half of the first millennium AD, these Neolithic farmers grew increasingly dependent on cultigens and dwelt in subterranean pitstructures. Most groups were fairly small and mobile; villages reached a maximum size of 20–35 houses during the late Basketmaker III period (400–700 AD). During the Pueblo I period (700–900 AD), site size continued to increase, and earth and masonry dwellings were constructed above the ground. Pitstructures – subsequently called kivas – continued to be constructed for use as gathering places.

Between the late Pueblo I and early Pueblo III periods (ca. 850–1150 AD), the Ancestral Puebloans built spectacular masonry buildings in Chaco Canyon and surrounding areas (figure 9.1). Pueblo Bonito is a well-known example (figure 9.2). These massive *great houses* are visually imposing, planned structures. Many are multi-storied; all exhibit very thick walls built in a distinctive core-and-veneer masonry style. The scale and intensity of this construction is different from anything seen before in this area. Chacoan great houses often are associated with architectural and landscape features such as great kivas (circular subterranean chambers), earthen mounds or berms, and cleared linear alignments, or roads. There are also hundreds of one-story *small sites* from this era exhibiting agglomerated layouts, simple masonry, and small rooms. Within approximately 100 miles of Chaco Canyon, at least 75 outlying great houses were built, usually in the midst of existing communities of small sites; great kivas, earthworks, and road segments are often also present (figure 9.1). Great houses, great kivas,

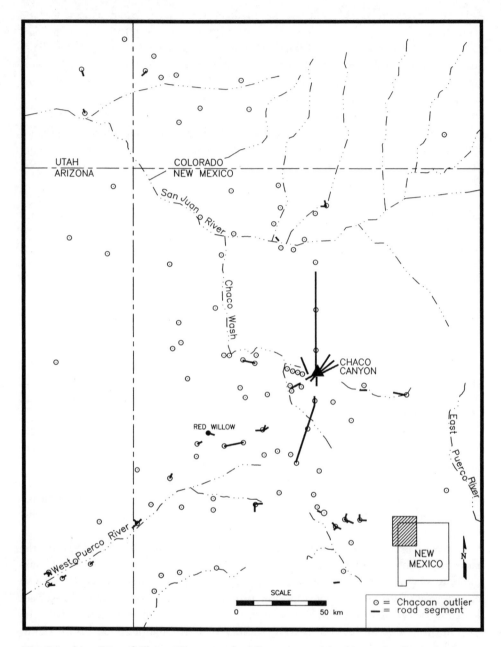

Map 9.1   Locations of Chaco Canyon and outlier communities (drawn by the author)

earthworks, and road segments are referred to collectively as *Bonito-style architecture* (Gladwin 1945).

Small sites are clearly habitations, but the purposes of *Bonito-style architecture* are less straightforward (see, for example, interpretations offered by Judge 1989; Kantner 1996;

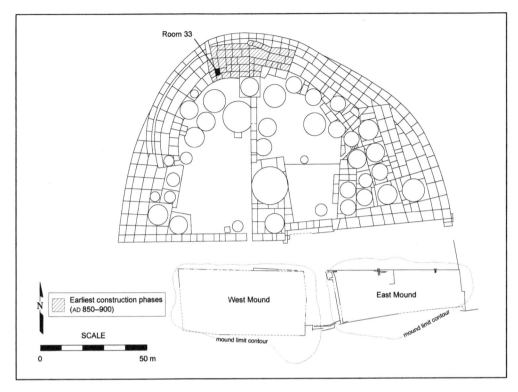

Figure 9.1   Plan of Pueblo Bonito, showing the two mounds and the early construction stages. (Modified from Judd [1964: Figures 2 and 23]; redrawn by the author and Chuck Riggs)

Lekson 1999; Mills 2002; Saitta 1997; Sebastian 1992; Toll 1985; Vivian 1990; Wills 2001). They are variously argued to be large habitations, storehouses, empty stages for ceremony, or assorted combinations thereof; evidence for these explanations is contradictory and inconclusive. Like many, but by no means all of my colleagues, I contend that great houses were erected within a context of social inequality, because construction required substantial planning and investment of labor, and because the buildings visually dominate their surroundings by means of massive size, exaggerated height, or commanding topographic position. The precise nature of social power at Chaco has proved difficult to understand, in part because the Chacoan evidence does not fit Western notions of direct associations between material wealth and power. Aside from the architecture itself, two anomalous burials, and a number of caches of beads and mystery objects, there is little to suggest material inequality. Power is not always expressed in terms of wealth, however, especially in societies where there are strong sanctions against glorification of individuals or families. Social hierarchies within historic and contemporary Puebloan communities are based on unequal access to farmland and other resources, but they find expression in exclusive access to ritual knowledge and control of ceremonies rather than in disparate distributions of material wealth (Brandt 1977, 1980, 1994; Levy 1992; Ortiz 1969; Whiteley 1985, 1986).

If similar values pertained in the past, this helps to explain the relative dearth of materially rich leaders at Chaco juxtaposed with the presence of large-scale architecture that obviously required, and embodied, significant social inequalities. Although major construction projects in Chaco were planned and completed in relatively rapid bursts of activity, the impetus to create monumental buildings did not appear overnight. As at some Mississippian sites (Pauketat and Alt, this volume), the architecture at Chaco represents the cumulative result of group and individual decisions made over several centuries. Those who contributed time, energy, or other resources to early, small-scale ritual events could not have anticipated the development of social asymmetries centuries later.

The three earliest great houses in Chaco Canyon – Una Vida, Pueblo Bonito, and Peñasco Blanco – were initiated during the late 800s AD in the three best spots for farming. Inhabitants of these sites were able to practice run-off and irrigation agriculture, and thus would have been consistently more successful than their dry-farming neighbors. Perhaps they seemed to have supernatural assistance, and these early great houses became the foci of agricultural rituals. Inhabitants may have shared surplus with neighbors, creating debt to be repaid with labor. By the 1000s AD, great house construction took off exponentially. During the Classic Bonito phase (1040–1100 AD) massive, formalized additions were made at five existing great houses, and two new great houses were built. Massed blocks of rooms and multiple stories lent great houses a dominating air. A shift towards institutionalized inequality is implied (Sebastian 1992:120–32). By the end of the eleventh century, the great houses of Chaco Canyon were loci for periodic gatherings that were probably ritual in nature and may well have involved feasting (Judge 1989; Sebastian 1992; Toll 1985). Participation in construction projects as well as in ritual activities and feasting would have contributed to a sense of social cohesion among the disparate groups who gathered at Chaco. Artifact evidence indicates that people came to the canyon from a wide range of surrounding areas. For example, ceramic and lithic materials were pouring into the canyon from the slopes of the Chuska Mountains 75 km to the west; these patterns led to early models depicting Chaco Canyon as a center for regional distribution (e.g., Judge et al. 1981), but such models have since been discarded, as the materials were not redistributed to outlying communities, nor were other tangible items returned in exchange.

The regional scale of Chacoan influence is evidenced by the appearance of Bonito-style architecture in *outlier* communities, dispersed across an area nearly 200 miles in diameter encompassing northwest New Mexico and neighboring portions of Utah, Colorado, and Arizona. Communities across this wide area probably shared similar beliefs and ritual practices (Lekson 1991). As in Chaco Canyon, social inequalities in the outliers may have been grounded in unequal access to good farmland. Small groups of people are likely to have been moving around the landscape during this period, and great houses may have functioned, in part, to attract new settlers to a community. Bonito-style construction in some settlements is likely to have been directed by people from Chaco, whereas in other situations, Bonito-style architecture appears to have been the result of local emulation (Van Dyke 1999b, 2000). Local leaders may have availed themselves of the opportunity to enhance prestige through participation in events at Chaco. By the late 1000s AD, Chaco Canyon had grown into a major venue for ritual activities, and the center of the Puebloan ideological universe.

Ritual, Landscape, and Memory

It is notoriously difficult to access prehistoric ideologies, yet many clues suggest the nature of Chacoan ritual and beliefs. As in contemporary Puebloan societies, landscape, myth, and ritual likely formed an interconnecting cosmological whole. Puebloan descendants of the Chacoans such as the Zuni, Tewa, and Keresans divide their physical, social, and spiritual worlds into horizontal and vertical dimensions (Cushing 1883, 1896; Ortiz 1969; White 1960). Horizontal divisions correspond to cardinal directions, and vertical divisions include upper and lower worlds. Nested layers or symmetrical quarters are connected at a center place – the pueblo village. Multiple levels are inscribed on the landscape by mountains and shrines, and the pueblo itself represents this organization in microcosm. Directional affiliations and boundary shrines are known from the Ancestral Puebloan archaeological sites of Los Aguajes and Kotyiti (Snead and Preucel 1999).

Horizontal and vertical divisions of the universe, and the notion of a center place, are likely to have been important at Chaco as well. As at Los Aguajes and Kotyiti, these beliefs were expressed spatially, on the landscape. Cardinal directions and astronomical alignments have long been recognized as important in the layout of Chacoan buildings and roads (e.g., Sofaer 1997). Road segments – which do not consistently connect sites to other sites, do not link sites with resources, and do not improve mobility on this flat terrain where people had no wheeled vehicles or draft animals – were almost certainly symbolic rather than economic in function (Roney 1992). The two most prominent road alignments extend due north and nearly due south out of Chaco Canyon (map 9.1). The North Road ends rather abruptly at Kutz Canyon, a dramatic area of bad-lands some 50 km north of Chaco. The South Road extends toward Hosta Butte, a prominent peak. Marshall (1997) has pointed out that the two roads fix Chaco both horizontally and vertically as a center place, midway between north/down, and south/up. The roads would have been ideal for ritual processions, which would have drawn active spatial experience into the cosmographic picture.

Astronomical events also were involved in the spatial configuration of the Chacoan world. We know that Chacoans watched the skies; petroglyphs atop Fajada Butte at the east end of the canyon mark solstices, equinoxes, and lunar events (Sofaer et al. 1979; Sofaer et al. 1982; Sinclair et al. 1987). Astronomical alignments also extend to some great houses. For example, Pueblo Bonito was positioned to dramatically show-case patterns of shadow and light that correspond with the equinox – the midpoint of the sun's journey on the horizon – reinforcing the position of this canyon great house as a center place within the larger universe, as well as within Chacoan quo-tidian experience (Sofaer 1997).

I argue that cosmological beliefs and ritual knowledge were expressed through architecture and landscape features, as ritual was formalized by aspiring leaders during the Classic Bonito phase (Van Dyke 2000, 2003). This process involved the use of social memory to legitimate new social structures and to help forge a Chacoan social identity. Social memory was employed in a manner similar to that described by Hobsbawm and Ranger (1983:9), in "establishing or symbolizing social cohesion or the membership of groups, real or artificial communities, (and in) establishing or legitimizing institutions, status, or relations of authority."

Connerton (1989) and others have usefully distinguished between inscribed, or materially visible, memory practices and embodied, or transitory, memory practices. Earlier in this volume (Van Dyke and Alcock), we broke down these categories further into ritual behaviors, narratives, representations and objects, and places. In the Chacoan world, connections to the past are most visible through places. Architecture and land-scape features, such as great houses, earthworks, great kivas, and road segments invoked memory to bolster social authority and social identity. There is also a good deal of circumstantial evidence to suggest that Chacoan ritual behaviors such as processions, feasting, and great kiva ceremonies likely referenced the past, but in this prehistoric setting, the specifics of these activities must remain conjectural.

Great houses

Over their three centuries of occupation, the great houses in Chaco Canyon must have represented many social ideas for different audiences. During the Classic Bonito phase, at least one of the functions of great houses seems to have involved memory. As noted above, there are several well-defined construction phases in the canyon (Lekson 1984; Windes and Ford 1992). Late eleventh-century construction patterns in Chaco Canyon are marked not so much by new construction as by repeated, formal, massive additions to existing great houses, some of which were established as much as 135 years earlier. Sebastian (1992) argues that these new construction patterns correspond to the rise of institutionalized leadership at Chaco. Clearly those who directed construction were concerned with maintaining and enhancing buildings initiated in an earlier time.

A direct link between memory and social power is suggested by the burial of two individuals beneath Room 33 in Pueblo Bonito (figure 9.2). There are relatively few burials at Chaco overall, and most contain little in the way of grave goods. These two men, however, were buried with thousands of pieces of turquoise and shell jewelry (Judd 1954:338–9; Pepper 1909, 1920). The two were interred during the late eleventh century, but they were placed in a room in the original late ninth-century section of Pueblo Bonito, which was at that time nearly 200 years old. These men were accorded special treatment with respect to grave goods; their placement in the oldest part of the central great house in Chaco Canyon is likely to have had special meaning.

The continued use and embellishment of great houses that were centuries old indicate concerns with conservatism and continuity that fit hand in hand with legitimation of authority through unbroken connections with the past. But great houses, with their shifting, myriad possible functions and uses, are somewhat unwieldy venues at which to examine the construction of memory. Let us turn now to other

Bonito-style architectural features – earthworks, great kivas, and road segments – where this process is evidenced even more clearly.

Earthworks

Earthworks at Chacoan great houses come in two varieties. Formal mounds are located in front of some canyon great houses such as Pueblo Bonito (figure 9.2) and Pueblo Alto. Encircling berms built of sterile earth, trash, and construction debris are found around some outlier great houses, particularly in the southern part of the San Juan Basin. The relationship between the two is not clear, but both are likely to have symbolic importance that involves memory.

Trash middens are part of a formal spatial arrangement visible at habitation sites from Pueblo I times onward, when occupants began routinely placing their garbage in front of dwellings, to the southeast. Congruent with worldviews that emphasize cyclicality and continuity with ancestors, many contemporary Puebloan peoples believe refuse must be carefully returned to the earth and treated with respect. Thus, middens are sacred space, and shrines are often located there (Cameron 2002; Ellis 1966, Ortiz 1969). In Ancestral Pueblo times, human burials often were placed within middens (e.g., Akins 1986; Roberts 1939).

By contrast, the formal mounds in front of many eleventh-century Chaco Canyon great houses are in the right location for trash middens, but their contents do not resemble domestic garbage (Windes 1987). Unlike trash middens at small domestic sites, these mounds rarely contain burials. Their stratigraphy suggests intermittent, perhaps annual, episodes of intense deposition. Mounds such as those in front of Pueblo Alto contain unusually high concentrations of broken utility jars, providing some of the strongest evidence for periodic feasting at canyon great houses (Toll 1985, 2001; Windes 1987; but see Wills 2001 for a different view). Given the sacred nature of refuse in contemporary Puebloan contexts, and the formal construction of some mounds at canyon great houses, it is likely that these features were connected in some way with ritual activities or beliefs. And given that refuse is material that was used in the immediate past, it is likely that trash mounds served as tangible reminders of specific past ritual events.

The second type of earthwork – encircling berms, or nazha – is found at some outlier great houses (Cameron 2002; Stein and Lekson 1992). Berms are often discontinuous, with breaks to admit road segments (figure 9.3). They have been speculated to demarcate sacred space, or to represent the walls of Chaco Canyon (Stein and Lekson 1992). It is often unclear from surface indications whether berms are continuous with midden deposits or are separate earthen constructions. This is true of the berm at the Andrews great house in the southern San Juan Basin, where an earthwork is covered with dense trash deposits, yet appears more formalized and distinct from earlier, amorphous middens nearby (Van Dyke 1999a). In the rare instances where outlier berms have been excavated, the earthworks have been found to consist of a confusing array of trash, ash, sterile earth, stone spalls and construction debris (Cameron 2002).

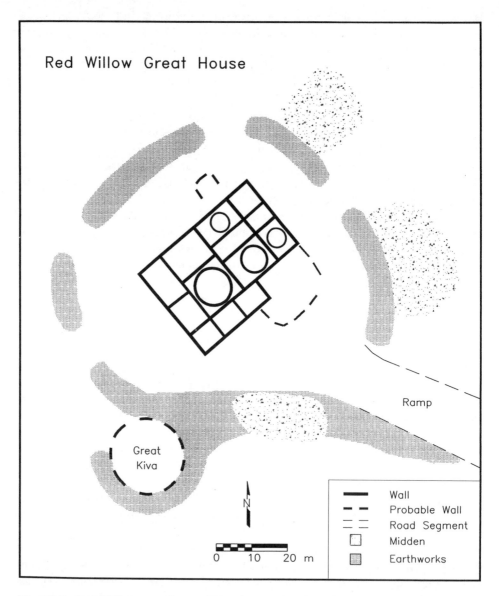

Figure 9.2 Red Willow great house. (From base map by Marshall and Sofaer [1988]; modified and redrawn by the author)

As noted, outlier great houses often appeared during the eleventh century in the midst of older, established communities. If, as I have argued above, the appearance of these structures is related to a shift towards inequality in the social order, great house builders seeking legitimacy could have profited from symbolic references to long-term continuity. Following this notion, John Roney (personal communication, 2000) offers the intriguing speculation that some outlier berms might represent false midden deposits. Earthworks in front of the great house, where the trash midden is *supposed* to be, could have been constructed largely of sterile earth and great house construction debris, and then covered with a thin veneer of trash. The construction of large, formalized, "fake" refuse deposits is the literal construction of a past where none existed before. The landscape would have been manipulated to create, out of whole cloth, a semblance of social continuity.

The Classic Bonito phase great kiva revival

Great kivas are round, semi-subterranean structures considered to represent integrative spaces, where groups engaged in social, ritual, or economic activities (Adler 1989; Adler and Wilshusen 1990; Hegmon 1989). The earliest great kivas – very large, circular, slab-lined pitstructures – are documented in Basketmaker III (450–700 AD) communities in Chaco Canyon, the San Juan Basin, and adjacent areas (Reed 2000). The great kiva at Shabik'eschee Village, a Basketmaker III site in Chaco Canyon, is fairly typical (Roberts 1929; Wills and Windes 1989). Social organization is likely to have been cooperative and communal in the small farming villages of the Basketmaker III period. These circular spaces would have been good facilities for face-to-face interactions, community meetings, and ritual performances.

Great kivas were relatively scarce in Chaco Canyon during the Pueblo I period (700–900 AD), although they did continue in other parts of the Ancestral Pueblo world. In the Classic Bonito phase, however, there was a dramatic burst of great kiva construction in the canyon. During this period, 12 great kivas were built in association with six canyon great houses, and four more were built in "isolated" contexts more than 100 m from a great house (Vivian and Reiter 1960). The Classic Bonito phase great kiva is a revival and formalization of the antecedent architectural form.

Classic Bonito phase great kivas such as Casa Rinconada exhibit highly formalized, distinctive features (figure 9.4). Dimensions (15–20 m in diameter) are fairly uniform and are unrelated to surrounding community population size (Van Dyke 2002). When associated with a great house, great kivas are often located in an open space or plaza to the south or southeast. Walls are of the same core-and-veneer masonry used in great house construction. Great kivas were roofed by means of four timber or masonry pillars that supported a log framework overlain with layers of smaller posts, bark, and earth. Standardized floor and wall features include an encircling masonry bench, wall niches, paired masonry floor vaults, a central elevated masonry firebox, and four roof support seating pits. Great kivas usually are oriented on a north/south axis, with entry by means of an antechamber to the north. Floor vaults, seating pits, and niches generally express bilateral symmetry along the north/south kiva axis. Like great houses, earthworks, and road segments, great kivas were constructed during the Classic Bonito phase in outlier communities throughout the San Juan Basin and adjacent areas (Fowler et al. 1987; Herr 1994; Marshall et al. 1979:263–328; Powers et al. 1983; Van Dyke 2002). Most excavated examples exhibit the same uniformity in size, orientation, symmetry, and interior features noted

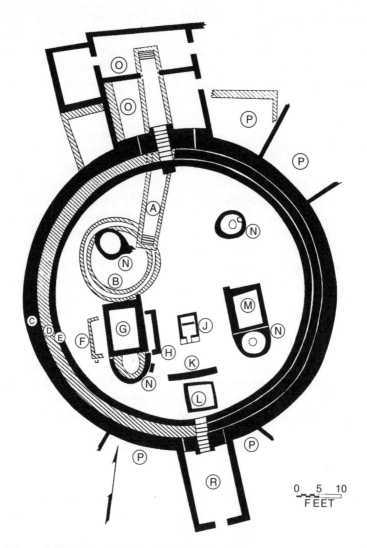

Figure 9.3 Plan of the great kiva Casa Rinconada, illustrating floor features. (A) subfloor passage, (B) circular trench, (C) outer wall, (D) original bench, (E) later bench veneer, (F) earlier partial vault, (G) west vault, (H) vault extension, (J) firebox, (K) fire screen, (L) subfloor enclosure, (M) east vault, (N) seating pits for roof support columns, (O) north antechamber, (P) partial peripheral rooms, (R) south antechamber. (From Vivian and Reiter [1960: 10, Figure 4], reproduced by permission of the School of American Research Press)

in great kivas in Classic Bonito phase Chaco Canyon (e.g., Eddy 1977; Irwin–Williams and Shelley 1980; Martin 1936; Morris 1921; Peckham 1958; Roberts 1932).

Multiple lines of evidence suggest the structures were venues for ritual. Contemporary kivas are used today for ceremonial purposes by Puebloan peoples. Caches of turquoise, beads, and other items found in sealed wall niches and at the base of seating pits in some great kivas are best interpreted as votive deposits. Some great kivas appear to possess acoustic properties that would have lent themselves well to ceremonial activities. Floor vaults may have been used as foot drums, overlain with wooden planks that would make a booming noise when people jumped or danced atop them. A subterranean passageway leading into a screened area in the great kiva at Casa Rinconada would have facilitated surprise entrances at dramatic moments (figure 9.4).

Perhaps the strongest evidence for the use of great kivas as stages for ritual events is found in the standardization of size, orientation, layout, and interior features described above. Religious architecture tends to be conservative, incorporating iconographic material symbols easily recognized by ceremonial participants and observers. Great kivas fit Adler and Wilshusen's (1990:135–6) conception of high-level integrative facilities, in which the area of a space used for ritual does not fluctuate with population size but is part of a suite of uniform characteristics. Abstract, religious ideas are often communicated through repetition in the inscribed memory processes discussed by Rowlands (1993). Thus it is likely that the repetitive, conservative, increasingly formalized iconographic form of the great kiva was more important to the builders than the mere need to establish a meeting space. Great kivas represented a shared idea and provided a locus for a suite of religious activities that crosscut other differences within the canyon as well as among the outliers.

The repetitive iconography inside great kivas is likely to have conveyed symbolic messages to ritual participants. One of these messages, I argue, involved the construction of a social continuum extending from the Classic Bonito phase back three hundred years or more. The boom in great kiva construction during the 1000s AD is an example of Chacoan leaders' use of architecture to reference the more egalitarian Pueblo I and Basketmaker III past. These circular, subterranean structures evoke earlier, communal ideologies and integrative practices, helping to naturalize new and unequal distributions of labor, surplus, and prestige.

The round shape of these structures would seem to have facilitated social interaction, which is why great kivas are often termed integrative spaces. This may well have been the case in earlier periods, but I contend an association between great kivas and social integration during the Classic Bonito phase may be intentionally misleading. Classic Bonito phase great kivas pose a curious contradiction between exclusionary and inclusive space: the structures would not have been ideal venues for open public events on the scale of those envisioned at Chaco which, using conservative population estimates, might easily have involved two thousand people (Lekson 1988). Ritual events accessible to thousands could have taken place in great house plazas, on roofs, or on top of mounds, but not in great kivas – using an estimate of 1 sq. m of floor space per person, only about 250 people could have fit in a great kiva with an 18 m diameter floor such as Casa Rinconada. The actual number may have been even smaller, as this estimate discounts the area taken up by the floor features and leaves no room for activities inside the structure, although people may have crushed together in tight proximity to witness events in the structure's center. There were up to ten great kivas in Chaco Canyon that may have been in contemporaneous use during the Classic Bonito phase; by the same calculations, canyon great kivas could have accommodated a more reasonable total of 2,500 people, if simultaneous events were held in all of them at the same time. If that was the case, however, which people visited which great kiva? Were all great kivas of equal status? It seems likely that there was an exclusionary character to the activities that took place in these structures. Ritual associated with great kivas may well have been part of a larger set of beliefs that drew people together, but this process was not uniform, nor was it monolithic.

Roads to ruins

One of the strongest illustrations of the use of landscape elements to construct social memory during the Classic Bonito phase is found in the Red Willow outlier community, approximately 70 km southwest of Chaco Canyon. In this community, a road segment was built to link a Classic Bonito phase great house with an abandoned early Pueblo II period great kiva several miles away (figure 9.5).

The Red Willow great house is an imposing structure built of core-and-veneer sandstone masonry (Marshall and Sofaer 1988:142–3). The collapsed building retains a topographic relief of at least 4 m. It contains an estimated seven large (24 sq. m or larger) ground-floor rooms, two second-story rooms, three enclosed ground-floor kivas, and one second-story kiva (figure 9.3). The surrounding landscape has been extensively modified. A trash-covered berm encircles the great house, and a great kiva 19 m in diameter is found immediately to the southwest. Several small room blocks are located on the mesa top behind the great house to the west. This imposing complex of features sits on the southeast edge of a small mesa overlooking the broad, gray-green expanse of Tohatchi Flats. Surface ceramics indicate that two temporal components are present at the great house. An early Pueblo II (900–1040 AD) ceramic group is dominated by Red Mesa Black-on-white and plain grayware. A Classic Bonito phase (1040–1100 AD) ceramic group is dominated by Gallup Black-on-white and indented corrugated, with small quantities of Chaco Black-on-white, Mesa Verde White Ware and White Mountain Red Ware. Mean ceramic dates for 1172 sherds from eight sample units cluster around 930 AD and 1090 AD, respectively. The ceramic evidence supports a picture of the Red Willow great house as a Classic Bonito phase structure established in the late eleventh century in the midst of an early tenth-century community, perhaps on top of an earlier building.

The great house berm articulates with a ramp that extends downslope off the edge of the mesa to the east. This ramp leads down to a road segment that extends across the valley for approximately 2.5 km, climbs a neighboring mesa, and ends at the isolated Los Rayos great kiva (Marshall and Sofaer 1988:42–5). The great kiva depression is 18 m in diameter. Associated features include three cairns, an extensive midden, and a number of discontiguous surface rooms. The ceramic assemblage is from the early Pueblo II period and is dominated by Red Mesa Black-on-white and plain gray ware.

It has not been possible to determine a direct date for the road segment itself. The high volume of sheet trash in this valley, from occupations ranging from Basketmaker III through early Pueblo III times, precludes dating the road by means of surface

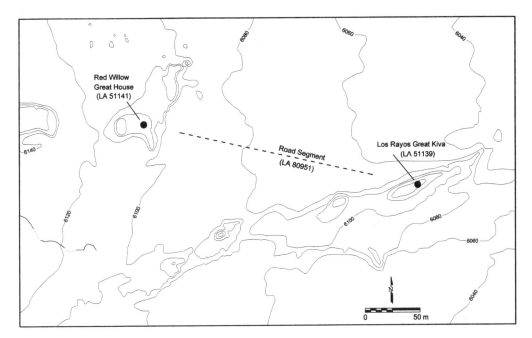

Map 9.2   The Red Willow–Los Rayos road on Tohatchi Flats (drawn by the author and Chuck Riggs)

ceramics. No subsurface road materials were discovered when a backhoe trench was excavated across this feature in 1991 (Kearns 1991). Given the ceramic dates for the sites at either end of the feature, one logical conclusion would be that the road was built during the early Pueblo II period to link the great kiva with the early Pueblo II settlement under Red Willow. However, the construction of Chacoan roads and road-related features is generally considered instead to date from the Classic Bonito phase. Furthermore, the Red Willow – Los Rayos road is articulated with the eleventh-century berm surrounding the Red Willow great house, arguing strongly for an eleventh-century road construction date. In either case, the Classic Bonito phase great house builders deliberately used or – more likely – outright created a physical link with the early Pueblo II great kiva across the valley.

What better way for great house builders to legitimate social inequality at Red Willow than through the construction of a physical connection with the community's past? Because the construction of Chacoan social power involved ritual, it would have made sense to appropriate ancestral ritual facilities as part of this process. The road, visible from both sites, would have been an ideal stage for processions that may have been an important part of Chacoan ritual. Construction of the Red Willow – Los Rayos road (or at the very least, the ramp and earthworks articulating with the road) during the Classic Bonito phase engaged the Early Pueblo II past to enhance authority in the Classic Bonito phase present. Furthermore, this connection to the past could have helped consolidate local social identity as inhabitants watched, or participated in, ritual processions. The population of outlier communities such as Red Willow probably fluctuated throughout the Chacoan era, as new people were attracted to the settlement and others left. Participation in ritual activities and processions would have been a useful way to draw disparate community inhabitants together while creating the illusion of a common past.

Summary and Discussion

During the Classic Bonito phase in Chaco Canyon and surrounding areas, peoples' experiences of architecture and landscape were integral to the recursive construction of ideologies that supported new social configurations. Spatial evidence indicates the Chacoan past was referenced in several ways as part of an appeal to social continuity that legitimated inequality and consolidated community identity. Additions to great houses in Chaco Canyon over the course of three centuries maintained physical continuity with past events and ancestors. Mounds and berms served as tangible reminders of the immediate past. Great kivas were formally incorporated into great house design as an overt reference to earlier, more communal forms of architecture. In at least one documented instance, a road segment linked the Chacoan present with a great kiva from a century before; other examples of this phenomenon surely await documentation. In these ways, architecture and landscape referenced social memory, creating both tangible and symbolic connections with ancestral spaces, events, and beliefs.

It is difficult in this prehistoric context to move beyond the simplistic argument, "memory was here," to contemplate diverse social messages, interpretations, and reactions. Here we have been concerned primarily with memory messages imposed "from the top down" in the interests of authority and identity, but it is unlikely that memory was constructed in such a monolithic fashion. Who led ritual processions between Red Willow and Los Rayos across Tohatchi Flats, and how were they chosen? Who had entrée into which great kivas, and what kinds of ceremonies went on inside? Who were the men buried under Room 33? What kinds of meanings – challenging, supportive, or both – did participants and observers ascribe to these moments of embodied memory? Although we may not be able to answer these questions, we should not forget to ask them.

Memory probably figured into the construction of social identity, but the process must have been complex and varied. While participation in ritual events may have helped consolidate a sense of identity among the disparate peoples who gathered periodically at Chaco, the exclusionary aspects of great kivas discussed above would have at the same time set some individuals or groups apart from others. At outliers, the appearance of Chacoan architecture seems closely related to the coalescence of community. And, at a regional level, the iconic, easily recognizable forms of great houses and great kivas, road segments and berms link together outlier settlements over a vast area. Outlier residents may have shared a bond of participation in annual or seasonal events at Chaco Canyon, but it seems unlikely that all members of Chacoan society participated in equal capacities in these events.

In some of the instances described here, Chacoans reused and appropriated places and architectural forms that had been abandoned for one or more centuries. Without texts, it is not possible to see whether memories of specific individuals or events were retained over this period. However, the Chacoan situation is unlikely to be an example of disjunctive memory, like Prent's Early Iron Age cult activities at Bronze Age sites, or Meskell's Roman burials in an Egyptian house (both in this volume). Puebloan culture was not static and unchanging, but there is a great deal of material continuity stretching from 450 AD through to the present. Threads of meaning undoubtedly were altered considerably across this time, but it is unlikely that they were snapped off entirely, to be replaced by new and invented memories.

Memory beyond Chaco

Spatial references to social memory in the Southwest are not limited to the Chacoan era. Chaco's influence continued well after the canyon had waned as a center; as with Vijayanagara (Sinopoli, this volume), references to Chaco are made through built features that I would argue constitute part of the continuing construction of social memory during post-Chacoan times. Kintigh (1994), for example, has argued that the great kiva form was used as a symbolic reference to Chaco during later periods of Puebloan aggregation. In the thirteenth century, in eastern Arizona some 200 miles southwest of Chaco, Herr (2001) speculates that very large, possibly unroofed great kivas were built to attract migrant settlers by reminding them of the Chacoan past. In Manuelito Canyon near Gallup, New Mexico, Fowler and Stein (1992) have documented a post-Chacoan road segment linking Atse'e Nitsaa, a thirteenth- to fourteenth-century structure, with Kin Hocho'i, a twelfth-century Chacoan great house. Additional roads linking Chacoan and post-Chacoan sites are known from eastern Arizona and the Four Corners area (Fowler and Stein 1992:117). In a rather controversial scenario, Lekson (1999) has postulated that the late thirteenth- to fourteenth-century center of Paquimé, located 630 km due south of Chaco Canyon in northern Chihuahua, was deliberately sited in spatial reference to the canyon along a north/south "Chaco meridian." Although Lekson's argument is problematic in a number of respects, his proposed linear, spatial association between sites across time is quite in keeping with the tenets of Classic Bonito phase Chacoan cosmographic expression as discussed here. As post-Chacoan social actors employed architecture and landscape to reference the Chacoan past, their aims and purposes undoubtedly shifted from those I have presented for the Classic Bonito phase – memory in the post-Chacoan world is a topic deserving its own due consideration.

Southwestern scholars are increasingly recognizing that spatial perception and experience are critical to interpretations of Chacoan society. Discussions around social power at Chaco have begun to move past the polarized debates of past decades as we begin to think more creatively about how inequalities were produced and legitimated. Although intangibles such as social memory are difficult to address prehistorically, I have demonstrated here that multiple lines of spatial evidence support

its meaningful presence in the Chacoan world. I encourage my colleagues to consider the role of memory in constructing interpretations for prehistoric societies
beyond Chaco in the North American Southwest.

References Cited

Adler, M. A. 1989: Ritual facilities and social integration in nonranked societies. In *The Architecture of Social Integration in Prehistoric Pueblos*, ed. W. D. Lipe and M. Hegmon. Cortez, Colo.:
Occasional Papers of the Crow Canyon Archaeological Center 1, pp. 35–52.

Adler, M. A. and Wilshusen, R. H. 1990: Large-scale integrative facilities in tribal societies:
cross-cultural and southwestern U.S. examples. *World Archaeology* 22, pp. 133–46.

Akins, N. J. 1986: *A Biocultural Approach to Human Burials from Chaco Canyon, New Mexico.*
Reports of the Chaco Center 9. Santa Fe: National Park Service.

Basso, K. H. 1996: *Wisdom Sits in Places: Landscape and Language among the Western Apache.* Albuquerque: University of New Mexico Press.

Bourdieu, P. 1977: *Outline of a Theory of Practice.* Cambridge: Cambridge University Press.

Brandt, E. 1977: The role of secrecy in a Puebloan society. In *Flowers in the Wind: Papers on
Ritual, Myth, and Symbolism in California and the Southwest*, ed. T. C. Blackburn. Socorro, N.
Mex.: Ballena Press, Anthropological Papers 8.

Brandt, E. 1980: On secrecy and the control of knowledge: Taos Pueblo. In *Secrecy: A Cross-
Cultural Perspective*, ed. S. K. Tefft. New York: Human Sciences Press.

Brandt, E. 1994: Egalitarianism, hierarchy, and centralization in the Pueblos. In *The Ancient
Southwestern Community: Models and Methods for the Study of Prehistoric Social Organization*, ed.
W. H. Wills and R. D. Leonard. Albuquerque: University of New Mexico Press, pp. 9–23.

Cameron, C. M. 2002: Sacred earthen architecture in the northern Southwest: the Bluff great
house berm. *American Antiquity* 67(4), pp. 677–95.

Casey, E. S. 1996: How to get from space to place in a fairly short stretch of time: phenomenological prolegomena. In *Senses of Place*, ed. S. Feld and K. H. Basso. Santa Fe: School of
American Research Press, pp. 13–52.

Connerton, P. 1989: *How Societies Remember.* Cambridge: Cambridge University Press.

Cushing, F. H. 1883: Zuni fetiches. In *Second Annual Report of the Bureau of American Ethnology
for the Years 1880–1881.* Washington, D.C.: Government Printing Office, reprinted (1966) by
KC Publications, Flagstaff, pp. 3–45.

Cushing, F. H. 1896: Outlines of Zuni creation myths. In *Thirteenth Annual Report of the Bureau
of American Ethnology for the Years 1891–1892.* Washington, D.C.: Government Printing Office,
pp. 321–447.

De Certeau, M. 1984: *The Practice of Everyday Life*, trans. S. Rendall. Berkeley and Los Angeles:
University of California Press.

Eddy, F. W. 1977: *Archaeological Investigations at Chimney Rock Mesa, 1970–72.* Boulder: Memoirs
of the Colorado Archaeological Society 1.

Ellis, F. H. 1966: The immediate history of Zia Pueblo as derived from excavation in refuse
deposits. *American Antiquity* 31(6), pp. 806–11.

Ellis, R. (ed.) 1997: *Stories and Stone: Writing the Anasazi Homeland.* Boulder, Colo.: Pruett
Publishers.

Fowler, A. P. and Stein, J. R. 1992: The Anasazi great house in space, time, and paradigm. In
Anasazi Regional Organization and the Chaco System, ed. D. E. Doyel. Albuquerque: Maxwell
Museum of Anthropology Anthropological Papers 5, pp. 101–22.

Fowler, A., Stein, J. R. and Anyon, R. 1987: *An Archaeological Reconnaissance of West-Central New Mexico: The Anasazi Monuments Project*. Albuquerque: Office of Cultural Affairs, Historic Preservation Division.

Gladwin, H. S. 1945: *The Chaco Branch: Excavations at White Mound and in the Red Mesa Valley. Medallion Papers* 33. Globe: Gila Pueblo.

Gosden, C. 1994: *Social Being and Time*. Oxford: Blackwell.

Hegmon, M. 1989: Social integration and architecture. In *The Architecture of Social Integration in Prehistoric Pueblos*, ed. W. D. Lipe and M. Hegmon. Cortez, Colorado: Occasional Papers of the Crow Canyon Archaeological Center 1, pp. 5–14.

Heidegger, M. 1962: *Being and Time*, trans. J. Macquarrie and E. Robinson. Oxford: Blackwell.

Herr, S. A. 1994: Great Kivas as Integrative Architecture in the Silver Creek Community, Arizona. M. A. thesis, Department of Anthropology, University of Arizona, Tucson.

Herr, S. A. 2001: *Beyond Chaco: Great Kiva Communities on the Mogollon Rim Frontier*. Anthropological Papers of the University of Arizona 66. Tucson: University of Arizona Press.

Hobsbawm, E. J. and Ranger, T. (eds.) 1983: *The Invention of Tradition*. Cambridge: Cambridge University Press.

Irwin-Williams, C. and Shelley, P. H. (eds.) 1980: *Investigations at the Salmon Site: The Structure of Chacoan Society in the Northern Southwest*. Portales: Eastern New Mexico University Printing Services.

Judd, N. M. 1954: *The Material Culture of Pueblo Bonito*. Washington, D.C.: Smithsonian Miscellaneous Collections 124.

Judd, N. M. 1964: *The Architecture of Pueblo Bonito*. Washington, D.C.: Smithsonian Miscellaneous Collections 147(1).

Judge, W. J. 1989: Chaco Canyon – San Juan Basin. In *Dynamics of Southwest Prehistory*, ed. L. S. Cordell and G. J. Gumerman. Washington, D.C.: Smithsonian Institution, pp. 209–61.

Judge, W. J., Gillespie, W. B., Lekson, S. H. and Toll, H. W. 1981: Tenth century developments in Chaco Canyon. In *Collected Papers in Honor of Erik Kellerman Reed*. Papers of the Archaeological Society of New Mexico 6. Albuquerque: Archaeological Society Press.

Kantner, J. 1996: Political competition among the Chaco Anasazi of the American Southwest. *Journal of Anthropological Archaeology* 15, pp. 41–105.

Kearns, T. M. 1991: *Pipeline Archaeology Revisited: Anthropological Investigations along the El Paso Natural Gas San Juan Expansion Project, New Mexico and Arizona. Division of Conservation Archaeology Technical Report #2504*. Farmington, N. Mex.: San Juan County Museum Association.

Kintigh, K. W. 1994: Chaco, communal architecture, and Cibolan aggregation. In *The Ancient Southwestern Community: Models and Methods for the Study of Prehistoric Social Organization*, ed. W. H. Wills and R. D. Leonard. Albuquerque: University of New Mexico Press, pp. 131–40.

Lefebvre, H. 1991: *The Production of Space*, trans. D. Nicholson-Smith. Oxford: Blackwell.

Lekson, S. H. 1984: *Great Pueblo Architecture of Chaco Canyon, New Mexico*. Albuquerque: University of New Mexico Press.

Lekson, S. H. 1988: *Sociopolitical Complexity at Chaco Canyon, New Mexico*. Ph.D. dissertation, University of New Mexico, Albuquerque.

Lekson, S. H. 1991: Settlement patterns and the Chaco region. In *Chaco and Hohokam: Prehistoric Regional Systems in the American Southwest*, ed. P. L. Crown and W. J. Judge. Santa Fe: School of American Research, pp. 31–55.

Lekson, S. H. 1999: *The Chaco Meridian: Centers of Political Power in the Ancient Southwest*. Walnut Creek, Calif.: Altamira Press.

Levy, J. E. 1992: *Orayvi Revisited: Social Stratification in an "Egalitarian" Society*. Santa Fe: School of American Research Press.

Marshall, M. P. 1997: The Chacoan roads: a cosmological interpretation. In *Anasazi Architecture and American Design*, ed. B. H. Morrow and V. B. Price. Albuquerque: University of New Mexico Press, pp. 62–74.

Marshall, M. P. and Sofaer, A. 1988: *Solstice Project Investigations in the Chaco District 1984 and 1985: The Technical Report*. Ms. on file, Laboratory of Anthropology, Santa Fe, New Mexico.

Marshall, M. P., Stein, J. R., Loose, R. W. and Novotny, J. E. 1979: *Anasazi Communities of the San Juan Basin*. Albuquerque: Public Service Company of New Mexico.

Martin, P. S. 1936: *Lowry Ruin in Southwestern Colorado*. Chicago: Field Museum of Natural History Anthropological Series 23(1).

Merleau-Ponty, M. 1981[1962]: *Phenomenology of Perception*, trans. C. Smith. London: Routledge and Kegan Paul.

Mills, B. J. 2002: Recent research on Chaco: changing views on economy, ritual, and power. *Journal of Archaeological Research* 10(1), pp. 65–117.

Morris, E. H. 1921: *The House of the Great Kiva at the Aztec Ruin*. New York: Anthropological Papers of the American Museum of Natural History 26, Part II.

Ortiz, A. 1969: *The Tewa World: Space, Time, Being, and Becoming in a Pueblo Society*. Chicago: University of Chicago Press.

Peckham, S. L. 1958: Salvage archaeology in New Mexico 1957–1958: a partial report. *El Palacio* 65(5), pp. 161–4.

Pepper, G. H. 1909: The exploration of a burial room in Pueblo Bonito, New Mexico. In *Anthropological Essays Presented to Frederick Ward Putnam in Honor of His Seventieth Birthday*. New York: G. E. Stechert and Company, pp. 196–252.

Pepper, G. H. 1920: *Pueblo Bonito*. Washington, D.C.: Anthropological Papers of the American Museum of Natural History, Volume 27.

Powers, R. P., Gillespie, W. B. and Lekson, S. H. 1983: *The Outlier Survey: A Regional View of Settlement in the San Juan Basin. Reports of the Chaco Center* 3. Albuquerque: U.S. Department of the Interior, National Park Service.

Reed, P. F. (ed.) 2000: *Foundations of Anasazi Culture: The Basketmaker – Pueblo Transition*. Salt Lake City: University of Utah Press.

Renfrew, C. 2001: Production and consumption in a sacred economy: the material correlates of high devotional expression at Chaco Canyon. *American Antiquity* 66(1), pp. 14–25.

Roberts, F. H. H., Jr. 1929: *Shabik'eschee Village: A Late Basket Maker Site in the Chaco Canyon, New Mexico*. Washington, D.C.: Bureau of American Ethnology Bulletin 92.

Roberts, F. H. H., Jr. 1932: *The Village of the Great Kivas on the Zuni Reservation, New Mexico*. Washington, D.C.: Bureau of American Ethnology Bulletin 111.

Roberts, F. H. H., Jr. 1939: *Archaeological Remains in the Whitewater District, Eastern Arizona. Part I: House Types*. Washington, D.C.: Bureau of American Ethnology Bulletin 121.

Roney, J. R. 1992: Prehistoric roads and regional integration in the Chacoan system. In *Anasazi Regional Organization and the Chaco System*, ed. D. E. Doyel. Albuquerque: Maxwell Museum of Anthropology Anthropological Papers 5, pp. 123–32.

Rowlands, M. 1993: The role of memory in the transmission of culture. *World Archaeology* 25(2), pp. 141–51.

Saitta, D. 1997: Power, labor, and the dynamics of change in Chacoan political economy. *American Antiquity* 62(1), pp. 7–26.

Sebastian, L. 1992: *The Chaco Anasazi: Sociopolitical Evolution in the Prehistoric Southwest*. Cambridge: Cambridge University Press.

Sinclair, R. M., Sofaer, A., McCann, J. J. and McCann, J. J., Jr. 1987: Marking of lunar major standstill at the three-slab site on Fajada Butte. *Bulletin of the American Astronomical Society* 19, p. 1043.

Smith, W. 1972: Prehistoric kivas of Antelope Mesa, Northeastern Arizona. *Papers of the Peabody Museum* 39, p. 120.

Snead, J. E. and Preucel, R. W. 1999: The ideology of settlement: ancestral Keres landscapes in the northern Rio Grande. In *Archaeologies of Landscape: Contemporary Perspectives*, ed. W. Ashmore and A. Bernard Knapp. Oxford: Blackwell, pp. 169–97.

Sofaer, A. 1997: The primary architecture of the Chacoan culture: a cosmological expression. In *Anasazi Architecture and American Design*, ed. B. T. Morrow and V. B. Price. Albuquerque: University of New Mexico Press, pp. 88–132.

Sofaer, A., Sinclair, R. and Doggett, L. 1982: Lunar markings on Fajada Butte, Chaco Canyon, New Mexico. In *Archaeoastronomy in the New World*, ed. A. F. Aveni. Cambridge: Cambridge University Press, pp. 169–81.

Sofaer, A., Zinser, V. and Sinclair, R. M. 1979: A unique solar marking construct. *Science* 206, pp. 283–91.

Soja, E. W. 1996: *Thirdspace*. Oxford: Blackwell.

Stein, J. R. and Lekson, S. H. 1992: Anasazi ritual landscapes. In *Anasazi Regional Organization and the Chaco System*, ed. D. E. Doyel. Albuquerque: Maxwell Museum of Anthropology Anthropological Papers 5, pp. 87–100.

Thomas, J. 1996: *Time, Culture, and Identity*. London: Routledge.

Tilley, C. 1994: *A Phenomenology of Landscape*. Oxford & Providence: Berg.

Toll, H. W. 1985: *Pottery, Production, and the Chacoan Anasazi System*. Ph.D. dissertation, University of Colorado. Ann Arbor, Mich.: University Microfilms.

Toll, H. W. 2001: Making and breaking pots in the Chaco world. *American Antiquity* 66(1), pp. 56–78.

Van Dyke, R. M. 1999a: The Andrews community: an early Bonito phase Chacoan outlier in the Red Mesa Valley, New Mexico. *Journal of Field Archaeology* 26(1), pp. 55–67.

Van Dyke, R. M. 1999b: The Chaco connection: evaluating Bonito-style architecture in outlier communities. *Journal of Anthropological Archaeology* 18(4), pp. 471–506.

Van Dyke, R. M. 2000: Chacoan ritual landscapes: the view from the Red Mesa Valley. In *Great House Communities across the Chacoan Landscape*, ed. J. Kantner and N. Mahoney. Anthropological Papers of the University of Arizona 65. Tucson: University of Arizona Press, pp. 91–100.

Van Dyke, R. M. 2002: The Chacoan great kiva in outlier communities: investigating integrative spaces across the San Juan Basin. *Kiva* 67(3), pp. 231–48.

Van Dyke, R. M. 2003: *Lived Landscapes: Memory, Phenomenology, and Chacoan Society*. Santa Fe: School of American Research Press.

Vivian, G. R. and Reiter, P. 1960: *The Great Kivas of Chaco Canyon and Their Relationships*. Santa Fe: Monographs of the School of American Research and the Museum of New Mexico 22.

Vivian, R. G. 1990: *The Chacoan Prehistory of the San Juan Basin*. New York: Academic Press.

White, L. A. 1960: The world of the Keresan Pueblo Indians. In *Culture in History: Essays in Honor of Paul Radin*, ed. S. Diamond. New York: Columbia University Press, pp. 53–64.

Whiteley, P. M. 1985: Unpacking Hopi "clans:" another vintage model out of Africa? *Journal of Anthropological Research* 41(4), pp. 359–74.

Whitely, P. M. 1986: Unpacking Hopi "clans," II: further questions about Hopi descent groups. *Journal of Anthropological Research* 42(1), pp. 69–79.

Wills, W. H. 2001: Ritual and mound formation during the Bonito phase in Chaco Canyon. *American Antiquity* 66(3), pp. 433–51.

Wills, W. H. and Windes, T. C. 1989: Evidence for population aggregation and dispersal during the Basketmaker III period in Chaco Canyon, New Mexico. *American Antiquity* 54(2), pp. 347–69.

Windes, T. C. 1987: *Investigations at the Pueblo Alto Complex, Chaco Canyon, New Mexico, 1975–1979. Chaco Canyon Studies, Publications in Archeology* 18F. Santa Fe: National Park Service.

Windes, T. C. and Ford, D. 1992: The nature of the Early Bonito phase. In *Anasazi Regional Organization and the Chaco System*, ed. D. E. Doyel. Albuquerque: Maxwell Museum of Anthropology Anthropological Papers 5, pp. 75–86.

Part III
Caveats and Commentaries

10
The Familiar Honeycomb: Byzantine Era Reuse of Sicily's Prehistoric Rock-Cut Tombs

Emma Blake

In Sicily one might find, all within a few miles of each other, the castle of
some newly-created baron, an Arab village, an ancient Greek or Roman city
and a recent Lombard colony . . . (La Lumia 1867)

Introduction

Sicily's archaeological record testifies to the sustained ebb and flow of cultural waves
across the island. Bronze Age, Iron Age, Greek, Punic, Roman, Byzantine, Arab,
Norman – while these identifying labels occupy a temporal space within an un-
folding historical sequence, the material remnants of these periods often collide and
cannot be separated so neatly by dates. These remnants persist, anachronisms to be
encountered in subsequent periods. Nowadays these past materialities, be they buildings or field systems or cooking pots, are demystified through historical studies, rela-
beled as heritage, and institutionalized through government legislation, defining the
terms by which we experience them. We can well imagine that the interplay between
people and vestigial objects would have taken very different forms in the past in the
absence of the kind of contextual information of artifacts that we now possess. The
challenge is to interpret that interplay without projecting our modern-day experiences onto the past. Sicily's rich and varied assortment of remains from the diverse

I am grateful to Susan Alcock and Ruth Van Dyke for their invitation to participate in the
AIA session and subsequent volume, and for their extremely helpful editorial comments. I
would like to thank Lynn Meskell for reading and commenting on an earlier version of this
paper, Amy Papalexandrou for her illuminating suggestions, and Veronica Kalas for introducing
me to further reading on Byzantine troglodytism. Trinity Jackman deserves special mention for
accompanying me to Pantalica, suggesting useful comparative examples, and for her comments
on a draft. Research for this paper was conducted while I was at the Cotsen Institute of
Archaeology at UCLA and was completed at Stanford University. I would like to thank both
institutions for the support provided.

phases of its past afforded, indeed, *obliged* many such encounters. This study focuses on one incidence of contact with material of a previous period for the insights this offers into the preservation of meaning and memory in a particular locality.

In the Byzantine period, a number of Sicilian hypogea dating from the Bronze and Iron Ages were transformed into modest dwellings and Christian chapels. This reuse occurred after many centuries of abandonment, and in some cases involved reshaping the interior space, frescoing the tomb walls with Christian imagery, and carving a facade. That Christian peoples would voluntarily occupy pagan burial sites is, at first blush, surprising. This chapter explores the cultural context of this reuse and weighs possible explanations. Pantalica, the most famous and best-studied example of the phenomenon, serves as a case study in which the circumstances and nature of the reuse are examined in close detail.

Standard explanations, discussed below, attribute the tombs' later occupation to the poverty and desperation of the local peasantry, retreating in terror from the coasts because of pirate raids, while escaping the economic demands of the occupying groups: Byzantines, and later, the Arabs and Normans. Yet the data do not support this story. Given the evident symbolic power of past spaces, the reuse of these ancient pagan sites by Christian peoples begs several questions. Did some memory of the first use of the rock-cut tombs linger? If so, was this a deliberate referencing of the past, or even the symbolic absorption of a reviled pre-Christian heritage? If instead cultural ruptures had erased original meanings of the sites, was this reuse an attempt to appropriate the power of an unknown past? After weighing the evidence for these possible interpretations, this study offers an alternative approach. Rather than explaining the reuse in terms of either memory or forgetting, commemoration or devaluation, this paper highlights the familiarity of these older sites derived from their concrete presence in the landscape. It is argued that the situated materiality of the tombs, and their relevance in the spatialized practices of subsequent peoples, were of greater importance here than any remembered original meanings. The phenomenon of Byzantine era reuse of Sicily's rock-cut tombs provides a salient example of what at first glance would seem to be an evocation of insular collective memory, but actually is quite the opposite: a sweeping new and cosmopolitan cultural practice, troglodytism, that demonstrates Sicily's participation in the Byzantine world.

Sicily's Rock-Cut Tombs

The Sicilian practice of hewing funerary cavities out of live rock has a long history. The geological conditions clearly played a critical role: limestone, a soft, porous, and easily carvable material, is widespread on the island. It is in those zones of limestone terrain, primarily in the southeast, the northern interior, and the west, that rock-cut tombs are known from the third millennium BC Copper Age, and possibly from as far back as the Middle Neolithic. Presumably the method of construction would have been the same in prehistory as in later periods, with workers roughly hacking out a central cavity then shaping more carefully from within, adding decorative features and so on. There is great variety in the tombs: some are underground, accessed vertically, while others are dug into cliff faces with upright entrances. The tombs may be grouped or isolated, and their spatial relationships to settlements vary. Some tomb chambers housed no more than one or two bodies, while other, possibly later tombs were composed of multiple chambers linked by corridors. However they all share this funerary or, in some places, possible cult function: there is no evidence of hypogea used as residences in the prehistoric period. Burials were primarily inhumations, with a few items such as pottery and objects of adornment included as grave goods.

These tombs were used for centuries, and this longevity possibly reinforced ancestral ties (Leighton 1999:79). In this respect they are seen to serve a social function similar to that proposed for megalithic tombs. Indeed in some areas, such as Sardinia and certain zones of Southern Italy, both types of burial sites were in use at the same time (Whitehouse 1981:45). It was in the Bronze Age (2500–900 BC) that Sicily's rock-cut tombs reached their apogee in size, elaboration, and variety. They continued to be used well into the period of Greek colonization up to the sixth century BC, concurrently with newer burial practices such as jar inhumations and cremations in urns. While the hollows of these tombs still dot the hillsides of Sicily, tombs with intact contents are exceedingly rare. Though this tampering in later periods is an obvious source of frustration for archaeologists, it is proof that the tombs have been put back in circulation in later times.

Pantalica in Prehistory

The site of Pantalica is the largest example of these rock-cut necropoli in Sicily (Plate 10.1). It consists of over five thousand tombs carved into the steep slopes of a limestone plateau along the Anapo River Gorge in the southeastern part of the island. The site and associated settlement were apparently founded around 1250 BC, during the Middle to Late Bronze Age transition, and continued into the Iron Age.

Our knowledge of the site derives largely from the excavations of Paolo Orsi at the turn of the century (Orsi 1898, 1899a). Though the excavation reports of the time are frustratingly incomplete from our present-day perspective, Orsi's writings are nonetheless informative. The tomb size and form vary widely, including circular, semi-circular, and quadrangular forms. The hundred or so tombs that still contained deposits when excavated yielded mostly multiple interments, though some single burials are known. Bodies were apparently added over time, with older burials rearranged, possibly even removed in some cases, in order to make room for the new ones. There was a notable variety of grave goods including bronze tools and weapons and items of adornment, some gold and silver pieces, and pottery. Among the pottery, there were both local fine wares (including large pedestalled basins) and transport vessels, a number of which seem influenced by Mycenaean prototypes (Leighton 1999:167–8). One copy of a Mycenaean vase most resembles the LHIIIB-C type, dating to 1250–1000 BC, which fits the broad time frame of the site's use: this classification, however, is not secure and the vessel could be older (Leighton 1999:150). Variation in grave goods across tombs points to social stratification within the living community.

Plate 10.1 Pantalica view (photo by the author)

Domestic artifacts found on the summit of the plateau indicate the location of the settlement associated with these tombs. However, the largest structure, previously thought to be a monumental building contemporary with the necropolis, is now strongly suspected to be a Byzantine era farmstead superimposed on the prehistoric settlement. Pantalica continued in use through the Early and Middle Iron Ages, with a spread of tombs from the north slope to the south. Interestingly, the number of burials rose in the final phase of the site's use, in the late eighth and early seventh centuries BC, before activity at both the necropolis and settlement was curtailed around 650 BC. The timing coincides with the emergence of the Greek colonies nearby and perhaps corresponds to the Greek incorporation of Pantalica into the hinterland of Syracuse (Leighton 1999). Apart from a few fourth century BC finds pointing to some limited Hellenistic period activity, Pantalica's settlement thereafter apparently remained unoccupied for around 1300 years (Orsi 1899a:87). However, this site's abandonment would not have meant its disappearance: the site is dramatic enough that, visited or not, it would have certainly been a well-known sight and a landmark of the area.

Byzantine Sicily

After this long hiatus, in the Byzantine period we witness the phenomenon of sustained and extensive reuse of Pantalica's tombs. Before discussing this reuse, however, the historical context of Byzantine Sicily requires elaboration. In the political sense, Byzantine Sicily begins in 535 AD, when the island passed easily under Byzantine control as the general Belisarius annexed it on his way to the Italian mainland. The island remained part of this political system for almost 350 years, until the Arab takeover in 878 AD (Finley, Smith and Duggan 1987:51). Despite this extended occupation, information on Byzantine administration and culture in Sicily is surprisingly limited, particularly in the early years. Apart from some functionaries, troops, and a few traders, the Byzantine presence appears to have been slight. Contemporary sources do not mention Eastern immigrants, and there is little to suggest that the takeover had much initial impact on the island's social fabric, though it did usher in a period of peace for a hundred years, until the mid seventh century (Finley, Smith and Duggan 1987:48; Giunta 1974).

With time, however, Byzantine culture and art took hold in Sicily, and continued to be felt for several centuries after the political rule was over. The island's population was, from its Greek heritage, predisposed to Byzantine culture, and seems to have absorbed more and more of it over time. From their foundation (beginning in the late eighth century BC, the Greek colonies had interacted with local populations, resulting in a hybridized Greco-Sicilian culture that took different forms throughout the island. Preserved during the Roman period, Greek remained the dominant language in Byzantine times. That this language signaled a corresponding ethnic identification is suggested by the fact that native-born Sicilians who became popes were referred to in the annals as the "Greek" popes. And if Sicilians felt particular ties to the east, these appear to have been reciprocal. The city of Syracuse in particular played an important role in the Byzantine Empire. The center of Byzantine administration on Sicily, and the site of a Byzantine mint, Syracuse even briefly replaced Constantinople as capital of the Byzantine Empire from 663–8 AD (Christie 1989:262; Finley 1968:183).

Although the island itself was politically controlled from the East, the Sicilian church was allowed to remain under Western papal direction. The result was an interesting blend of eastern and western elements in Sicilian Christianity. Monasticism was introduced from the east. The eastern influence is also noted in the widespread resistance to the rule of celibacy among the clergy, a western innovation. Though a western-styled basilican plan predominated in Sicilian churches, architectural fragments suggest the popularity of design elements typical of the so-called Byzantine artistic style, in some cases imported wholesale from the east (Finley 1968:175–8). All in all, the evidence was such that Moses Finley (1968:178) in his history of Sicily was able to write that "By the second half of the seventh century the Sicilian church was Eastern in every important respect, including the liturgy and the ceremonies, other than its administrative attachment for a while longer to Rome." Clearly the religion, ethnicity, and practices of the island's inhabitants were imbued with hellenism, new and old. Thus the characterization "Byzantine" extended far beyond politics to encompass religion, language, art, and ideology.

The Byzantine Empire, of course, was only one of several foreign powers to control Sicily in the early Middle Ages. Byzantine political power was under threat from the second quarter of the ninth century, when the Arabs began their conquest of the island in earnest. This process ended fifty years later with Arab takeover, but Byzantine cultural influences on Sicily continued for many centuries after the Arab victory. The Arabs were tolerant towards other religions. They exacted a tribute from non-Moslem populations, and they generally allowed Byzantine practices to continue and Byzantine churches and liturgy to be maintained. Similarly, the Normans, who took over under Roger I in the late eleventh century AD, interfered little with established Byzantine practices. Though the Normans were merciless in their takeover of the island, once it was fully under their control, a period of peace and prosperity reigned that permitted Byzantine and Moslem cultures to flourish alongside the culture of the Latin west. While hostilities between the Norman rulers and the Byzantines to the east were quite common, Sicily maintained contact with the Byzantine Empire during the Norman period. Indeed, by all accounts the kingdom of Sicily was an incredibly culturally diverse place. The incorporation of many Greek and even Arabic elements into Norman churches testifies to this mix of influences (Norwich 1992:448–58). This ongoing cultural influence means that a "Byzantine" object may in fact belong to these subsequent political phases. Therefore, the reuse of the tombs may be said to be "Byzantine" in character while possibly belonging in some cases to periods after Byzantine rule had ended.

Byzantine Pantalica

After more or less bypassing the site for over a millennium, people returned to Pantalica in the Byzantine era. On the plateau itself, stone structures point to a large fortified farmstead with multiple rooms (Leighton 1999:155–7). On the slopes of the plateau, three separate agglomerations of dwellings and associated chapels were all carved into the cliffs alongside or incorporating the earlier tombs (Plate 10.2). Details of these settlements, and particularly of the chapels, are distinctly Byzantine.

The largest of the three settlement groupings – Filiporto – lay in the southwest of the complex and consisted of some 150 habitations. Interiors varied considerably, from multiple adjoining chambers, to single cells, with individual rooms ranging from 6.25 sq·m to 34 sq·m (Orsi 1898:19). The rooms in most cases had niches carved into the walls. Some structures were two stories high. Filiporto's chapel, known locally as S. Micidiario, has a central apse with two arched niches on either side (Plate 10.3). An irregular room flanks the church, which in turn is joined by a second room, possibly used as a latrine (Messina 1979:108). The wall paintings are in extremely poor shape, but traces of a Christ figure and two angels remain. A fragmentary inscription in Greek is visible – naming St. Merkourios, a popular subject of Byzantine wall paintings (Messina 1979:107–8).

The second and third groupings of dwellings are much smaller though each had its own chapel. The settlement grouping of S. Nicolicchio lies on the south slope of the plateau and consists of twenty or so living units (Orsi 1898:25–7). Though the chapel of S. Nicolicchio opens to the south, the apse is in fact east facing, placed at a right angle from the entrance. Its irregular form is explained by the fact that it occupies an older space that has been restructured. Despite the limitations imposed

Plate 10.2   Pantalica, Filiporto settlement complex: prehistoric tomb entrances with expanded Byzantine era doorway on the left (photo by the author)

by the aspect of the cliff face or the shape of the extant chamber, a majority of rock-cut churches share this eastward orientation, suggesting that a degree of conformity was sought, despite restrictions (Caprara 1970:110). The central apse and side niches of S. Nicolicchio resemble the arrangement of S. Micidiario described above. The frescoes are clearer here. Saints Elena and Stefano are depicted, with their names in Greek, along with another unidentified saint. The third chapel, the Grotta del Crocifisso, is composed of two attached rooms, with a rectangular apse, which, unusually, faces west. There are traces of frescoes of the crucifixion, a female figure, and Saint Nicola (Messina 1979:105–8).

While Orsi provides very little information on the dwellings themselves, his description of one chamber complex, Grave 56, characterizes the oddity of this reuse.

Plate 10.3 Pantalica: chapel of S. Micidiario, interior. Apse with niches and modern-day graffiti visible (photo by the author)

Grave 56 consisted of a large trapezoidal room with eleven cells fanning off it, positioned at two levels. In subsequent times, the outer door to the central chamber had been expanded and reshaped. Orsi here found a quantity of coarseware sherds and fragments of glass cups which he dates to the Byzantine period. But what was most extraordinary was that in the cell opposite the entrance, the prehistoric contents were still *in situ*. Skeletal remains were accompanied by sherds of what Orsi describes as red and brown burnished pottery, probably Pantalica's Early Iron Age wares (see Leighton 1999:203–4). In addition, a simple bow fibula and two small blades were present (Orsi 1899a:58–9). Orsi expresses surprise that these "poor mountain people of the seventh and eighth centuries had transformed a noble tomb of almost 2000 years earlier into a habitation, clearing out the cells and leaving some modest but eloquent relics" (Orsi 1899a:58; my translation). This inconsistent treatment of the older materials, selectively preserving some and discarding the rest, eludes immediate comprehension.

The exact chronology of Pantalica's reoccupation is open to debate. A hoard of gold jewelry and coins, found in 1903 in the courtyard of the fortified structure on the plateau, provides a possible date for the occupation (Orsi 1910; Uggeri 1974:201). The gold coins bear the images of the emperors Constantine II through Constantine IV, thus covering a range of 641–85 AD, dating the hoard's contents, and probably its deposition, to the end of the seventh century. The hoard could indicate fears of an

Arab raid, or simply served as a way of storing wealth. Unfortunately we cannot corroborate this date with a close dating of associated pottery, as this period of Sicily's history lacks an adequate ceramic typology (Christie 1989:263). The Byzantine and Arab pottery of earlier centuries has not been sufficiently differentiated from the later "Arab-Norman" pottery of the mid eleventh century and after (Wilson 1985:329). Again, the frescoes in the chapels fall into a stylistic range between the seventh to ninth centuries, but this dating is by no means secure. Though the frescoes tell us that the churches were in use at least by the seventh to ninth centuries, we do not know how much earlier the churches themselves may have been established. The first mention of the medieval settlement of Pantalica comes in a church document of the diocese of Syracuse from 1093 AD. Pantalica is mentioned in subsequent documents in 1104, 1145, and 1151 AD. The site was evidently used during the Norman period. However, a document listing the possessions of the diocese of Syracuse in 1169 makes no mention of Pantalica, suggesting that perhaps it had been abandoned by then. There are no subsequent references to it (Messina 1979:104–5). In 1555, a visitor to the site described it as deserted (Uggeri 1974:201). All this disparate evidence suggests that the period of reuse at Pantalica dates from the end of the seventh to the mid twelfth century. What can we make of this reuse? To feel at ease with such utterly remote material culture suggests that perhaps these artifacts and localities were not so remote after all: perhaps the preservation of a memory of the site's significance, however dim, across the centuries, made this "honeycomb," as Vincent Cronin (1959:255) called it, a welcome place of refuge. The subsequent portions of this paper will fill out the context of the phenomenon, and weigh the validity of this theory against alternate interpretations.

Troglodytism and Tomb Reuse: Identifying the Inhabitants

By placing Pantalica's reuse against the cultural backdrop of early medieval Sicily, we are better equipped to explain it, and in turn, gain insight into other cases of reuse. If this reuse entailed remembering the older sites, then it is crucial to determine *who* is doing the remembering, and how the identities of those people may be coloring any preserved memories. Pantalica, while an exceptional site for its size and importance, was by no means unique. For example, Cassibile, the second most extensive rock-cut necropolis, also in the environs of Syracuse but along the south coast at some remove from Pantalica, was also reused in the Byzantine period, and contains two rock-cut villages (Orsi 1899b:118). Further, this reuse fits into the larger phenomenon of troglodytism, or occupation of cavities, whether carved out or natural. Establishing a chronology of this practice is a challenge. It is not known when the first rock-cut dwellings appeared on Sicily. Underground funerary catacombs were found in Sicilian cities such as Syracuse, Marsala, and Agrigento by the third century AD. But these rock-cut spaces' funerary function and urban context differentiate them from the phenomenon discussed here (Bonacasa Carra 1986). Rock-cut dwellings and churches in rural contexts appear later and would seem to be a distinct practice.

There are several indirect pieces of evidence by which to date the latter practice. While pottery of the early medieval period is difficult to pin down chronologically, the lack of late antique wares at the rock-cut sites is informative. The total absence of such pottery from any of these troglodyte settlements strongly suggests that they do not predate the late sixth or seventh century (Christie 1989:259–60). In the case of the troglodyte churches, their proliferation and small size are typical of the Byzantine emphasis on private worship. Greek inscriptions and Byzantine church forms and wall paintings would seem to confirm their characterization as Byzantine. However, the conservatism of Byzantine architecture makes the churches difficult to date with precision. Ousterhout (1999:27) gives the example of two virtually identical churches, one built in 907 AD, one built in 1080. Moreover, we must be hesitant to date a church by the inscriptions or frescoes in it, which can always be added later. Whatever we may infer from the indirect evidence, the earliest piece of direct evidence of troglodytism dates from 841, when an Arab chronicler described the sacking of the *Fortezza delle Grotte*, the name given to forty inhabited caves in the interior (Uggeri 1974:211). This dates the inception of this phenomenon to the end of the period of Byzantine control of the island, at the latest.

Rock-cut churches did not end when the Byzantines lost political control of the island. Indeed, the Arabs permitted both Byzantine and Latin practices to continue, and under the Normans, new rock-cut structures were built and older ones reactivated (Messina 1979:14). In western Sicily troglodyte settlements are not thought to appear until as late as the fourteenth century (Mirazita 1988:74–5).

For the island as a whole, no systematic study has determined how many of these rock-cut settlements incorporate prehistoric structures. It is often difficult to tell if the cavity is new or a case of reuse, because the reuse may entail the widening of doorways and cavities, leaving little of the original surfaces. The reuse was not limited solely to prehistoric features: it also took place at the Greek quarries of Syracuse and at Passolatello (Uggeri 1974:204), and several early Christian tombs were later turned into churches (Messina 1986:248). However, the prehistoric tombs were the most common objects of appropriation, and so cannot be dismissed as anomalous incidents as easily as one might do with these other cases.

Who were the inhabitants of these troglodytic sites? The extent to which the troglodyte settlements were related to monasticism is an ongoing debate. In central Turkey, Cappadocia, the famous Byzantine troglodyte settlement has long been interpreted as a vast monastic complex, and this explanation has been applied to other such settlements (Rodley 1985). The rock-cut residences were thought to have appealed to monastic sensibilities, representing the symbolic abandonment of worldly concerns. Messina suggests that the monastic communities preferred to inhabit earlier burial sites in order to simulate death (Messina 1979:14). For the Sicilian examples, there is little scholarly tradition of attributing a monastic function to them. Orsi interprets the site of S. Marco near Noto in Sicily as being a monastic settlement, given the rows of small "cells" carved in the rock, but he does not venture this interpretation for other sites (Orsi 1898:16–17). However, because in nearby Apulia and elsewhere in the Byzantine Empire this has been the standard explanation, the monastic connection warrants consideration here.

Monastic communities in the west are usually depicted as foreigners from the east. If this were true of Pantalica's residents, it would be highly unlikely that they brought with them the memory of a site they had never seen, so the identity of the inhabitants is critical here. Transplanted Greek monastic communities are known from the mid seventh century in Ravenna and Rome, some consisting of refugees fleeing Arab invasions from the Levant and Egypt (Christie 1989:258). The extent to which such refugees also settled on Sicily is unknown, and has almost certainly been overstated with regards to southern Italy. This interpretation derives from the widely held belief that some 50,000 monks fled Greece for Southern Italy to escape persecution. The story comes from a historian of the last century, Lénormant, whose claim, though unfounded, has become dogma. This supposed monastic colonization has colored all considerations of troglodyte settlements, and pins down the date to ca. 1000 AD (Caprara 1970:113–15). Although there is no secure proof of such a movement, it is possible that a migration of religious orders did occur. Yet if we are going to pursue the idea of an influx of people from the east, there is nothing to suggest this took place in 1000 AD. There are many other moments when similar migrations may have occurred. One author dates Greek migration earlier, in the eighth century, in response to the persecutions of the iconoclastic period that sent eastern immigrants in flight to Sicily (Messina 1975:394). The Moslem threat in Africa and Syria in the seventh century would warrant a flight as well. Indeed, this explanation of flight fits many periods: the early sixth-century people could have fled the Vandals in Africa (Caprara 1970:114–15). This last story is told to explain the troglodyte settlements on Sardinia, which include reused hypogea (Kirova and Saiu Deidda 1984). Each account sounds plausible, but the structural similarities – the recurring flight of religious orders westward and northward across widely different time periods – call them all into question. In prehistoric contexts, explanations of new material culture patterns that rely on purported movements of peoples have come under scrutiny, and we may be equally skeptical here.

The theory of foreign monastic orders settling in these rock-cut sites is further weakened by recent claims that the phenomenon of monasticism at the source – the east – has been overstated. Scholars have recently been rethinking the monastic character of Cappadocia, the iconic troglodyte monastic locality. Kalas argues that while some of the settlements at Cappadocia were inhabited by monastic orders, not all were. Kalas differentiates the settlements' function based on the presence of a refectory and other architectural features (Kalas 2000; see also Mathews and Mathews 1997:298). More plausible than the picture of thousands of monks perpetually on the move is that *ideas* of monasticism were circulating, instead of peoples. The flow of information around the Mediterranean was enough to account for the spread of at least certain elements of these eastern monastic practices, if not the monks themselves. It seems likely, then, that the idea of troglodytism originated in Eastern monasticism but was diffused into secular settings (Messina 1972–3:234). Because Pantalica lacks a refectory or other obvious indicators of monastic activity, we can consider this to be a secular settlement.

Though we may feel confident that these were secular sites, the vexing issue of identity of the rural inhabitants remains. Were they Greek immigrants, or former city-dwellers, or longtime rural populations? The Moslem geographer Ibn Hawqal, visiting Sicily in the 970s, was shocked by the intermarriage between Christians and Moslems in rural areas, resulting in both religions being practiced by members of the same families (Hawqal 1964:128). As this observation (however biased) is contemporary with the proposed occupation of the troglodyte settlements, it hints at a more complex identity for the residents of those settlements, and suggests the messiness of the identities behind the labels.

Troglodytism and Reuse: Explanations

Given then that Pantalica was not a monastic site, we cannot see in the choice to settle there a formalized commitment to asceticism. Other explanations are necessary, for Pantalica and for the phenomenon of Byzantine troglodytism more generally. The most common explanation casts troglodytism as a form of *incastellamento*, the wholesale abandonment of the coastal cities, a retreat to defended high points of the hinterlands, in reaction to general insecurity and specifically to a fear of seaborne raiders (e.g. Uggeri 1974:200). In this vein, Orsi (1898:1) describes rock-cut settlements in the southeast of the island as "hidden" and assumes that they were where the population gathered for protection from the onslaughts of the Moslems. Yet how dangerous was Sicily at this time? Certainly in the early years of Byzantine control of the island, Sicily was relatively safe, remaining removed from the upheavals of the mainland brought on by the power struggles between Franks, Ostrogoths, Lombards, and Byzantines. The recorded flight of Roman senators to their Sicilian estates during the first half of the sixth century is evidence that this region was stable compared to the mainland (Christie 1989:254). By the seventh century it is true that Sicily was threatened by Arab incursions. The southeast coast was a popular target: the city of Syracuse was sacked by the Arabs in 669 AD, and the historian Paolo Diacono's account of the event, written approximately one hundred years later, notes that the inhabitants took refuge in the hills (Messina 1979:8). However, there is nothing to suggest this was anything more than a temporary flight, for the people returned to the city soon after. On an island-wide scale, urban decline on Sicily is not evident until the eighth or ninth century, so there is at the very least a time lag in the impact of this raiding on settlement patterns. *Incastellamento*, though already occurring in northern and central Italy, did not really get under way in Sicily until the ninth to eleventh centuries (Christie 1989:261–81), at the end of the Byzantine period or after the island was already under Arab control, at which point presumably the raids had stopped. Moreover, these protected hilltop settlements did not entirely replace the more exposed dispersed settlements of the countryside: several surveys indicate that individual farmsteads and small villages in the lowlands carried on, only truly disappearing in the thirteenth century (Wilson 1985:329–31). The Monreale survey in inland western Sicily, for example, yielded evidence of occupation of hill towns and abandonment of villages, but a full 56 percent of the villages nevertheless still showed use during the Arab occupation (Johns 1985:220).

Another threat may have been greater than that of the Arabs: the wrath of the Byzantine ecclesiastical authorities during the iconoclastic period (726–843 AD). Human representations in art were forbidden, and this law was enforced strictly, so much so that artistic production in the empire is said to have fallen during that era. In support of this theory, an early ninth-century document mentions that during the period of iconoclast persecution, people sought refuge in mountains and *caves* (Uggeri 1974:212 n.62; my italics). Perhaps these caves were carved rather than natural. In Pantalica's chapels, a pictorial manifestation may have been a safe act of defiance, as the chapels were less distinguishable from the habitations than free-standing churches, and thus may have escaped notice (Messina 1979:108–11).

One theory sees a direct correlation between economic conditions and the emergence of rock-cut habitations. The claim is that poverty and desperation obliged the site's residents to avail themselves of the older structures, as they did not have the resources to construct a settlement from scratch (Caprara 1970:115). This theory is in keeping with the traditional picture of economic collapse in late antiquity. The decline of Mediterranean trade that had begun in the centuries prior to the Byzantine takeover was in no way checked by their arrival, as the virtual disappearance of imports by the seventh century in Italy attest. Limited coinage points to a barter economy and a general shift toward self-sufficiency, though frequent coin finds indicate that Sicily's monetary system persisted longer than on the mainland (Christie 1989:261–2).

It is true that it takes far less time to carve out a room in the soft limestone than it does to build a free-standing stone structure of comparable size. An ethnographic account from Turkey in the nineteenth century recorded that one person was able to excavate a room 25 feet by 13 feet by 10 feet high in a month. A fairly elaborate church was noted as being completed in six months (Rodley 1985:224–5). Reusing older structures would have required even less energy. One scholar thus explains the reuse of Pantalica as a simple matter of convenience (Agnello 1975:8). Support for this argument comes from the fact that troglodytism does coincide with periods of economic hardship. Another suggestion is that the peasantry left the coastal cities for the countryside to avoid the heavy burden of taxation imposed by the Byzantine authorities (Uggeri 1974:212). All these accounts see troglodytism in general as the prosaic response of a society reduced to a primitive state, with reuse being the sign of true destitution.

However, in the case of Pantalica, these explanations are insufficient. The three villages, decorated churches, free-standing structures, and valuable hoard together contradict the picture of a population in desperate straits. As one of the most prominent sites in the region, the inhabitants would hardly have been hidden from view and could still have been targeted for taxation. Indeed, the site's appearance in the twelfth-century church documents indicates that it was not overlooked. Thus the standard functionalist explanations cannot account for the specific choice to occupy ancient tombs, and we must look elsewhere.

This leaves us with analyzing the reuse of the hypogea as a cultural choice, as two scholars have done (Messina 1972–3:234; Turco 1990:76). If we view reuse as a cultural phenomenon, several interpretations are possible. Of particular interest here is the possibility that it was the endurance of local practices through time, or at least the memory of those practices, that drew people back to this site. Indeed, this theory has been put forth to explain troglodytism in general. Apulian rock-cut dwellings, for example, have been seen as a continuation of prehistoric practices (Tinè Bertocchi 1964). However, the later frequenting of the site is in all respects different from its initial use. There is no evidence to suggest that there was any cultural continuity or residual meaning at Pantalica to attract these later peoples to the site. Their casual disregard for the older tombs, neither avoiding them, destroying them, nor privileging them, would seem to demonstrate an absence of any affinity or common bond with the earlier peoples. Nor does this disregard suggest the opposite: that these older pre-Christian sites were abhorrent to the Christian population and were purposefully destroyed. Some cavities were reused, some were not. Some were cleared out, some were left intact. A systematic erasure of the past cannot be detected in these actions. After 1,300-odd years and numerous cultural transformations, it is almost certain that the Byzantine residents of the site knew less about it than we do now from archaeological research. We cannot detect a memory of this site, in the literal sense of the word, in this reuse.

Indeed, there is something inherently problematic with such stories of cultural continuity, because they tend to naturalize complex social processes. Paolo Orsi even went so far as to claim troglodytism to be an "ingrained trait" of the Sicilians (Orsi 1902:635)! Although such claims are rarely made now, there is a lingering romantic tendency in Mediterranean anthropology to identify the timeless community whose millennia-old practices have survived the waxing and waning of imperial powers and economic fortunes (see Horden and Purcell 2000:463–84 for a fuller discussion of this). Implicit in the descriptions of these traditional communities are notions of backwardness, stasis, and isolation. It is increasingly clear, however, that the Mediterranean has always been a zone of connectivity and dynamism, with evident variability within regions over time.

If the theory that the sites were somehow remembered is untenable, one other possibility is that the residents were reacting to the remnants of a past that they did not know, but whose power they were attempting to draw on. The discursive role of ancient sites and the supernatural, other-worldly power attributed to them in the past is well-recognized. Recently there has been a spate of studies of people exploiting an indigenous past to create or reinforce their own origin myths, as a way of underpinning a local identity that is under threat (e.g., articles in Bradley and Williams 1998; Kotsakis 1998; Mamani Condori 1996). At first glance, the circumstances would seem ripe in Sicily for such a gesture, as a foreign culture was being imposed on the populations. In this scenario, the flight from the classical city to the preclassical autochthonous locale would have been a clear statement of cultural resistance on the part of the subject peoples to their foreign rulers. By occupying these older spaces they would be reaffirming their cultural integrity and finding in them a source of strength. Such a narrative resonates in this postcolonial era, when the agency of subaltern groups in cultural contact zones has been brought into sharp relief.

And yet such a foreign/local binary doesn't work here. The people who constructed Pantalica's villages and chapels and who reused other sites were themselves heavily steeped in Byzantine culture, and these sites are examples of a Mediterranean-wide practice. Hawqal's description of intermarriage between Moslems and Christians, together with what we know of the incredible cultural diversity of this region, make it clear that this was a population long accustomed to, and characterized by, cultural pluralism. Such an opposition between foreign and native would have been meaningless. Understanding the reuse therefore must take into account not simply the isolated history of Sicily at the local scale, but its place in broader cultural currents.

One such current was the Byzantine penchant for troglodytism. Troglodytic practices across the Byzantine world offer important grounds for comparison and demonstrate the extent of this generalized phenomenon. Rock-cut dwellings and churches are found throughout the Byzantine Empire, with notable and numerous examples in Turkey, Algeria, Macedonia, Serbia, Cyprus, and North Africa. Rock-cut habitations and cult centers are mentioned frequently in ecclesiastical documents, including one manual of procedures for consecrating a rock-cut church (Messina 1979:8–9). These rock-cut churches must have been so widely accepted that twelfth-century church documents generally do not differentiate between free-standing and rock-cut churches. Formerly these sites were seen as marginal to built architecture of the period, but in the past few decades it has been acknowledged that they constitute a key component of Byzantine culture (Fonseca 1978:16). Far from being exclusive to Sicily, the nearby regions of Apulia and Calabria in Southern Italy have numerous rock-cut structures. Indeed the phenomenon seems to be even more developed there than in Sicily, and the towns tend to be quite large. In Apulia 96 major sites and many other lesser ones are recorded (Uggeri 1974:214). In the district of Matera alone, 105 rock-cut churches are recorded, including restructured Bronze Age hypogea (Caprara 1970:104–5).

Byzantine era reuse of non-Christian rock-cut tombs is also attested in Jerusalem, though the circumstances are slightly different as there was no change in function. There, Jewish tombs of the first century AD were first reused, after a brief interruption, for pagan burials in the late first or early second centuries up until the fourth century. In the fifth and sixth centuries, the tombs were then used for Christian burials. Nearby, surveys in the lower Kidron Valley have found that earlier Jewish burial caves were reused intensively by monks as hermitic cells in the lower Kidron Valley (Avni 1993:271). Interestingly, in many cases the earlier burials are preserved intact alongside the later burials, though there are also cases of extensive restructuring of burial chambers that must have destroyed prior burials (Avni 1993:270–5). This haphazard approach to the earlier material and the absence of a cultural affiliation between the original and secondary users recalls the case of reuse at Pantalica. Thus, in different cultural and geographic contexts, troglodytism and reuse of older sites were both practiced around the same time, suggesting a Mediterranean-wide phenomenon.

It would seem then that Pantalica's residents were expressing not a local identity through this reuse, but that their choice was outward-looking, derived from a far-flung cultural network that happened to coincide with a local past. This last point is not unimportant: after all, they did choose to reuse the older structures instead of starting anew, and this brings us back to detecting a sort of link with these older places. That link, I argue, was familiarity. The peoples would have grown up aware of these places, without needing to know their history. In the absence of any shared culture, it must have been the place itself that was significant. The similarity of the locality-making projects opened up a conceptual space for encountering these older sites, not based on a preserved meaning but on a recognition of these old places in a new light. Though the early use of the site was entirely different from the later one, the likeness of the spatial project and the familiarity of the site itself apparently made the pagan burials palatable. Thus, when people reused the sites, they were availing themselves of a familiar local place from which to engage with broader contemporary cultural currents. In this respect, the phenomenon is akin to the one Meskell describes in this volume, where the materiality of place demanded a response from later inhabitants, who then fabricate a social "memory." In the case of Pantalica, this familiarity did involve *memory*, but only in the immediate, short term sense of life-histories and localized habits, through which the sites would have been absorbed and stored with the other repeated experiences of landscape.

Far from a gesture of isolation and tradition, the act of reuse was cosmopolitan and forward-looking, as the site's residents forged a pan-Mediterranean Byzantine identity through their own version of troglodytism. With more secure contextual evidence than is available in prehistoric cases of reuse, this study contributes to our understanding of the impact of pre-existing constructed spaces on people in the past, and may help us to distinguish between cases of collective memory and unstudied familiarity.

Conclusion

The topic of peoples' encounters with objects of the remote past has received considerable attention of late, and it is increasingly recognized that these encounters often entailed an evocation of the past in contemporary social negotiations. Often these narratives concerning "the past in the past" are hampered by a sparse material record. Armed with extensive information on Byzantine religion and practices, we know the cultural context in which the people experienced these tombs, and thus are better equipped to make sense of their actions. In stark contrast to the easily recognizable and "consumable" Greek temples and baroque churches of the island, this visually arresting honeycomb evokes the exotic otherness of a foreign culture. It comes as a surprise, then, to learn of the site's extensive reuse in the Byzantine period. In the case of Pantalica, paradoxically, the act of retreating into the embodiment of the local past was in fact a gesture of cosmopolitanism. Recent work on the deployment of older sites as signifiers of local identity offers fruitful lines of inquiry, though the Sicilian cases do not fit these theories satisfactorily. Instead, focusing specifically on the example of Pantalica, I have argued that this phenomenon of reuse resulted from a fortuitous convergence of the older site's familiar local presence and new pan-Mediterranean cultural currents. This familiarity would have been grounded in the present life of the site, not in its past. The recognition of the flexibility of tradition and of the strategic uses to which the past may be put has opened up an analytical space for the study of the reuse of older places, practices, and objects. Apparent traces of cultural continuity and collective memory must be examined very carefully, therefore, to see if they are real or imagined.

References Cited

Agnello, G. 1975: Nuove indagini sui santuari rupestri della Sicilia. *Byzantino-Sicula II: miscellanea di scritti in memoria di G. R. Taibbi*, ed. B. Lavagnini and S. M. Ganci. Palermo: Istituto Siciliano di Studi Bizantini e Neoellenici Quaderno 8, pp. 1–9.

Avni, G. 1993: Christian secondary use of Jewish burial caves in Jerusalem in the light of new excavations at the Aceldama tombs. In *Early Christianity in Context: Monuments and Documents*, ed. F. Manns and E. Alliata. Jerusalem: Franciscan Printing Press, pp. 265–76.

Bonacasa Carra, R. M. 1986: Nota su alcuni insediamenti rupestri dell'area Palermitana. *La Sicilia Rupestre nel contesto delle Civiltà méditerranée*, ed. C. D. Fonseca. Lecce: Galatina Congedo Editore, pp. 213–26.

Bradley, R. and Williams, H. (ed.) 1998: The Past in the Past: The Reuse of Ancient Monuments. *World Archaeology* 30(1).

Caprara, R. 1970: Una chiesa rupestre controabsidata in territorio di Mottola. In *Puglia Paleocristiana*. Bari: Adriatica Editrice, pp. 103–17.

Christie, N. J. 1989: The archaeology of Byzantine Italy: a synthesis of recent research. *Journal of Mediterranean Archaeology* 2(2), pp. 249–63.

Cronin, V. 1959: *The Golden Honeycomb*. London: Granada.

Finley, M. I. 1968: *A History of Sicily: Ancient Sicily to the Arab Conquest*. New York: Viking Press.

Finley, M. I., Smith, D. M. and Duggan, C. 1987: *A History of Sicily*. New York: Viking Penguin.

Fonseca, C. D. 1978: Habitat-strutture-territorio: nuovi metodi di ricerca in tema di civiltà Rupestre. In *Habitat-Strutture-Territorio: Atti del Terzo Convegno Internazionale di Studio sulla Civiltà Rupestre Medioevale nel Mezzogiorno d'Italia*, ed. C. D. Fonseca. Lecce: Galatina Congedo Editore, pp. 15–24.

Giunta, F. 1974: *Bizantini e Bizantinismo nella Sicilia Normanna*. Palermo: Palumbo.

Hawqal, I. 1964: Kitab Surat Al-Ard. In *Configuration de la Terre*, trans. J. H. Kramers and G. Wiet. Paris: Editions G.-P. Maisonneuve e Larose.

Horden, P. and Purcell, N. 2000: *The Corrupting Sea: A Study of Mediterranean History*. Oxford: Blackwell.

Johns, J. 1985: The Monreale survey: indigenes and invaders in medieval west Sicily. *Papers in Italian Archaeology IV, part iv. Classical and Medieval Archaeology*, ed. C. Malone and S. Stoddart. Oxford: BAR International Series 246, pp. 215–23.

Kalas, V. 2000: *Rock-cut Architecture of the Peristrema Valley: Society and Settlement in Byzantine Cappadocia*. Ph.D. dissertation. Ann Arbor: University Microfilms.

Kirova, T. K. and Saiu Deidda, A. 1984: L'uso cristiano delle grotte e delle architetture rupestri. *Sardegna. Atti del VI Congresso Nazionale di Archeologia Cristiana. Pesaro-Ancona 19–23 settembre 1983*. Florence: La Nuova Italia Editrice, pp. 151–70.

Kotsakis, K. 1998: The past is ours: images of Greek Macedonia. In *Archaeology Under Fire: Nationalism, Politics and Heritage in the Eastern Mediterranean and the Middle East*, ed. L. Meskell. London and New York: Routledge, pp. 44–67.

La Lumia, I. 1867: *History of Sicily under William the Good*. Florence.

Leighton, R. 1999: *Sicily Before History*. Ithaca, N.Y.: Cornell University Press.

Mamani Condori, C. 1996: History and prehistory in Bolivia: what about the Indians? In *Contemporary Archeology in Theory: A Reader*, ed. R. Preucel and I. Hodder. Oxford: Blackwell, pp. 632–45.

Mathews, T. F. and Mathews, A.-C. D. 1997: Islamic-style mansions in Byzantine Cappadocia and the development of the inverted T-plan. *Journal of the Society of Architectural Historians* 56, pp. 294–315.

Messina, A. 1972–3: *Paolo Orsi e la "civiltà rupestre medievale della Sicilia."* Archivio Storico Siracusano, n.s. 11, pp. 229–36.

Messina, A. 1975: La cripta di "Santa Lania" (Lentini) e il problema delle arcate cieche nell'architettura altomedievale. In *Byzantino-Sicula II: miscellanea di scritti in memoria di G. R. Taibbi*, ed. B. Lavagnini and S. M. Ganci. Palermo: Istituto Siciliano di Studi Bizantini e Neoellenici Quaderno 8, pp. 385–94.

Messina, A. 1979: *Le chiese rupestri del Siracusano*. Palermo: Istituto Siciliano di Studi Bizantine e Neoellenici, Monumenti 2.

Messina, A. 1986: Forme di abitato rupestre nel Siracusano. *La Sicilia Rupestre nel contesto delle Civiltà méditerranée*, ed. C. D. Fonseca. Lecce: Galatina Congedo Editore, pp. 245–50.

Mirazita, I. 1988: L'habitat rupestre nella Sicilia occidentale nei secoli XIV–XVI. Fonti Notarili. In *Il Popolamento rupestre dell'area Mediterranea: la tipologia delle fonti gli insediamenti rupestri della Sardegna*, ed. C. D. Fonseca. Lecce: Galatina Congedo Editore, pp. 73–9.

Norwich, J. J. 1992: *The Normans in Sicily*. London: Penguin.

Orsi, P. 1898: Chiese Bizantine del territorio di Syracuse. *Byzantinische Zeitschrift* 7, pp. 1–28.

Orsi, P. 1899a: Pantalica. *Monumenti Antichi* 9, pp. 33–115.

Orsi, P. 1899b: Cassibile. *Monumenti Antichi* 9, pp. 117–44.

Orsi, P. 1902: Timpa Ddieri. *Notizie di Scavi di Antichita*, pp. 631–5.

Orsi, P. 1910: Byzantina Siciliae. *Byzantinische Zeitschrift* 19, pp. 63–90.

Ousterhout, R. 1999: *Master Builders of Byzantium*. Princeton: Princeton University Press.

Rodley, L. 1985: *Cave Monasteries of Byzantine Cappadocia*. Cambridge: Cambridge University Press.

Tinè Bertocchi, F. 1964: *La pittura funeraria apula*. Napoli: L'Arte Tipografica.

Turco, M. 1990: Cassibile. Appunti per una carta archeologica del territorio. *Sicilia Archeologica* 23(72), pp. 67–78.

Uggeri, G. 1974: Gli insediamenti rupestri medievali: problemi di metodo e prospettive di ricerca. *Archeologia Medievale* 1, pp. 195–230.

Whitehouse, R. 1981: Megaliths of the central Mediterranean. In *The Megalithic Monuments of Western Europe*, ed. C. Renfrew. London: Thames and Hudson, pp. 42–63.

Wilson, R. J. A. 1985: Changes in the pattern of urban settlement in Roman, Byzantine and Arab Sicily. *Papers in Italian Archaeology IV: The Cambridge Conference. Part I, the Human Landscape*, ed. C. Malone and S. Stoddart. Oxford: BAR International Series 246, pp. 313–44.

11
The Translation of Time

Richard Bradley

The most famous book about memory is a work of fiction. Marcel Proust's *A la recherche du temps perdu* was first published in eight volumes between 1913 and 1927, and soon afterwards it was translated into English by C. K. Scott Moncrieff. More recently this version has been revised by Terence Kilmartin. Each of them renders Proust's title in a different way. Scott Moncrieff quotes from a Shakespeare sonnet and calls the novel *Remembrance of Things Past*. Kilmartin stays closer to the author's own words, which he translates as *In Search of Lost Time*.

Those English titles have quite different connotations. One is directly concerned with remembering the past, whilst the other talks of searching for a past that is lost. *Remembrance of Things Past* suggests that recollection is an almost involuntary process, as indeed it is in the first part of Proust's novel, but *In Search of Lost Time* evokes a deliberate effort to remake a past that is out of reach. Both these processes are relevant to the concerns of archaeology and, most particularly, to the contents of this book.

Remembrance of Things Past

This version of Proust's title raises several important issues. How long could social memories remain intact? How effectively were they preserved through different practices or different kinds of material culture? And did those memories decay simply through the passage of time, or were they erased deliberately though what Forty and Küchler (1999) have termed the "art of forgetting?"

The first question is addressed quite explicitly in Meskell's paper, in which she comments that the inhabitants of Deir el Medina do not seem to have remembered events over much more than two generations. Studies of oral history reveal something similar. They certainly suggest that memories may become unstable within a surprisingly short space of time, although precise estimates vary between one hundred and two hundred years (Henige 1974; Vansina 1985). Memories become increasingly inaccurate until they are so corrupt that they can hardly be distinguished from myth

(Gosden and Lock 1998). Of course the loss of information can be delayed by specialized techniques, but it would be unusual for oral traditions to retain their integrity across the lengthy sequences discussed in several of the papers. Following Henige (1974), one might suggest that memories could have been transmitted fairly accurately over the time spans discussed by Sinopoli, Joyce, and Van Dyke, but not for much longer than that.

The process of attrition can be arrested in several ways. The most obvious is through the codification of social memories in writing, and in that case it is important to investigate the circumstances in which people first decided to record the events of the past in a durable medium. A good example of this is found in Prent's paper, in which she notes that the conscious reuse of the Mycenean palaces of Crete took place during the period when the works of Homer were popular. Both could have been intended to emphasize a particular version of history.

Just as personal memories become unstable, it is clear that oral texts can change their contents over time, even when the performers intend to reproduce them accurately (Lord 1968). Some of the characteristic devices employed in composing these texts are specifically designed as mnemonics. Thus the genealogies of the Anglo-Saxon kings were codified in alliterative verse to make them easier to recall, yet they still included a strange mixture of well documented ancestors from the recent past, supplemented by more remote figures from the Classical world and the Old Testament (Sisam 1990). For Goody (1977), the "domestication of the savage mind" happened because writing made it possible to construct a new kind of history and to compare different versions of the same events. Even so, written sources may still record traditions whose contents had altered over the generations. When they were set down in writing, that process of interpretation would not end. This is surely the premise of literary theory (Eagleton 1983: chapters 2 and 4).

Memories could be codified in other ways. Lillios describes how portable artifacts may have been employed to convey quite specific information about the past. In Portugal, stone plaques were apparently used to record genealogies, yet such accounts were first encoded in material form when those artifacts were buried with the dead. The decoration on the plaques cannot have been created incrementally, and for that reason it is not clear whether they presented an accurate version of the past. Joyce's study of heirlooms offers another perspective, for here the objects themselves had circulated for a long time before they were deposited. They carried inscriptions setting out their histories and associations with particular people. In this case two rather different ways of recording memories seem to have been combined.

Perhaps a closer analogy to the codification of oral traditions in writing is the construction of monuments, and this process plays a large part in these papers. Monuments are extremely conspicuous statements about the world and were often built on a large scale because they were meant to last. Not only did these constructions leave a distinctive mark on the landscape, they made such extravagant demands on human labor that enormous numbers of people would have participated in their creation. This point is illustrated by Pauketat and Alt.

At the same time, the studies in this book make it abundantly clear that monuments did change over time. In fact they were modified and rebuilt, abandoned and replaced. Whatever the intentions of the people who first designed them, these structures were subject to the same instability as oral narratives (Bradley 2002: chapter 4). Like public rituals, such monuments might have been represented as immutable, yet the contexts in which they were used may have altered dramatically over time (Bloch 1986). There was a certain tension between the enduring character of these buildings and the changing ways in which they were actually used. Out of that tension archaeologists compose their own versions of history.

This is no easy task, and it is made still more difficult by the emphasis on establishing a sequence that is so central to modern research. The close attention paid to stratigraphy and absolute dating results in a strictly linear conception of time. That makes it harder to account for what seem to be anomalies, like the road in Van Dyke's paper that connects a newly built monument to a ruin, or the prolonged circulation of antiquities described by Joyce. It is difficult to accommodate the interplay between different time scales, and the patterns of citation and cross-reference that are described at monument complexes like Vijayanagara, Pueblo Bonito and Cahokia raise special problems, for they seem more characteristic of post-modern architecture. Indeed, there appears to be a certain tension between the archaeologist's ambition to construct a linear narrative and the kinds of narrative that were contrived by the people who built these monuments in the first place. As a number of the authors point out, individual buildings may have been physically linked to others surviving from the past. Perhaps that is because of the very nature of these projects. Even today, ritual and ceremonial can present an unchanging image to the world: one in which the past has entirely merged with the present. At the same time, such projects clearly formed part of the politics of their own time. This is clear from several of the chapters. For instance, Sinopoli points out that the most massive projects in her study area were undertaken during a period when the political structure was vulnerable. Similarly, Pauketat and Alt demonstrate the enormous scale on which building projects like Cahokia were conceived but show that those monuments were really quite short lived.

In other words, time was a flexible medium. Memories might only retain their integrity for a limited period, yet the progressive distortion of history could form an integral part of the political process. In some ways, that makes it more important than ever to understand why particular versions of the past were captured in a permanent form. The problem is reflected in the composition of this volume, for many of the studies consider the points of contact between writing and other kinds of material culture. This has advantages and disadvantages. It certainly helps to shed light on the reasons why the past assumed so much importance in specific societies and even on the strategies that were adopted by particular actors. On the other hand, the very fact that some of this information was written down may limit the wider relevance of these case studies. Writing is a specialized kind of communication which may be adopted in quite specific circumstances. To return to an earlier example, it has even been suggested that writing was first adopted in Greece in order to set down the origin myths contained in the works of Homer (Morris 1986). There may have been more variety among the ways in which memory operated in less complex societies. This is particularly clear from the contributions by Lillios and Van Dyke.

The politics of the ancient world involved forgetting as well as remembering. This has two distinct aspects. The first is the rather paradoxical process of "remembering by forgetting." This describes the situation in which an object or an event is remembered as a spectacle although no trace of it remains. Sometimes that transaction may have involved a conspicuous act of destruction. This model has been advocated by Küchler (1987) in her account of the traditional wood sculptures known as *malangan*. These are effigies which are displayed at public ceremonies in New Ireland. After the ceremony is over, *malangan* are abandoned and allowed to decay like the bodies of the dead, so that only a memory survives. It is not easy to use this model in archaeology, but that process has been compared with the destruction of statue menhirs at Copper Age sites in the southern Alps (Keates 2000). Another example may be found in the chapter by Pauketat and Alt, who describe the cyclical creation and destruction of specialized buildings on the top of the mounds at Cahokia.

The other possibility is more akin to iconoclasm. It involves a deliberate attempt to obliterate all trace of the past and to remove it from human consciousness. Again, this process is hardly represented among the papers in the book, although Christian reactions to the remains of paganism sometimes took this course. At first the church dictated that the remains of older religions should be eliminated, and this resulted in a campaign of deliberate destruction. In time, however, this attitude was relaxed and people were permitted to integrate the traces of a pagan past into the fabric of the new religion. In Northern France, where these policies were determined by the Synod of Nantes, both these approaches to the past are evidenced by archaeology. Some of the megalithic tombs surviving from the Neolithic period were completely destroyed, but the remains of others were converted into churches and graveyards (Billard et al. 1998). As a result, their original roles could no longer be recalled. Beyond the limits of memory, another approach was required.

In Search of Lost Time

The second, more accurate translation of Proust's title has a quite distinct emphasis. Past time is lost to the present and can only be recalled by an effort of will. That is an active process. Again, it suggests important questions for an archaeology of memory. Could past events or ideas be recreated in their original forms, or were they reinterpreted using whatever clues could be found? Why was it so important to relate the present to the past at particular junctures, and was that past reconstructed, or was it entirely remade?

The most important point is that beyond the limits of human memory any reuse of ancient material remains must have involved an act of interpretation. In some cases that interpretation could be influenced by written sources surviving from the past, so that the process was reasonably well informed. An interesting example is discussed by Papalexandrou who considers the use of spolia in Byzantine churches. In this case it is clear that such relics were given a special significance because of their historical associations, but there are many other cases in which no such clues were available. As a result, people in the past would have been compelled to interpret extinct material culture in the same way as archaeologists do today. The materiality of ancient remains would have posed a problem to past communities just as they did to early antiquarians, and the process of learning about these survivals might have taken a rather similar course. Guided by oral traditions, literary sources and their own prejudices about the past, people would have tried to explain the material traces of antiquity. But they needed to understand them in their own terms.

That does not mean that every coincidence between ancient and more recent material culture need have posed a challenge. Blake makes this point most effectively by studying the Byzantine use of caves in its wider cultural setting. She shows that the association between certain of these sites and prehistoric burials in Sicily need not be significant. By contrast, Iron Age reuse of older palaces in Crete took place at a time when other changes were happening, and they add weight to Prent's argument that these sites were a source of political and spiritual legitimacy. Again her case depends on practicing a kind of contextual archaeology.

It would be too simple to leave the discussion here, for it supposes that people in the past would have had the necessary knowledge to interpret what survived. Sometimes this was not possible. It may not have been easy to identify the traces of past activity with any confidence, for it has taken careful research to establish which phenomena are cultural and which are of natural origin. Until a subject like geology was fully developed, it would not have been easy to distinguish between human creations and elements of the unaltered topography. Both may have enjoyed a similar significance in antiquity, but geological features like rock outcrops could well have been mistaken for ancient ruins (Bradley 1998).

In other cases, people may have tried to assimilate the remains of the past into their own creations, but were simply mistaken in the ways in which they understood them. Meskell's chapter provides a good example of this process, for when the Romans employed Deir el Medina as a cemetery they apparently confused the ruins of an ordinary domestic building with those of an ancient tomb – and reused it accordingly. The history of archaeology is filled with errors of this kind.

It is not enough to pursue this comparison between the reuse of the past in the past and a primitive kind of field archaeology, for that says little or nothing about the reasons why particular places, monuments, and landscapes were so carefully selected for this purpose. For the most part the chapters in this book consider the use of the past as a source of political legitimation. That is a process that can be observed today; indeed, it often provides the justification for state archaeology. Much is made of the "invention of tradition" (Hobsbawm and Ranger 1983) and this idea underlies the papers by a number of the authors including Papalexendrou, Prent, Pauketat and Alt, Meskell, and Van Dyke. On the other hand, it would be wrong to restrict the argument to this approach. As Whitley (2002) has pointed out, not all antiquities were associated with ancestors or with sources of political power. Many were linked instead with the supernatural, and often they were feared. It may be as useful to consider when conspicuous monuments were shunned as it is to study the reasons why some of them were brought back into use.

Nor was it always the case that places were deliberately reused to draw on their associations with the past. Just as these could provide a source of legitimation, their connections might also pose a threat to society. As we have seen, one way of tackling this problem was iconoclasm. This would have been undertaken in order to eliminate a source of danger represented by the past, but another important process was *confrontation*: the creation of entirely new structures which were intended to modify, or even transform, existing interpretations of these places. A good example is the construction of Roman monuments to celebrate the defeat of subject populations. This process could be studied in more detail, for it involves the forcible substitution of one set of memories for another. Where the interpretation of ancient sites had involved an established version of history, that particular narrative was cancelled and another took its place.

Perhaps it is time for archaeologists to envisage something akin to "false memory syndrome." The term could cover a variety of different phenomena, many of which have already been discussed in this book. There is the progressive loss of memory experienced in traditional societies, and there are also the various techniques by which that process can be arrested. But at the same time there is much to suggest that such memories change even when this is not meant to happen. There is also evidence for the deliberate reuse of places associated with the past, but often it was a past whose contents could no longer be recalled. That required an act of interpretation, and in most cases people would have been unable to achieve this in terms that would satisfy the criteria of contemporary scholarship. Out of this mixture of confusion and fabrication, the past was renewed and reinvented, and ancient social life pursued its course. It would be a mistake to take all these connections literally, for it is more rewarding to investigate the circumstances in which they were devised. Even the falsest of memories can have enormous implications.

True to the theme of this collection, I conclude where I began. Like Proust's autobiographical novel, the remaking of the past in the past was both a creative act and an interpretation. Perhaps it is not so surprising that the most famous book about memory should be a work of fiction.

References Cited

Billard, C., Carré, F., Guillon, M., Treffort, C., Jagu, D. and Verron, G. 1998: L'occupation funéraire des monuments mégalithiques pendant la haut moyen age. Modalités et essai d'interpretation. *Bulletin de la Société préhistorique Française* 93, pp. 279–86.
Bloch, M. 1986: *From Blessing to Violence*. Cambridge: Cambridge University Press.
Bradley, R. 1998: Ruined buildings, ruined stones: enclosures, tombs and natural places in the Neolithic of south-west England. *World Archaeology* 30(1), pp. 13–22.
Bradley, R. 2002: *The Past in Prehistoric Societies*. London: Routledge.
Eagleton, T. 1983: *Literary Theory. An Introduction*. Oxford: Blackwell.
Forty, A. and Küchler, S. (eds.) 1999: *The Art of Forgetting*. Oxford: Berg.
Goody, J. 1977: *The Domestication of the Savage Mind*. Cambridge: Cambridge University Press.
Gosden, C. and Lock, G. 1998: Prehistoric histories. *World Archaeology* 30(1), pp. 2–12.
Henige, D. 1974. *The Chronology of Oral Tradition: Quest for a Chimera*. Oxford: Clarendon Press.
Hobsbawm, E. and Ranger, T. 1983: *The Invention of Tradition*. Cambridge: Cambridge University Press.

Keates, S. 2000: The ancestralisation of the landscape: monumentality, memory and the rock art of the Copper Age Valcamonica. In *Signifying Place and Space*, ed. G. Nash. Oxford: British Archaeological Reports, pp. 85–102.

Küchler, S. 1987: Malangan: art and memory in a Melanesian society. *Man* 22, pp. 238–55.

Lord, A. B. 1968: *The Singer of Tales*. New York: Athenaeum.

Morris, I. 1986: The use and abuse of Homer. *Classical Antiquity* 5(1), pp. 81–138.

Sisam, K. 1990: Anglo-Saxon royal genealogies. In *British Academy Papers on Anglo-Saxon England*, ed. E. Stanley. Oxford: Oxford University Press, pp. 45–204.

Vansina, J. 1985: *Oral Tradition as History*. Madison: University of Wisconsin Press.

Whitley, J. 2002: Too many ancestors? *Antiquity* 76, pp. 119–26.

Index

Index compiled by: Andrew L. Christenson